IMAGES
of America

ROBINSON AND CRAWFORD COUNTY

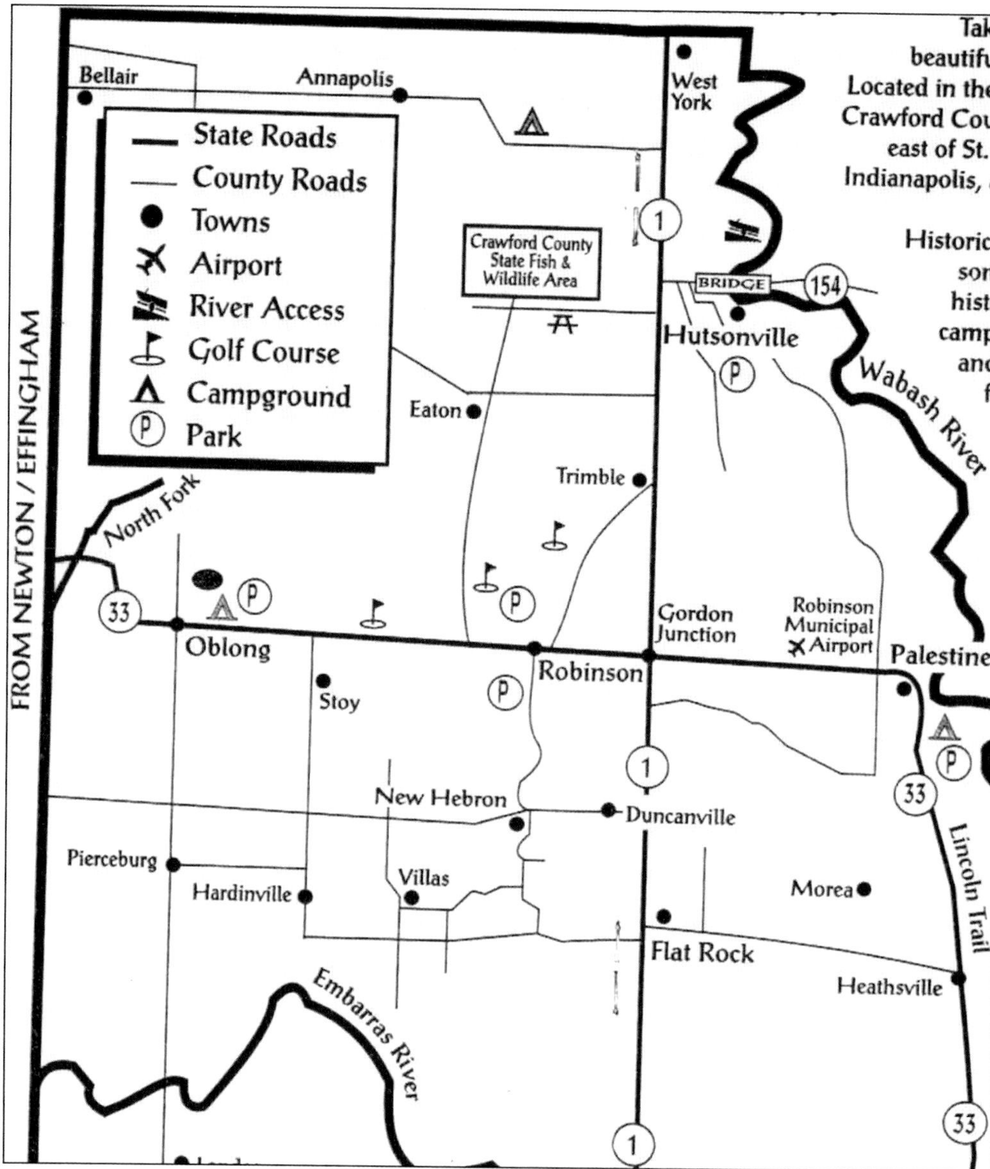

This Crawford County map indicates Route 1, a state highway, and the Lincoln Trail.

On the cover: The present Crawford County Courthouse was originally built in 1897 in High Victorian Gothic style. It was remodeled between 1949 and 1950, during which the high tower, gabled roof, a liberty statue, and the rooftops of the towers were removed. The magnificence of the original courthouse remains in the basic structure, although the appearance is quite different. (Sue Jones.)

IMAGES
of America

ROBINSON AND CRAWFORD COUNTY

Evelyn M. Wallace and Sue Jones

ARCADIA
PUBLISHING

ISBN 978-0-7385-4029-0

Published by Arcadia Publishing
Charleston, South Carolina

Printed in the United States of America

Library of Congress Catalog Card Number: 2006927508

For all general information contact Arcadia Publishing at:
Telephone 843-853-2070
Fax 843-853-0044
E-mail sales@arcadiapublishing.com
For customer service and orders:
Toll-Free 1-888-313-2665

Visit us on the Internet at www.arcadiapublishing.com

I would like to take this opportunity to extend heartfelt thanks to Susan-Marlene for her wonderful idea and Sue Jones for helping to make this book a reality. I would also like to thank the Livvix and Scott family for allowing me to be a part of their family and making me feel so welcome in their home, and the people of Crawford County for making me feel at home in their county.

—Evelyn M. Wallace

CONTENTS

ACKNOWLEDGMENTS

The dedication and tenacity of the Crawford County Historical Society (CCHS), Palestine Preservation Project Society, Hutsonville Historical Society, and many people of Crawford County are largely responsible for the photographs and historical content available in this book. Many of these historical society members are of the local Daughters of the American Revolution chapter, and they have served their county and country very well. Key people came forward with photographs that have become an integral part of the fascinating stories and people contained herein. Each individual or institution is credited by its respective initials throughout the text, after the photograph provided.

I would like to thank Sue Jones (SJ), currently secretary of CCHS, for saving a large part of the Argus photographs on compact disks and for her tireless efforts in securing more photographs and genealogical histories. Juanita Jochim (JJ) supplied me with the materials to write a voluminous amount of history for Palestine, and Scarlett Williamson (SW) kept a wonderful collection of photographs and knowledge of Hutsonville and Trimble. Contributors to this collection include Wendall and Ruth Evelyn Espy Goodwin for their photographs and recollections of Richwoods and the Shaners for their collection of the Mullens' photographs, along with country hospitality. Local historians who contributed photographs and knowledge were Richard Price (RP); Jim Finney (JF) in Oblong; Kay Young (KY), current president of CCHS for Oblong photographs; and Bill Millsap (BM) for saving the day with irreplaceable images of Palestine. I would also like to thank the people who may not have contributed photographs but were helpful in small and large ways for creating this book. Phyllis Moraga of Wonderland Antiques for her map-making ability, Village Framery (VF) in Palestine, Palestine Public Library for its historical Web pages, and Oblong Public librarians (OL) for their informative notebooks. I would like to acknowledge Mary Kindt, Linda Philippe, Ray Elliot, John Larrabee, Keith Waldrop, Cheryl Mefford, the Seyferths, and the Mannings.

INTRODUCTION

Crawford County in Illinois, along with several other counties and cities across the United States, honors William H. Crawford, a former Georgia senator and American minister to France. He became secretary of war, our seventh secretary of the treasury, and was a presidential nominee in the 1824 bid, but a massive stroke he suffered in 1823 dashed his chances. To be associated with such a venerable man is quite apt, because throughout history this county and many of its people have shown abilities beyond the usual while maintaining a charming and genuine modesty.

Palestine was Crawford County's beginning and one of Illinois's earliest continuous white settlements. A French trading post was erected around 1680. It was the obvious place to establish two forts, LaMotte and Foot, with the Wabash River nearby. During the War of 1812, the forts protected the inhabitants and traders from the Native Americans. By 1816, Crawford County became the 11th county in Illinois, and Palestine was consequently laid out by Edward N. Collum and Judge Joseph Kitchell. Collum laid out the east side, while Kitchell platted out the west side. The placement of the U.S. Land Office on May 11, 1820, later became a county seat for a large territory that reached as far north as Canada and stretched west to almost include Vandalia. Some years later, the Lincoln Trail forded by the Halls (Squire, Matilda, and son), Hankses (Dennis, Betsy, and four children), and Lincolns (Thomas, Sally, and Abraham) followed the Wabash through Palestine, as they camped there in 1830. Thomas and Abraham Lincoln paid visits to the land office around that period to purchase land in Macon and Coles County, and it is believed that on some occasions they stayed at the Dubois Tavern.

The first county courthouse was located in Palestine but was torn down early in the 19th century, and the bricks were used to build other homes, specifically the Lagow home, which was razed in 1918. Today, even though its population is one-fifth that of Robinson's, it thrives with the bulk of independent businesses and specialty stores for the county. J. D. Mullen's Dressings has been in business in downtown Palestine since 1948, but the oldest continuous business was the Miesenhelder Mill, which was established in 1852 by the Condit family.

On Christmas Day in 1843, ground was leveled in Robinson for a public square, and eventually a magnificent new county courthouse was erected there, in High Victorian Gothic style. Businesses were erected around the square, and many of those buildings still stand today. Ye Olde Candy Shoppe sells Heath Candy (and other Hershey products) in the same square where the Heath family took over an ice cream and confectionery in 1914. It is still manufactured in Robinson by Hershey and has maintained the original high standards.

When you drive into Robinson you will encounter a sign that says "Welcome to Robinson, home of author Jim Jones, 6700." The impact of the claim this sign produces gives any visitor a true and fair picture of the people that inhabit this quiet rural area. James Jones, author of *From Here to Eternity*, is a poster boy for a county that holds its veterans in high esteem, is industrious beyond usual expectations, and has, quite frankly, accomplished extraordinarily lasting achievements. From its sparse beginning as the fourth village with two residences, it has become well industrialized, with the largest population in Crawford County. There is every indication that the work of one generation paved the way for furtherance of the next. This is especially true in the case of A. H. Jones and James Jones (who were distantly related).

After being admitted to the bar in 1875, A. H. Jones rose quickly in the state's legislative bodies, and by 1898, he was able to get the Illinois State Food Law passed, becoming, in the process, the first food commissioner and president of the National Association of the State Food and Dairy Departments. For six years, he lobbied in Washington, D.C., until he secured a National Food Law. Even though he was doing work of widespread importance, his interest and influence in local affairs was prodigious. He was a member of Robinson's board of trustees, the school board, the city council, and the Illinois State Central Committee. He helped organize the company that brought the Big Four Railroad through Crawford County and was directly responsible, along with other movers and shakers of his day, for the building of the Robinson County Courthouse, the post office, and the beautiful Carnegie Library on Main Street.

Around 1924, the rough-and-tumble son of Ramon Jones, James, strode into the Carnegie Library and became a regular there, reading voraciously, and graduating to the adult books in his teens. He was third-generation Crawford County born, and his grandfather George W. was a wealthy lawyer who owned one of the most beautiful homes on Main Street. James's father was a dentist, and his uncle Charles was a state attorney for a time.

Generally speaking, James had a normal childhood, along with the rest of Robinson's children and his two siblings, Jeff and Mary Ann, and attended its public schools and graduated from Robinson High School. In 1939, he enlisted in the army before the onset of World War II and personally witnessed the bombing of Pearl Harbor while he was stationed there. He had a decorated military career and was awarded a Purple Heart and Bronze Star citations.

When James was sent back home from the war, he was initially sent to Memphis but made his way back to Robinson, where he met Lowney Handy, who helped him set his life on a writing track. He spent five years writing his first novel, *From Here to Eternity*, while residing in Handy's home, and they spent another two years trying to find a publisher for the book. Scribner published it in 1951 to great success. James went on to write a total of 11 books, many focusing on World War II. Other subjects he covered depict the tragedies he had the inner fortitude to overcome and deserve as much attention as his first novel.

Oblong, the only town so named in the United States, rose to worldwide importance shortly after oil was struck in a nearby town four miles south of Stoy, on the John Shire farm. The legend goes that a drilling site was marked by tossing an empty whiskey bottle into the air and drilling where it landed. After drilling 14 feet down, oil was struck. The Shire No. 1 well was shot with nitroglycerine and became a 2,500-barrel-a-day gusher. From 1908 to 1910, Crawford County became the largest oil-producing area in the world. John D. Rockefeller soon owned wells in the area, and Stoy and Oblong became a hub. Many of the prominent citizens prospered because of the oil boom, and the area population grew from 4,000 to 10,000 very quickly.

Naturally, back in 1961, a man by the name of Enos Bloom came up with the idea of starting a museum dedicated to the preservation of artifacts, tools, and written information solely on the subject of petroleum and oil production. The Illinois Oil Field Museum became a reality in 1967 and is one of a few such museums in this country. For a number of years, it was entirely funded by the community businesses through donations and taxes. In a relocated area west of Oblong, the museum comprises three buildings containing oil memorabilia, actual drilling equipment, tools, and small-scale models of existing oil refineries. It also houses a modern library on oil fields and petroleum, as well as books relating to the history of Crawford County.

The county's people take pride in their longevity, quality of life, and tight community. James Jones's article published in the *Ford Times* back in March 1957 quoted, "This kind of a community is the spine, the tough, straight resilient spine, from which we hang the rib case . . . of our 'economies' and our politics, our 'policies,' and from which dangle the appendages of our industries."

The Wabash

Beautiful river by Hutson, with the silvery sheet of blue;
Ever sluggishly moving onward like a panoramic view.

While now I trace thy meandering course, from the old town down to the bend,
A feeling of sadness comes o'er me, as the journey onward I wend.

To think of the scenes of my childhood, of the ones who used to stray
Along with me down the river's banks, where now I stroll today.

To watch for the landmarks of boyhood, and find that the river's surge
Swept them away- like the friends of youth, the winds sigh only the dirge.

Once gaily adown thee, old river, in his birchen bark canoe,
Floated the Indian warrior, with his maiden of dusky hue.

Upon thy banks where his councils, around brightly glowing fires;
The mossy mounds near the river's brink, the graves of ancestral sires.

The warrior has gone from thy forest, and his race is almost run;
Driven by white men westward, with the course of the setting sun.

But thy grand old oaks and thy elms, that were once his shelter and pride,
Still nod to the rippling waters, as they grow by the river's side.

Flow on, oh beautiful river! Flow gently to the sea;
I'll watch thy waters a little while- then the Master will summon me.

—W. C. Jones, from *Birch Rod Days*, 1892

One

PALESTINE
THE PIONEER CITY

John La Motte first spotted the land west of the Wabash River in 1678, according to his journal. In it, he proclaimed Palestine the "Land of Milk and Honey." He had become separated from the La Salle exploring party, who were French settlers looking for places to set up trading posts along the river. Some years later, the region was established with a French trading post.

In response to the Native American unrest, Fort LaMotte was constructed by Baptists between 1810 and 1812, and their meetings were held within its log walls. A few miles northwest, Fort Foot was also established by the Eatons when they moved out of Fort LaMotte. These were civilian frontier outposts, and the 90 rangers who were stationed there were under the command of Capt. Pierce Andrews.

Illinois was admitted to the union as a state on December 3, 1818, and the town was platted by Judge Joseph Kitchell and Edward N. Collum, with territorial court being held at Collum's home. After several attempts by others for a permanent structure, Presley Walters was contracted to build a courthouse/land office completed by him in December 1832. It quickly became a hub for Crawford County, parceling out land for a seemingly vast area. Land was sold to Abraham Lincoln's family through the office, and in February 1833, Robert Kinzie bought 102.29 acres for $127.86¼ as payment in full for the Chicago Loop, land that laid north of the Chicago River and east of State Street.

A portion of the original business district from the 1900s still stands and has been restored and listed in the National Register of Historic Places. The Fife Opera House is used as Palestine's historic center. An earlier opera house no longer stands. It was built by Robert A. Plunkett in 1891 on the southwest corner of the intersection of Main and Grand Prairie Streets, with 21-by-80-feet seating capacity, half the capacity of Fife's, at 350. Plunkett's Hall was not used for entertainment after Fife's was built across the street in 1898, and Fife's is still the tallest building in that district.

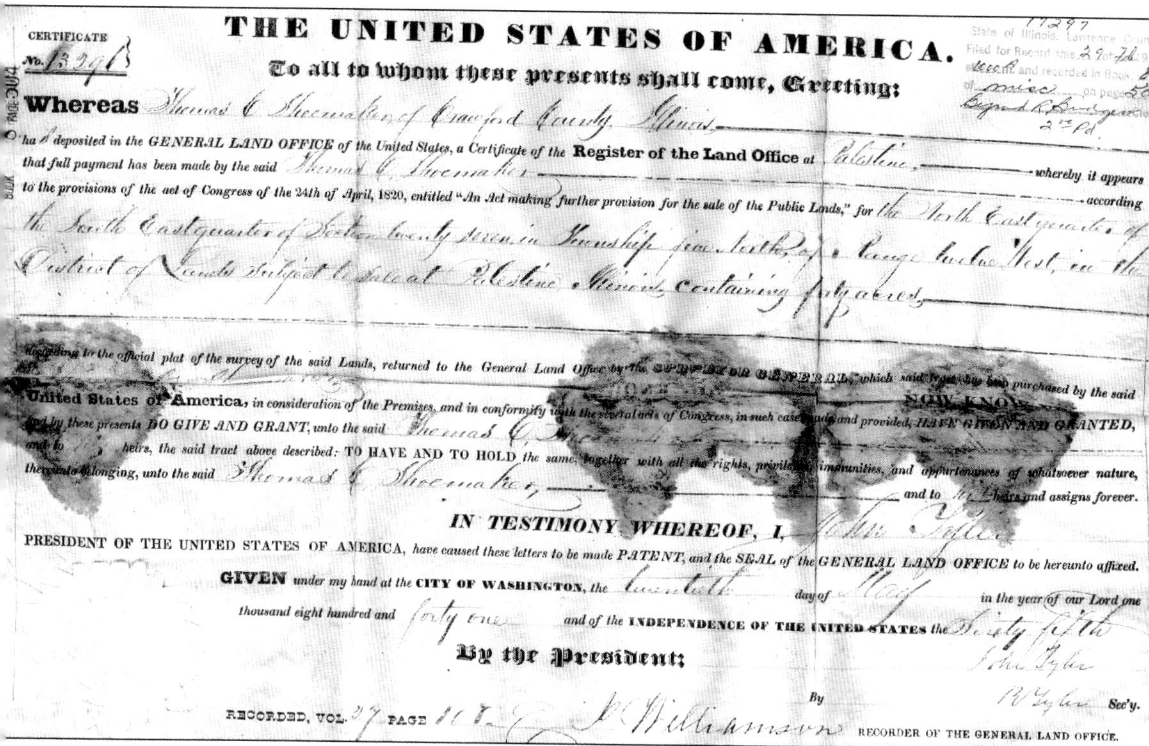

CERTIFICATE No. 13296

THE UNITED STATES OF AMERICA.

To all to whom these presents shall come, Greeting:

Whereas Thomas C. Shoemaker of Crawford County Illinois, has deposited in the GENERAL LAND OFFICE of the United States, a Certificate of the Register of the Land Office at Palestine, whereby it appears that full payment has been made by the said Thomas C. Shoemaker according to the provisions of the act of Congress of the 24th of April, 1820, entitled "An Act making further provision for the sale of the Public Lands," for the North East quarter of the South East quarter of Section twenty seven in Township five North of Range twelve West, in the District of Lands Subject to sale at Palestine Illinois, containing forty acres,

according to the official plat of the survey of the said Lands, returned to the General Land Office by the SURVEYOR GENERAL, which said tract has been purchased by the said Thomas C. Shoemaker

NOW KNOW YE, That the United States of America, in consideration of the Premises, and in conformity with the several acts of Congress, in such case made and provided, HAVE GIVEN AND GRANTED, and by these presents DO GIVE AND GRANT, unto the said Thomas C. Shoemaker and to his heirs, the said tract above described: TO HAVE AND TO HOLD the same, together with all the rights, privileges, immunities, and appurtenances of whatsoever nature, thereunto belonging, unto the said Thomas C. Shoemaker and to his heirs and assigns forever.

IN TESTIMONY WHEREOF, I, John Tyler PRESIDENT OF THE UNITED STATES OF AMERICA, have caused these letters to be made PATENT, and the SEAL of the GENERAL LAND OFFICE to be hereunto affixed.

GIVEN under my hand at the CITY OF WASHINGTON, the twentieth day of May in the year of our Lord one thousand eight hundred and forty one and of the INDEPENDENCE OF THE UNITED STATES the Sixty fifth

By the President: John Tyler

By R. Tyler Sec'y.

RECORDED, VOL. 27 PAGE 168 J. Williamson RECORDER OF THE GENERAL LAND OFFICE.

State of Illinois, Lawrence County. Filed for Record this 29 of Dec. and recorded in Book misc. on page

Palestine became the most important town in Illinois when the U.S. Land Office was located there in May 1820 and opened for business on July 23, 1821. Joseph Kitchell was the first registrar and receiver and parceled land out north, all of which was considered to be Madison County previously. There were several prominent men who served the office, among them, James McLean, Harmon Alexander, Guy W. Smith, David McGahey, and William and Robert C. Wilson. Augustus C. French (Joseph Kitchell's son-in-law), who became governor, served the land office from 1839 to 1842. This land sale certificate shows a sale of 40 acres to Thomas C. Shoemaker at $1.25 an acre for land in Lawrence County. The president's signature and his secretary, whose surname was also Tyler, is present. Before the official county courthouse/land office was built, record books, a desk, and money chest were kept in the home or place of business of the registrar. The land office was discontinued after the land had been entirely sold that lay south of the Danville district. By 1871, the only attorney that lived in Palestine was Judge J. C. Allen, but he only practiced in circuit courts. (JJ.)

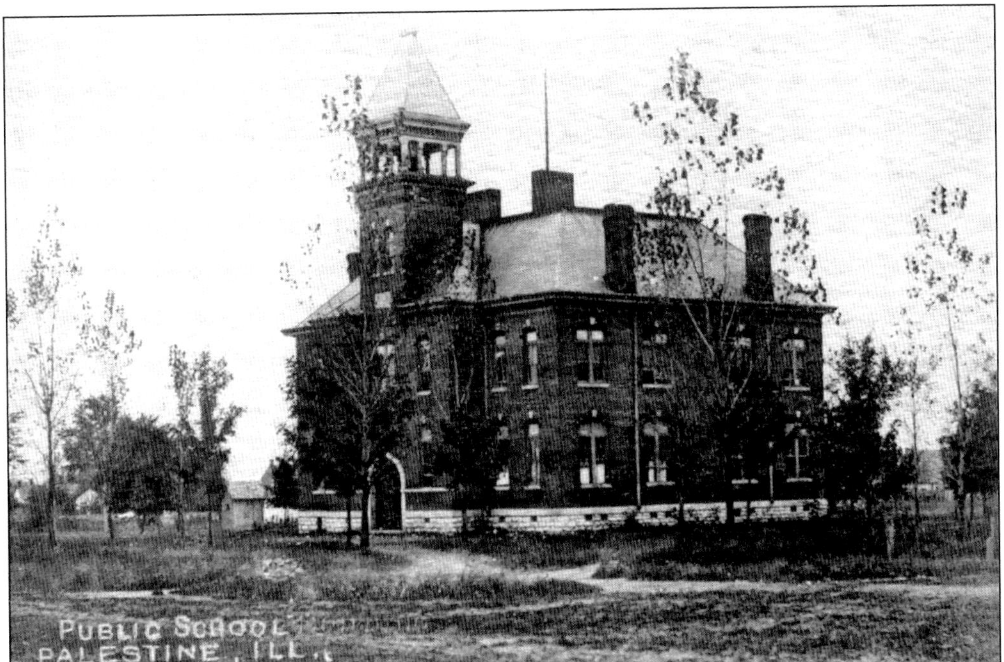

This two-story brick school was erected on the former site of the U.S. Land Office in 1892. It was built to replace the frame schoolhouse that was constructed only 20 years before, a short distance away. First- and second-grade classes continued to be held in the original frame building until 1920 because the school population increased after the railroad boom, which began in 1905. (SJ.)

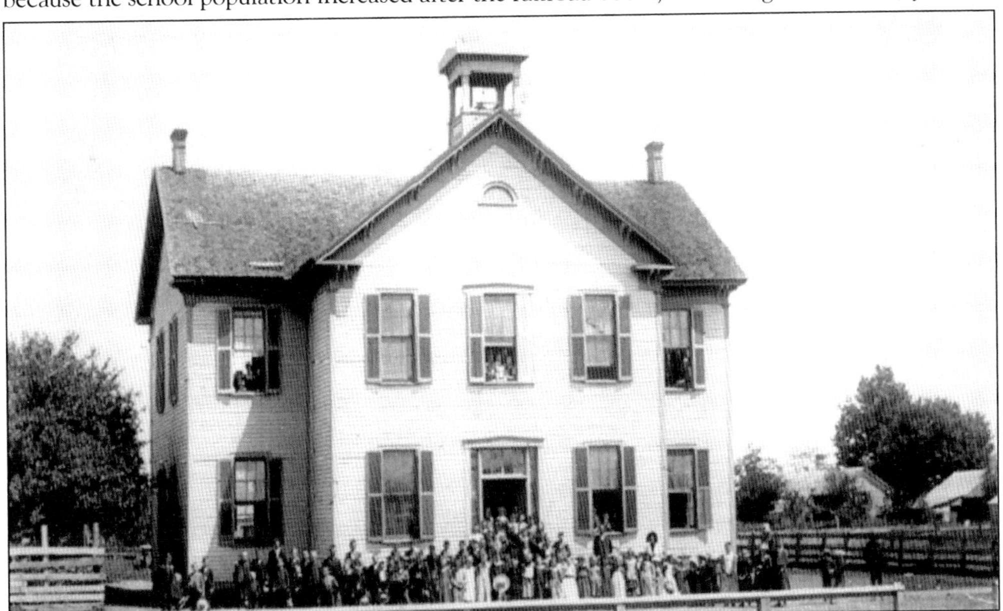

Prior to this first official elementary school, Palestine's youth were taught the rudiments in various buildings. This schoolhouse was built in 1872 and was located at the northeast corner of Main Street and Franklin Street. The principal, Orlando Greer Taylor, who was also a medical doctor, is standing among the students at the front entrance. When the new school building was finished, the bell tower was removed. (VF.)

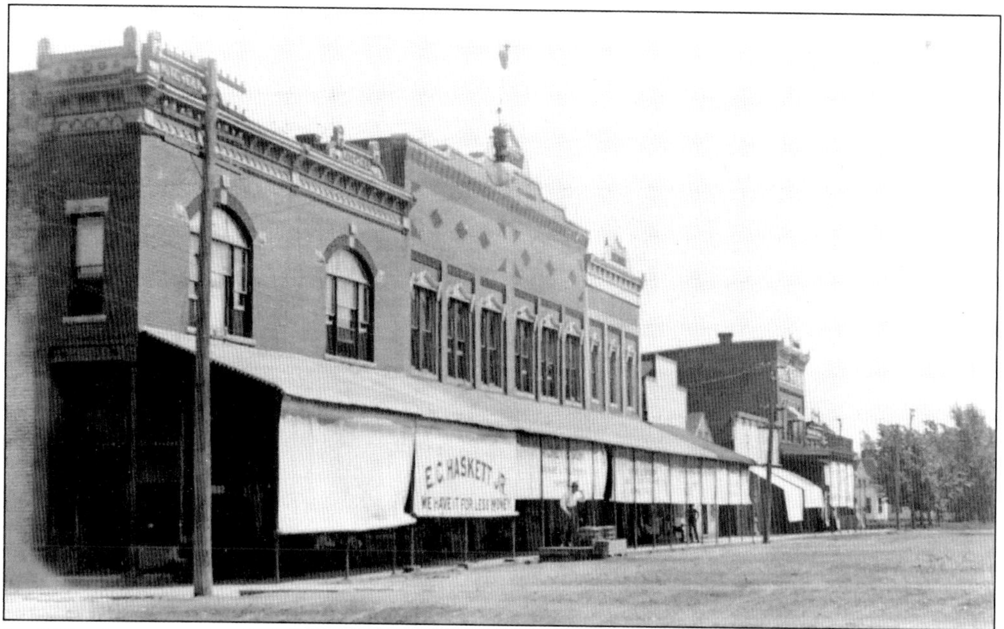

In 1873, the east side of Main Street had frame buildings and was a solid business district with the Boatwright store, Voke's Meat shop, Gus Fox General Store, and Purcell's Harness Shop, among many others. By 1900, as depicted in this photograph, the Kitchell building had changed the face of the second block. Dr. Orlando Greer Taylor built the northern half, and Ed Miller built the southern portion. Both men had married Kitchell daughters, Ola and Lena. (SJ.)

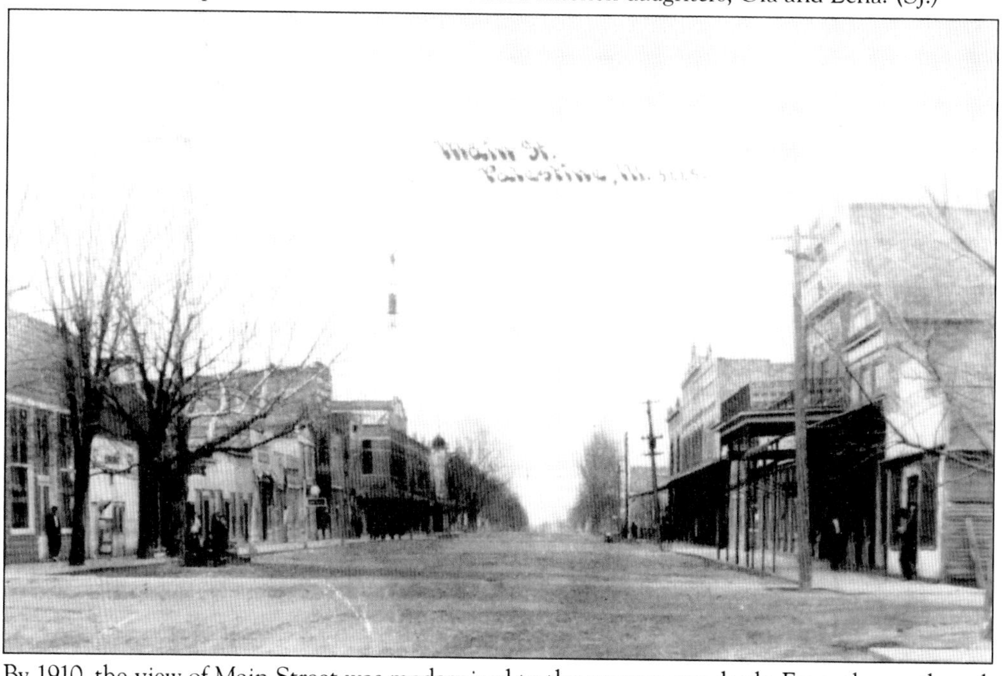

By 1910, the view of Main Street was modernized to the current standards. From the south end, all the major landmarks, some of which are still in existence, were in place. One exception was the Evening Star Theatre, the white building in the left foreground, which was the first nickelodeon in Palestine. (SJ.)

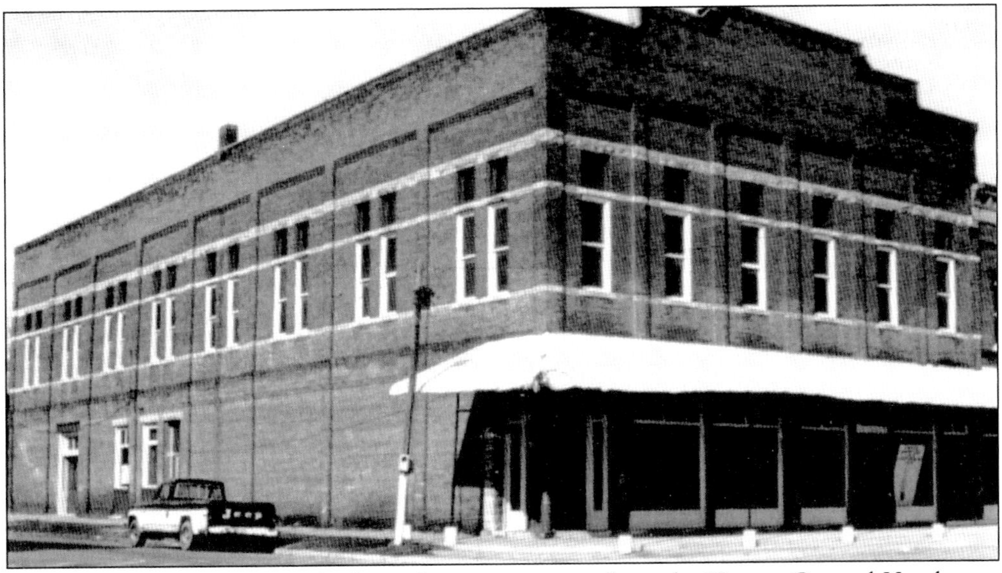

David Fife's opera house was built on the same corner where the Hunter Garrard Hotel once stood. His father was William Fife, an immigrant from Ireland, who met and married his wife Martha in Ohio, moved to Palestine in 1865, and had seven children. David graduated from Garvin Commercial College in Terre Haute, returned in 1893, and went into business with his brothers-in-law I. Buzzard and G. Dickinson. He bought them out in 1894. His opera house was completed in 1901 and is now the headquarters of the Palestine Preservation Project Society. (SJ.)

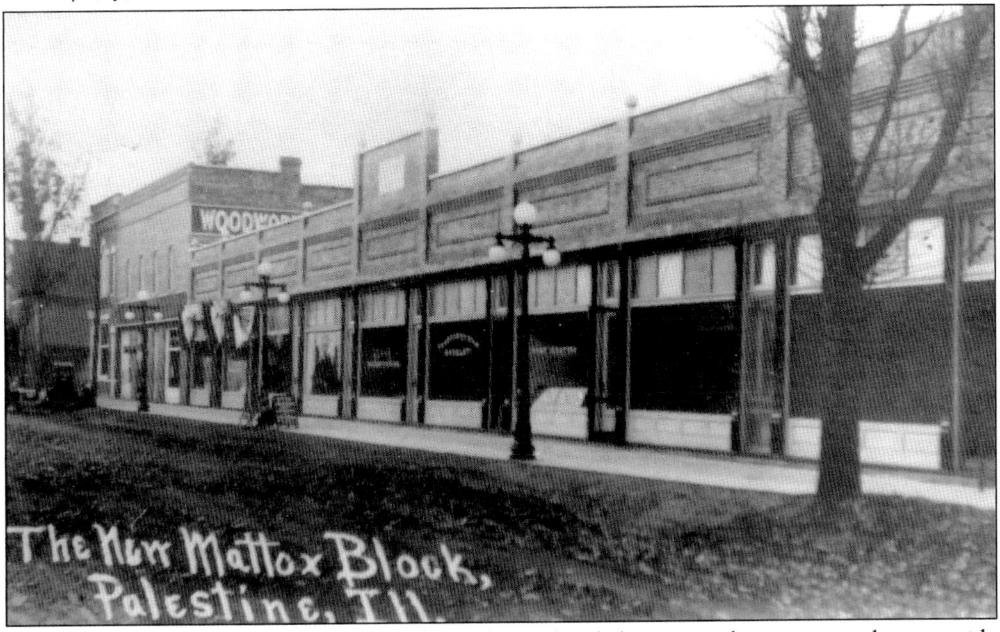

The addition of the new Mattox block (300) south of the original square on the east side comprised the First National Bank, Woodworth Motor Company, Royale Theatre (built 1921), McPherson's Bakery, and Sturgell's Ice Cream Parlor. It was built by Ed Mattox, who ran a meat market of his own on this block that was the best-equipped meat market in Crawford County. He married Lillie Heustis in 1895, and their home was on West Grand Prairie Street. (SJ.)

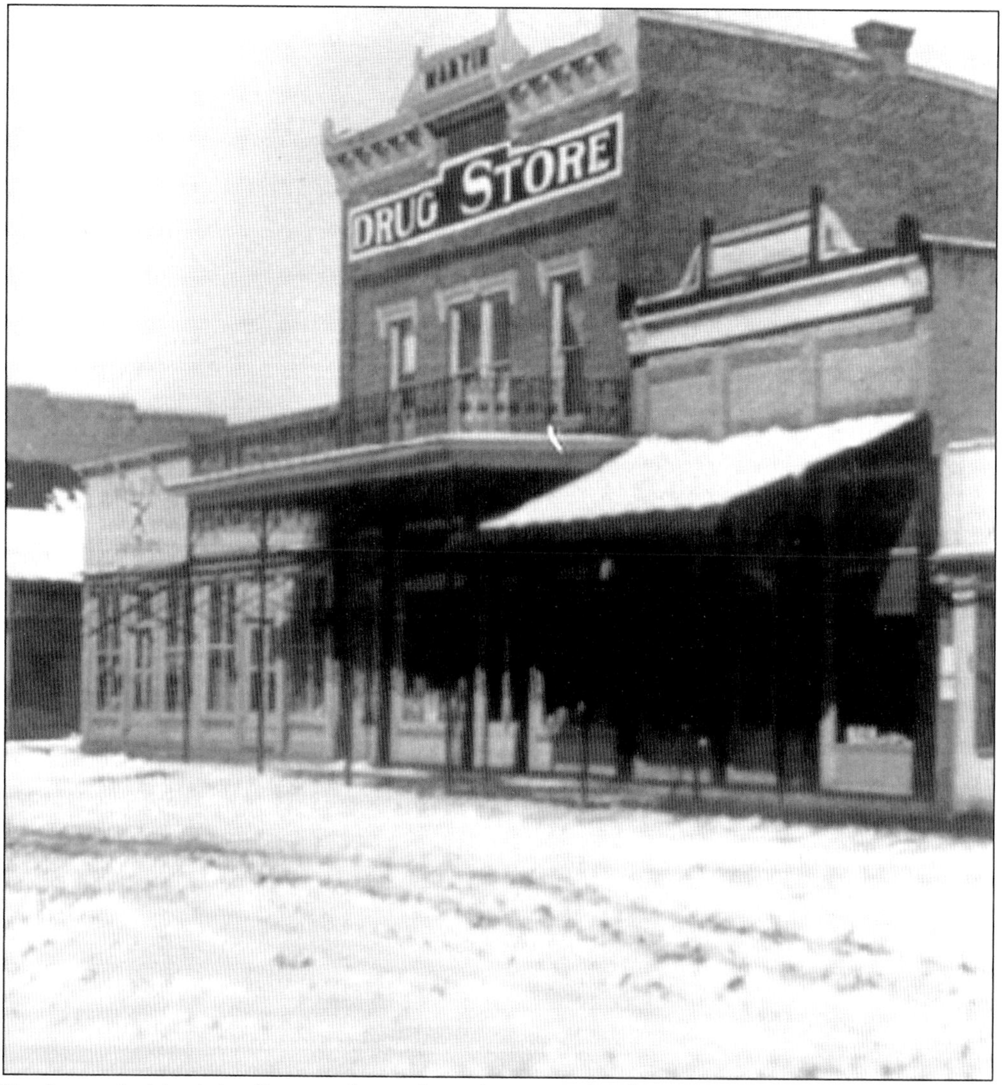

Dr. James A. Martin's office was located on the east side of Main Street, with the pharmacy, which he opened in 1888, on the ground floor. His brother, John, ran the pharmacy. At the age of 14, James clerked in a general store for three years and then attended medical school while apprenticing under Dr. T. N. Rafferty for a year and a half in Palestine. Dr. Martin was a popular doctor and was sorely missed after he died on February 26, 1916. (VF.)

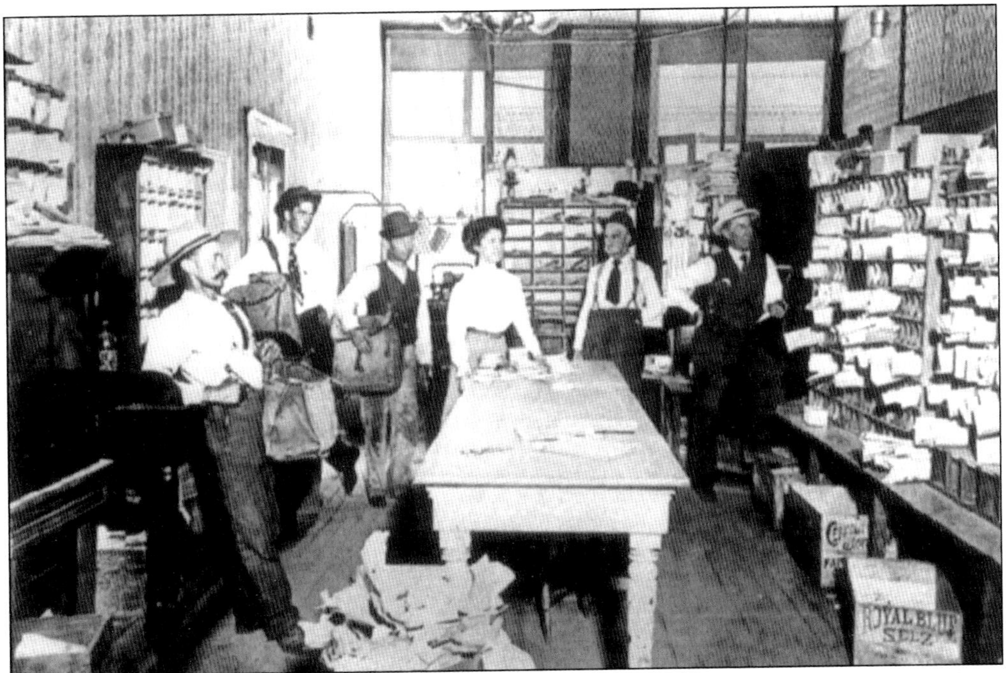

The original post office site was located on the north half of the Fife block between a clothing and shoe store and below a real estate/law office in a ground floor storefront operation. William Wilson was the first postmaster of Palestine. (VF.)

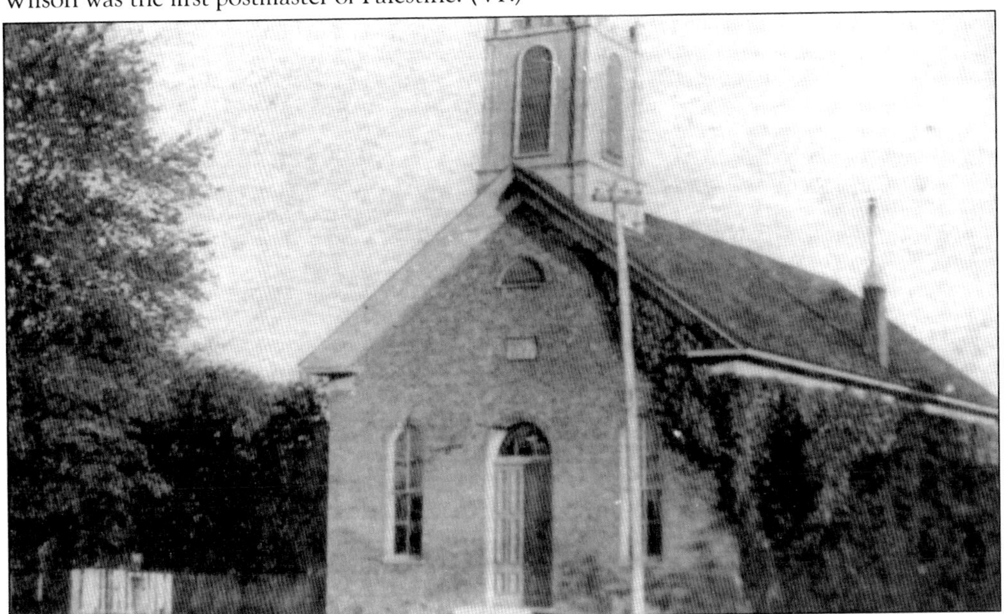

Erected in 1874 by members on East Grand Prairie Street, the First Christian Church was the second building after the first frame structure was destroyed by fire in 1855. The steeple bell was salvaged from a steamboat that sunk in the Wabash River. When a new church was built in 1916 at Jackson and Grand Prairie Streets, the church became the first indoor gymnasium for grade school students by 1918. After 1920, Fred Todd purchased it and used it as the office for the *Palestine Register* newspaper until December 31, 1964. (SJ.)

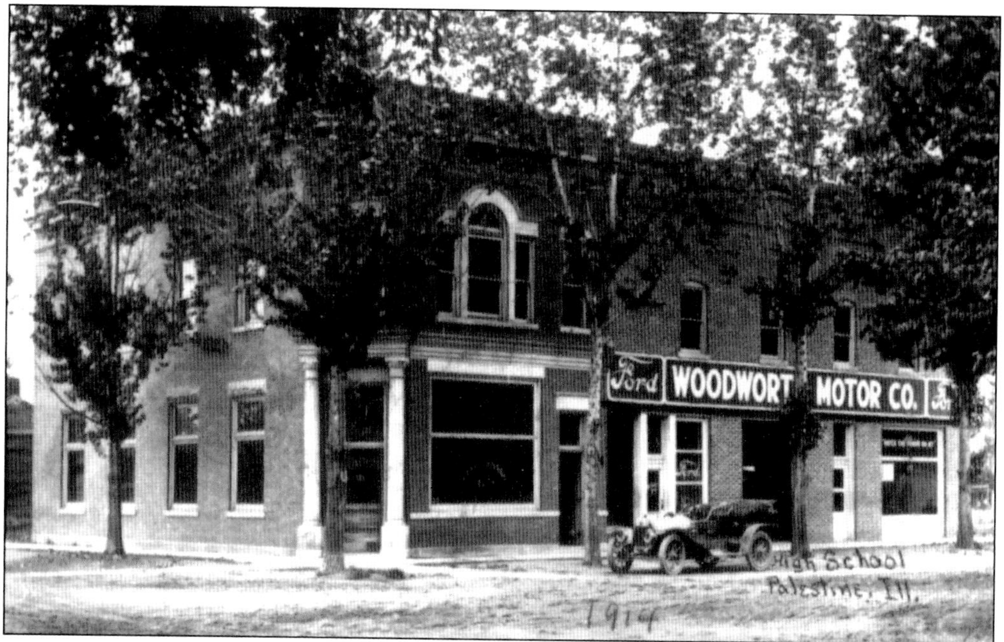

Dr. J. A. Ikemire's automobile is parked at the door to the building where his medical office was located. This structure also served as temporary classrooms for Palestine Township High School from 1914 to 1916, while a building was being constructed in the southwest corner of town. (VF.)

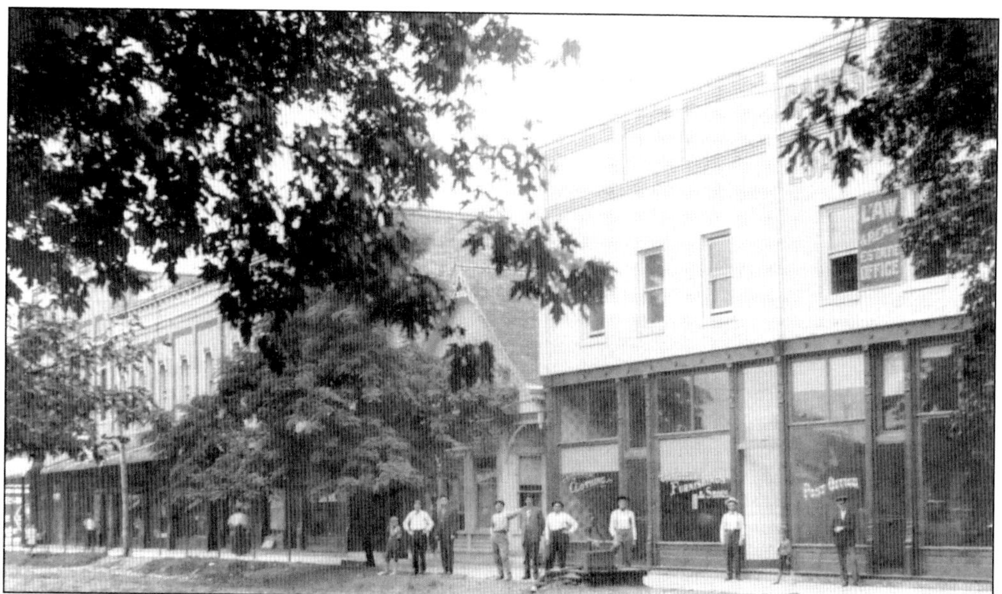

Fife's block was well named because on this first block on the west side of Main Street were the Fife Opera House, the Fife Bank, David and Alta Woodworth Fife's home, a dry goods store, the post office, and a real estate/law office above. The Palestine Bank was started by William and Robert Fife in 1899 and then reorganized later, including Matthew Fife on the board. They replaced David Fife's home into the middle of the square and built the Farmer's State Bank where it had been located. The facade of the Farmer's State Bank is striking and still stands today. (SJ.)

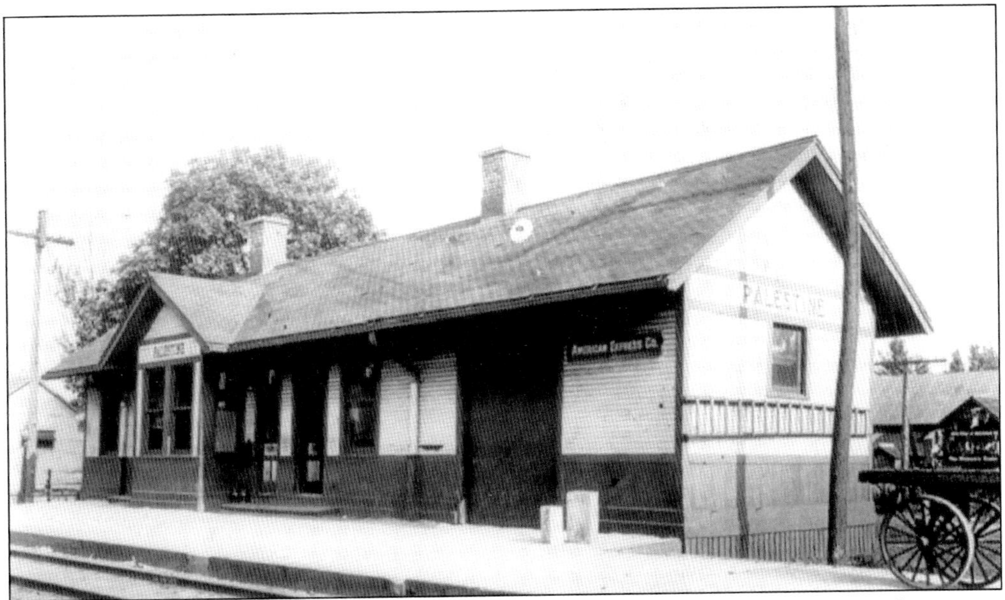

Passengers on the Illinois Central Railroad waited on this platform for ingoing and outgoing trains in 1910. The Illinois Central depot was built on the south side of the tracks between Main and Pike Streets. The Illinois Central ran three trains eastward and three trains westward each day, while Penn Central ran three trains south and three trains north each day. Chicago salesmen liked to go to Crawford County for a day, hustling business, and catch the red-eye back home overnight. (VF.)

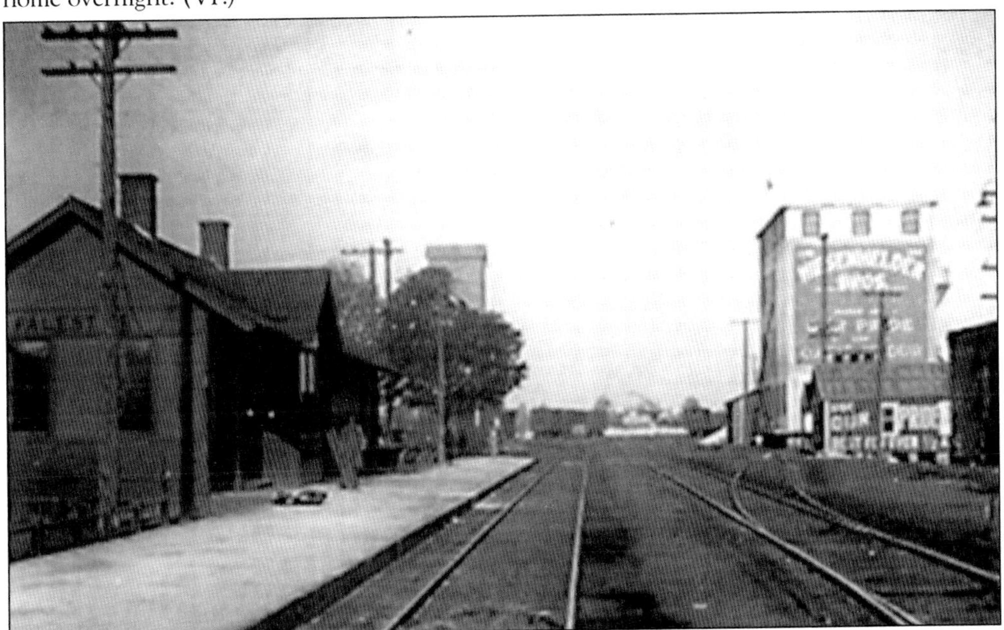

For many years, Palestine was of extreme importance along the Illinois Central division from Effingham to Indianapolis, as a trade route. Miesenhelder's mill enjoyed a longevity that has not yet been surpassed in Crawford County. It was established by the Condit family around 1850 as LaMotte Roller Mills and was bought by Amos Miesenhelder around the end of the Civil War. In 1915, the old mill was abandoned, and a new mill and elevator were built. (VF.)

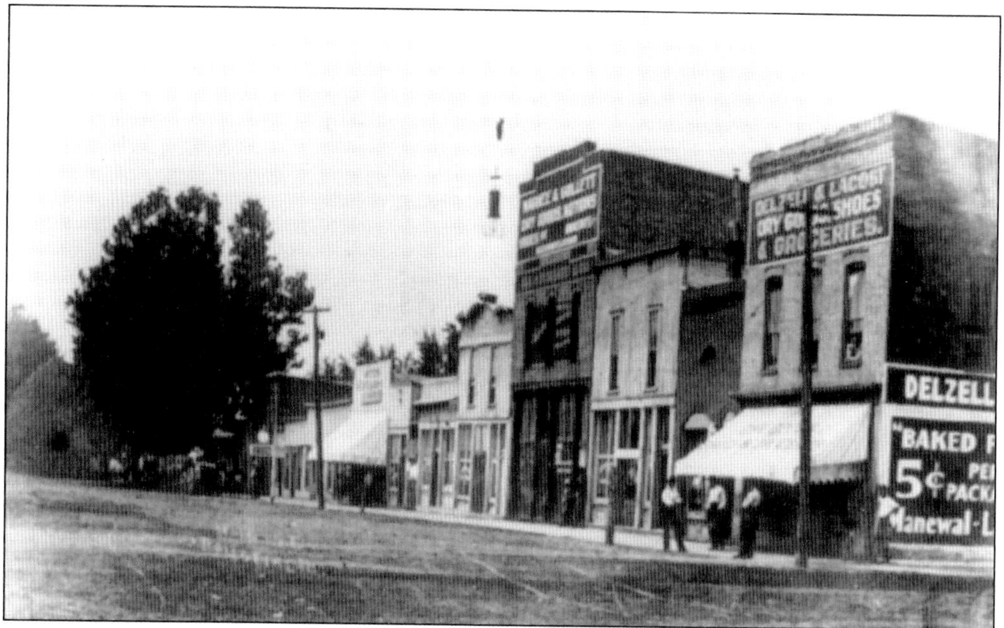

Facing the Kitchell block on the west side of Main Street were Delzell and Lacost, Ira Julian's Barber Shop, Harlan Haskett's (with Dr. Steele's office above), Markee and Gullett, Overholser and Hackett, Higgin's Meat Shop, Dietz Restaurant, and several other smaller businesses. In 1908, a fire leveled several of these businesses, but they were rebuilt later. (VF.)

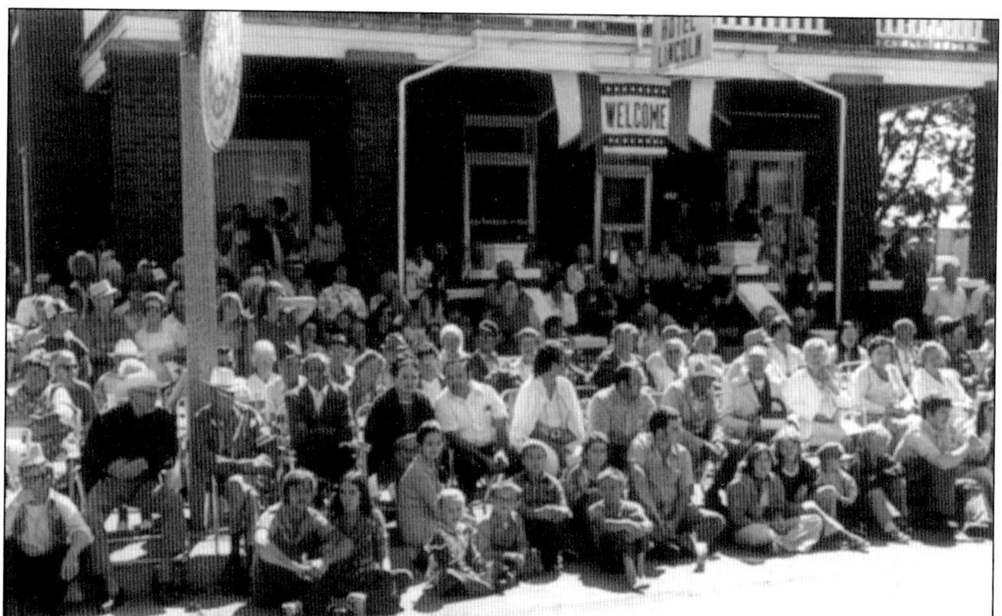

A Labor Day crowd is gathered in front of the Lincoln Hotel in this 1976 photograph at the corner of Main and Market Streets. This was the previous site of the Catterton Hotel. A doctor's office adjoined the south end of the Catterton Hotel, and William Catterton also owned a livery stable, extending the hotel to nearly a full block length. The hotel burned down on March 4, 1925. The Lincoln Hotel, pictured here, burned down on April 25, 1990. (VF.)

Auntie Gogin started out life as Mary Ewell. She married Enoch Gogin, who was the son of Thomas, one of the founding members and actual builder of Palestine's Wesley Chapel. Mary was a devoted church worker and a businesswoman. She bought lots 116 and 121, which were in the Kitchell block, to start her store, the Millinery, and was the first woman in Illinois to own and operate her own business. (VF.)

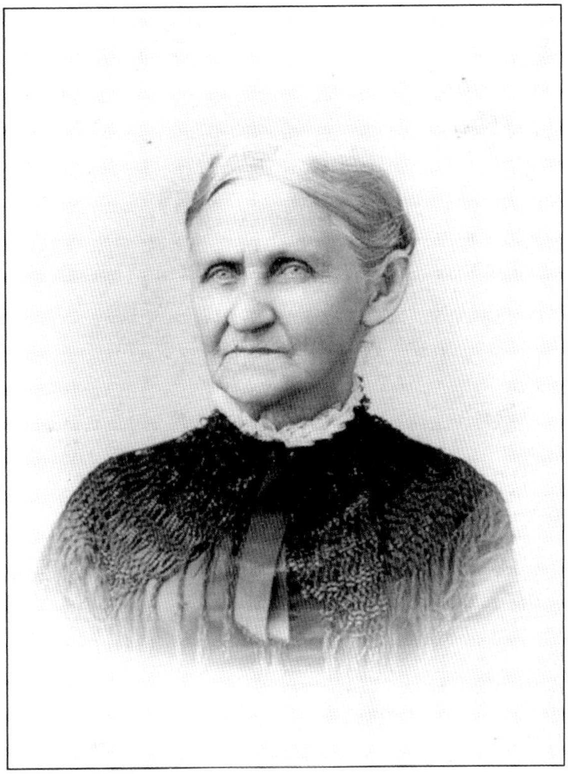

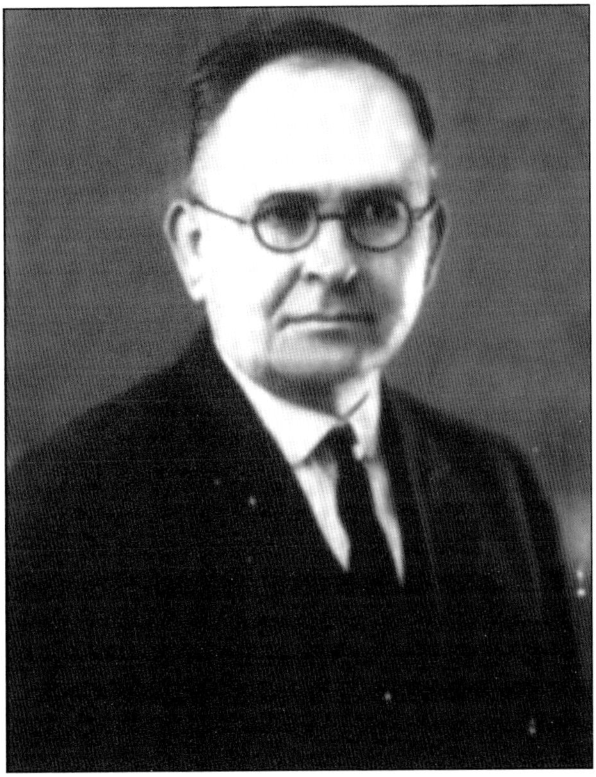

As president of the school board, J. A. Ikemire made provision for his office building on West Grand Prairie Street to provide temporary high school classes. They were held in rooms above the Woodworth Motor Company during the 1916–1917 school year. (VF.)

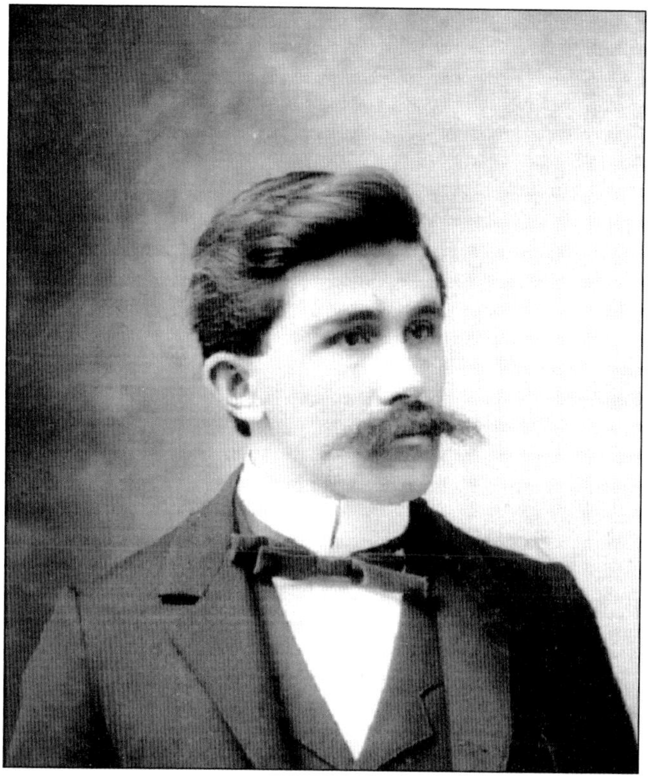

Dr. Levi Roscoe Illyes, born on December 22, 1872, was an obstetrician in Palestine and Heathsville from 1903 to the 1940s, but his career span was from 1898 to 1951. Illyes retired shortly before he died on June 12, 1952. (VF.)

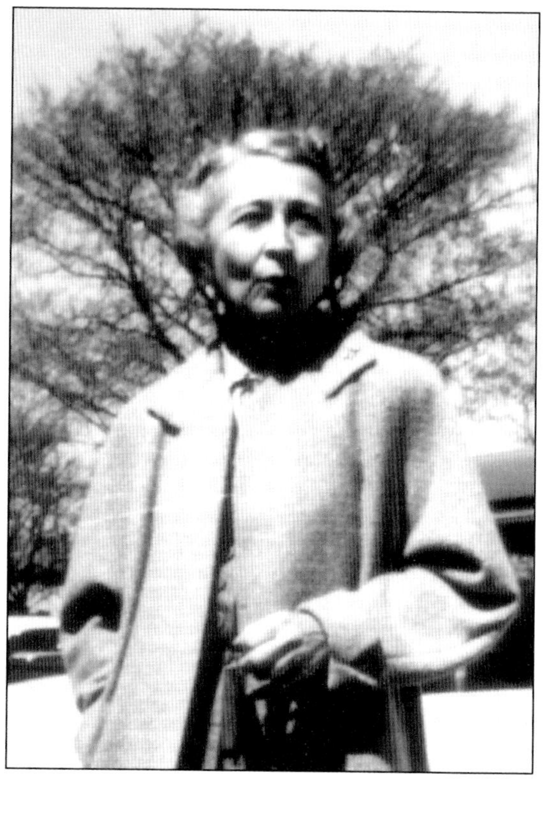

The daughter of J. A. Ikemire, Marjorie Louise, also practiced medicine in Palestine and in Vincennes, Indiana, as an allergist. In high school, Marjorie had been the tops on the debating team. She worked in her father's clinic and lived in Palestine all her life. (VF.)

Orlando Greer Taylor, born on November 1, 1862, started as principal of the frame grade school and then became superintendent of schools and married Ola Kitchell. He became trustee for the village board and was responsible for the establishment of all the major public works. He practiced medicine for 50 years and died on December 30, 1943. His son, John R. Taylor, practiced medicine in Palestine for 52 years and was an accomplished organist at the Presbyterian church. (VF.)

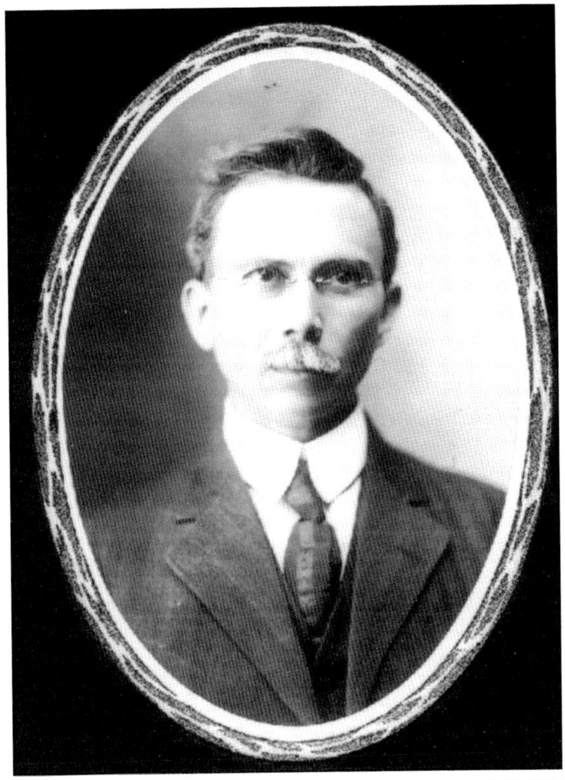

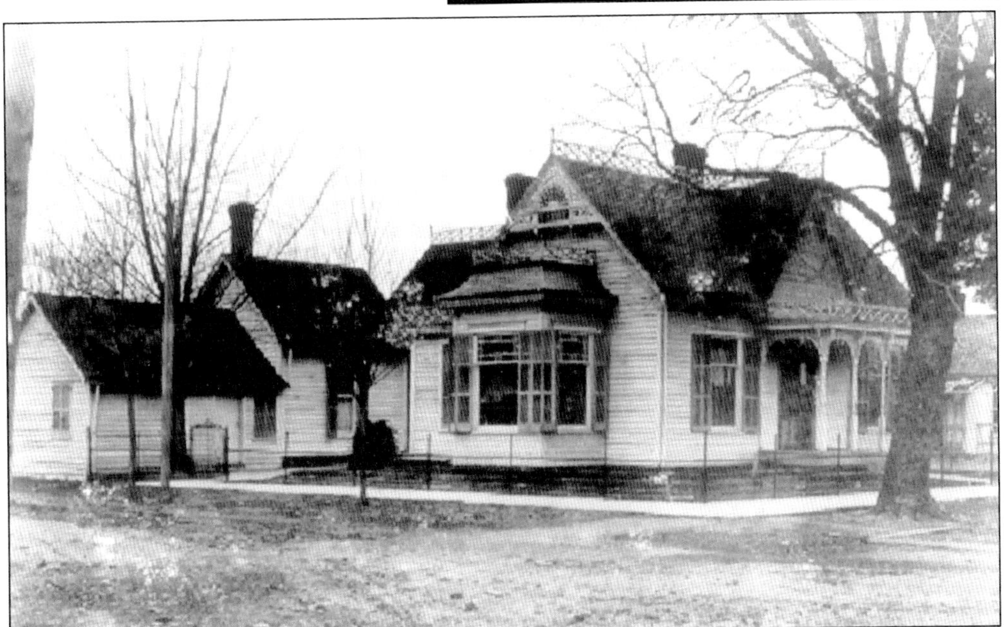

Many frame homes, like Dr. James A. Martin's from 1907, still stand in Palestine. Martin's home is at the northwest corner of Main Street and LaMotte Street. Martin was born in Barren County, Kentucky, on January 1, 1856, and came to Palestine with his parents in 1864. He finished medical college in Cincinnati, Ohio, in 1879, returned to Palestine, married Elizabeth Fife in October 1884, and set up a medical practice and pharmacy on Main Street. (VF.)

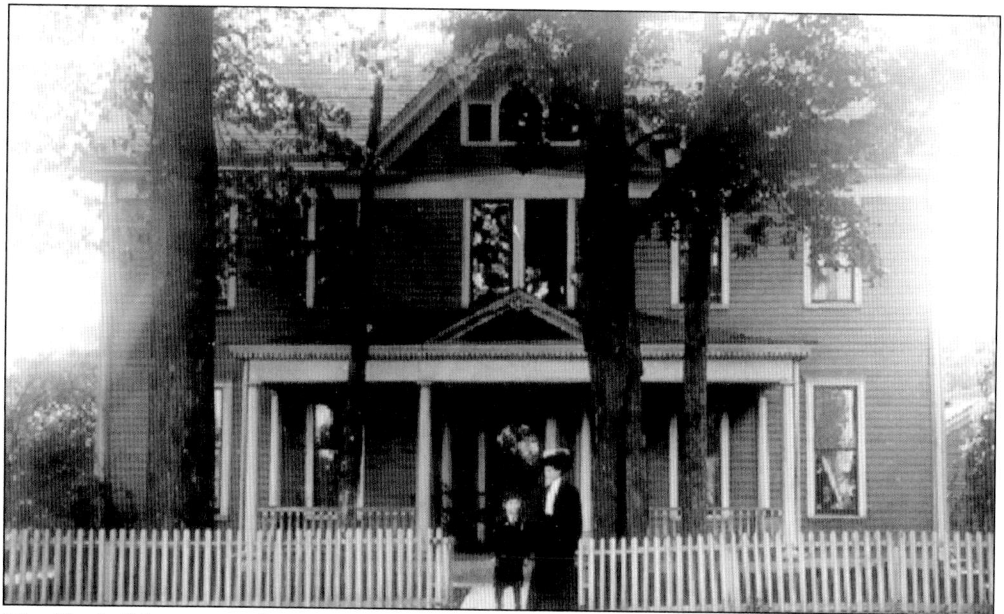

The Kitchell home stood at Main and LaMotte Streets and was one of the grander homes in Palestine. Standing out front at the gate is grandma Rachel Kitchell and grandson Miles Miller. Rachel was born on May 17, 1788, and died in 1867 at age 79. She is buried in the Kitchell cemetery. The family kept a general store on Main Street through three generations. Their store, Kitchell and Company, was last operated by Milo Haskett Kitchell, who died in 1947. (VF.)

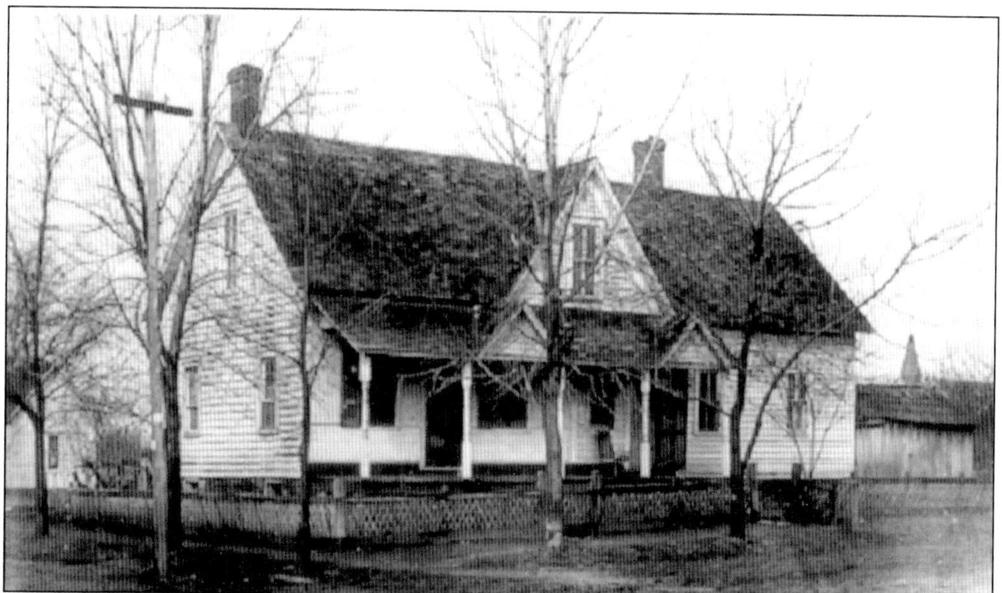

Augustus C. French's home in town once stood at the northwest corner of Pike and Grand Prairie Streets. It was built in 1845, shortly before French began to serve his first term as governor of Illinois. Prior to that, this New Hampshire native served as state representative for Illinois in the 10th and 11th general assemblies. He married Clarissa Kitchell on October 15, 1839, at the age of 31. Two years later, a son was born to them, but Clarissa died four months after giving birth, and by August 1, 1841, the baby died as well. Both are buried in the Kitchell cemetery. (VF.)

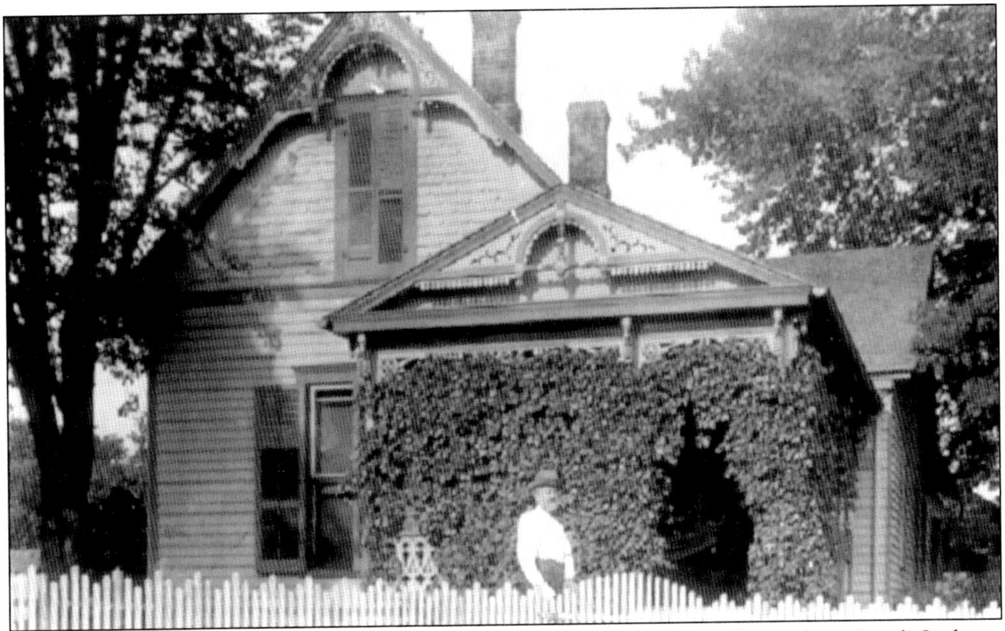

Amos Miesenhelder is shown standing outside his home, which was located on South Jackson Street on the east side. As owner of Miesenhelder Mill, he ran a 24-hour operation, milling wheat and corn. (VF.)

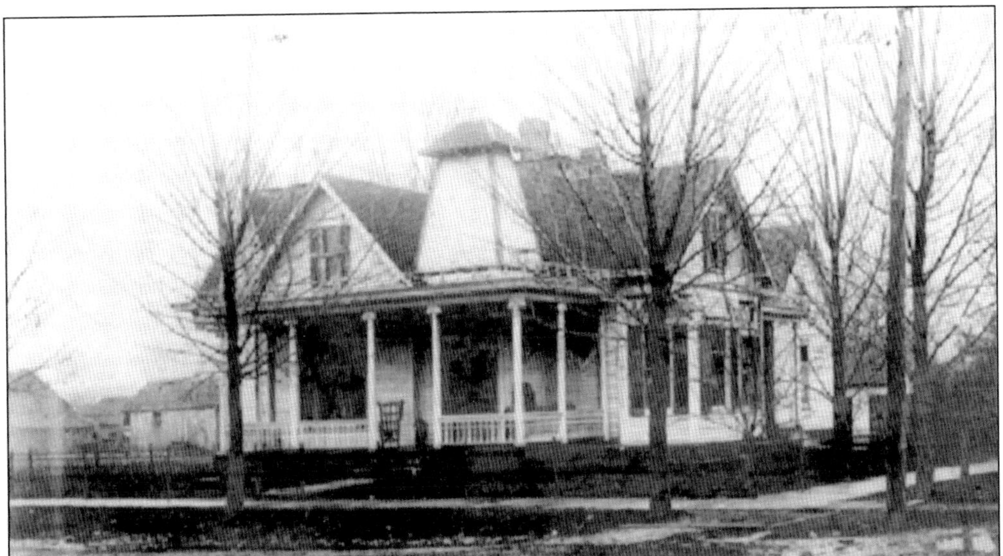

This was Robert Fife's first home, which was located on the northeast corner of Main Street and LaMotte Street. Later on, the Fifes had bigger and more palatial homes built on South Main Street. The homes of Mattie Fife Hughes, Robert, and Mathew Fife were within a very short walking distance. The Fife family also gained possession of Maplewood, Augustus C. French's country home, south of Palestine. (VF.)

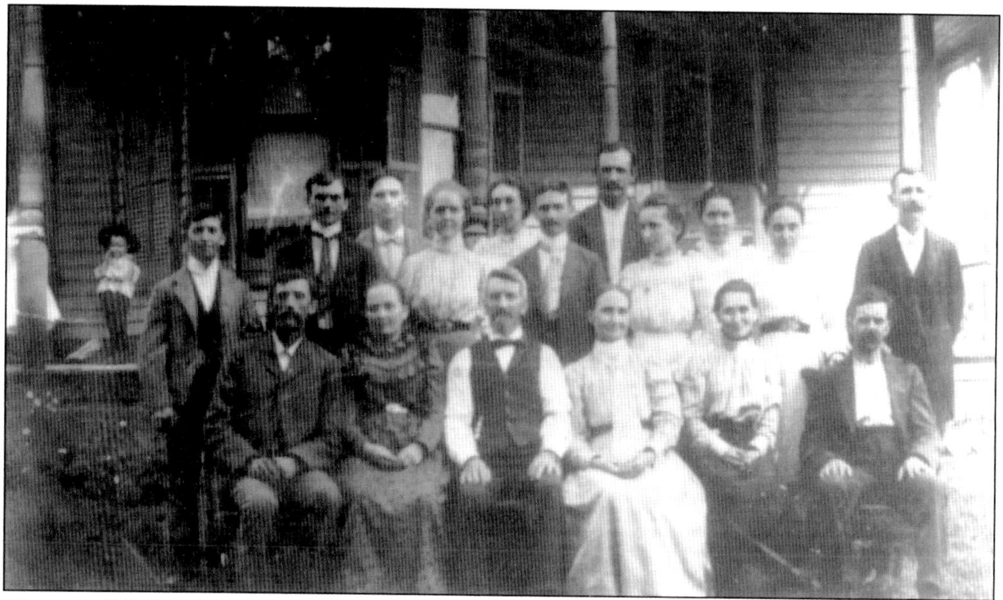

This is a Fife family portrait taken at Robert Fife's home. From left to right are (first row) Ira Buzzard, Jennie Fife Buzzard, William Fife, Martha Fife, Anna Fife Dickinson, and George Dickinson Sr.; (second row) William Fife Jr., Matthew Fife, Ora (Welsh) Fife, Robert Fife, Inez Fife, Elizabeth "Lizzie" Fife Martin, and James A. "Jim" Martin; (third row) David Fife, Alta Fife, James Marian Hughes, and Martha Fife Hughes. Little George Dickinson Jr. is standing on the porch with another child, who is hiding behind a porch rail. (VF.)

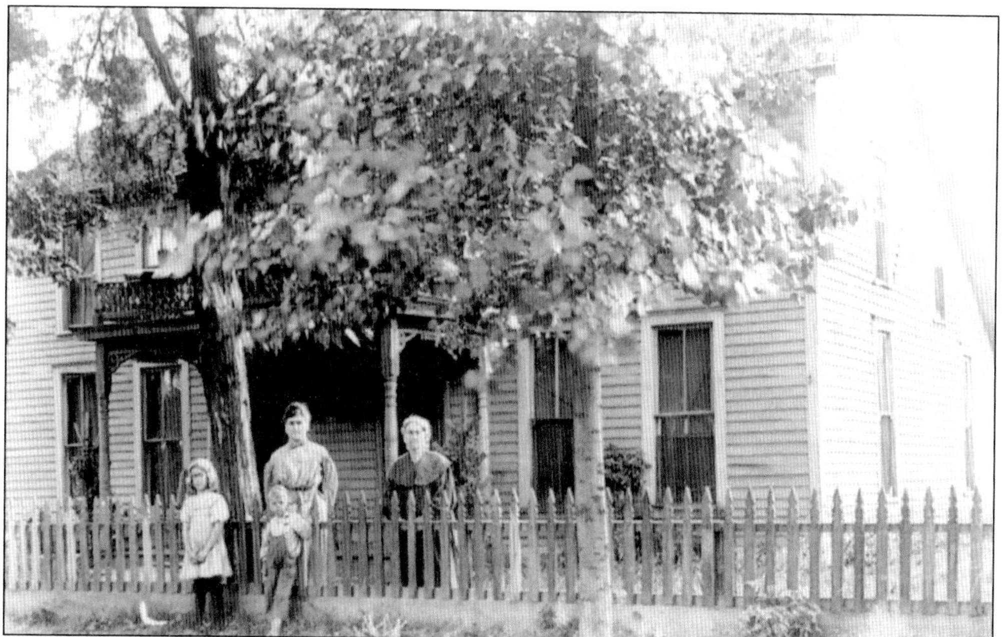

When this house, which was called "the old Beam place," was being torn down, they discovered an old log cabin underneath the exterior and estimated it to be around 150 years old. The owner at that time was Jim Gullett, who found the original size was 15 by 18 feet, built of hewn poplar logs and fastened with handmade iron nails. (VF.)

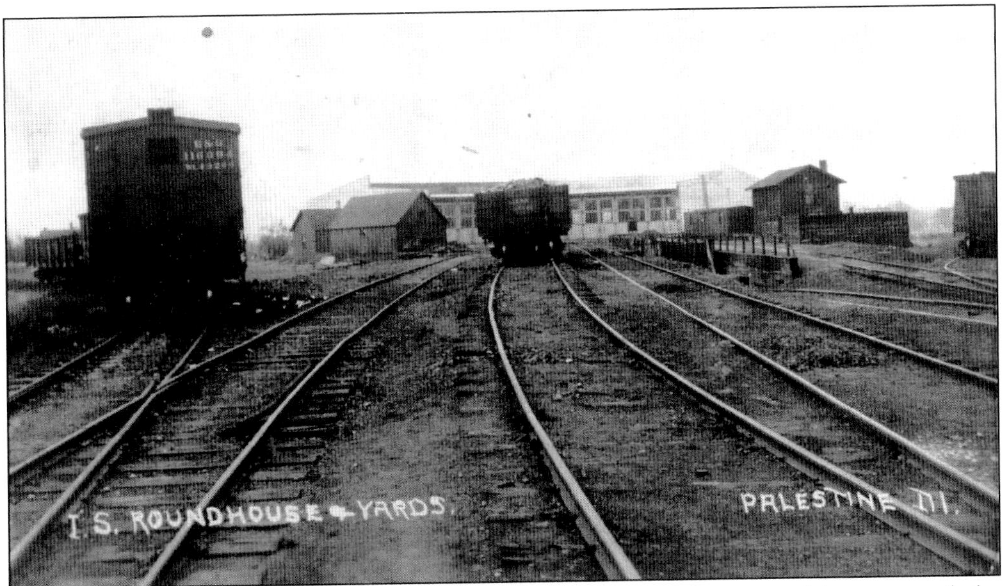

The first railroad roundhouse for Crawford County was in Palestine and incorporated the Indianapolis Southern. It was built between 1885 and 1887 and had 12 stalls where 180 men worked around the clock keeping the steam engines repaired and ready to be sent out. By 1955, the diesels were taking over, and the use of repairmen dwindled, eliminating the need for the roundhouse, which was later torn down. (BM.)

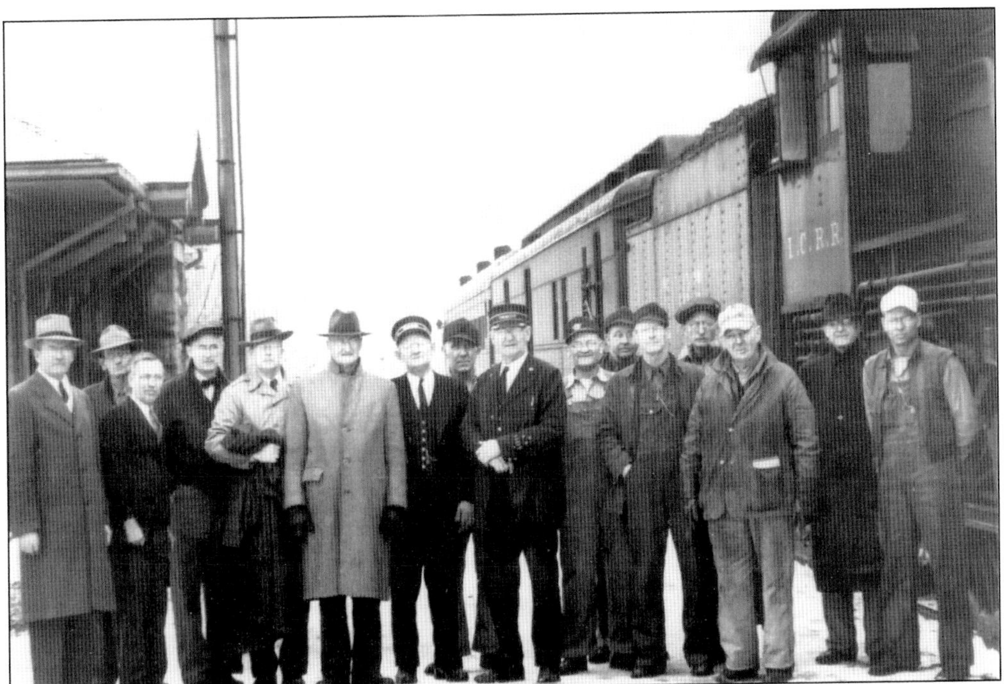

Pictured next to the last run from Palestine to Indianapolis (the 5065 about 1945 or 1946) are the engineer, conductors, and mechanics. The men in business attire are Palestine and Illinois Central Railroad executives. Well-known names of repairmen and mechanics were the Lougherys and Elders. (BM.)

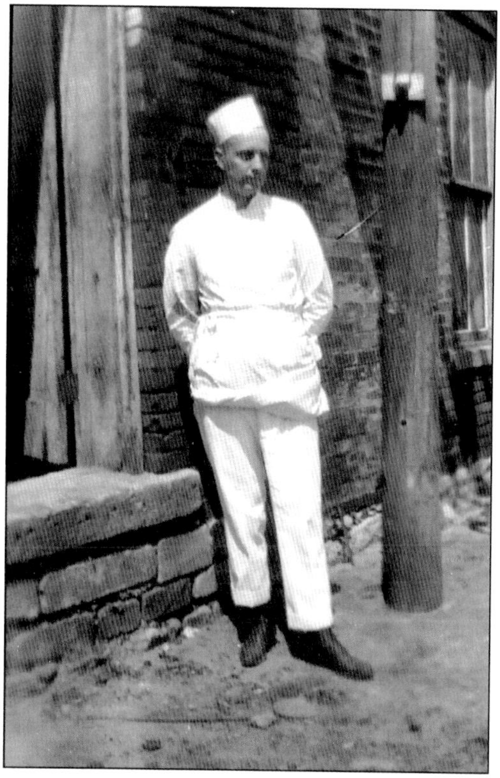

When John D. Mullen left Clark County, Illinois, at the age of 14 in the early 1900s, he had his eye on fortune and took up the trade of chef. During World War I, he served as a cook in Tours, France, where he discovered a special dressing at a café and liked it so well he began spending his free time working at the café to learn the ingredients. Mullen's Imitation French Dressing is a result of his discoveries and experimentation, and it has not been changed since 1926. (J. D. Mullen Company.)

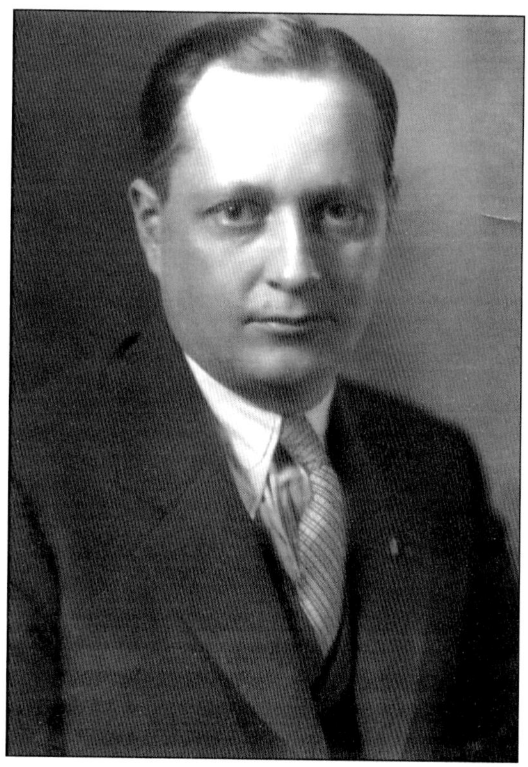

After the war, Mullen returned to Illinois, where he owned a succession of restaurants, all of which served the special dressing he had concocted, which resulted in patrons' questions about where they could buy the dressing and have it on their tables at home. In 1948, he opened the manufacturing and bottling plant located in the storefront on Main Street in Palestine. He ran the specialty company to great success until 1963, when he sold out to new owners. (J. D. Mullen Company.)

Clara Mullen was a schoolteacher in Robinson for 30 years. She was born in Sheffield and graduated from the university in Urbana. She met John D. Mullen in Robinson and married him on Christmas Eve in 1946. They made their home in Robinson on North Allen Street. They did not have children, and Clara passed away in 1991. (J. D. Mullen Company.)

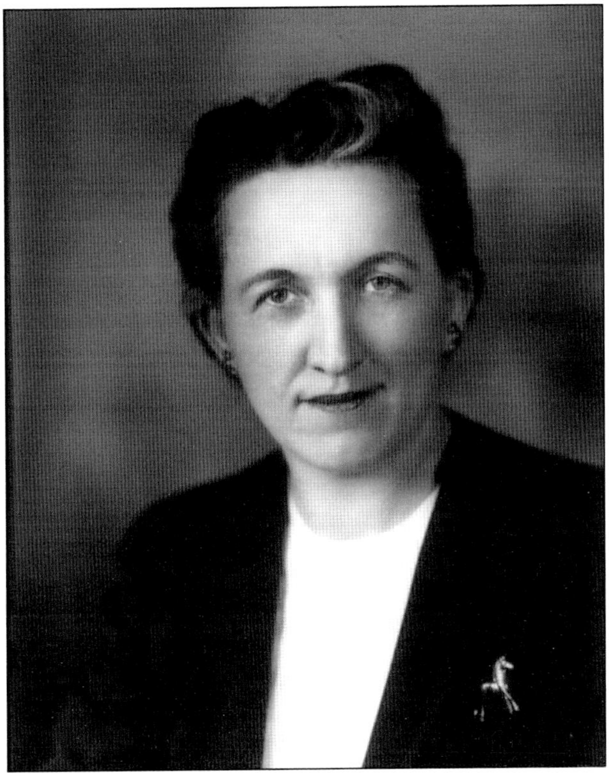

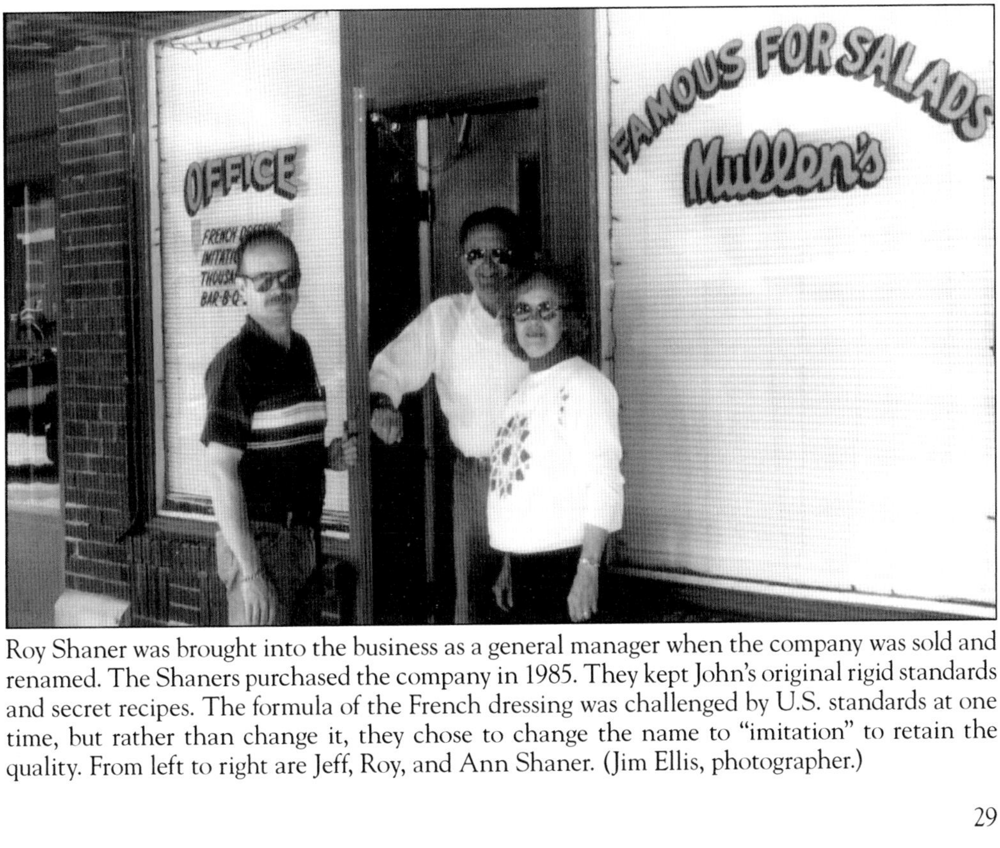

Roy Shaner was brought into the business as a general manager when the company was sold and renamed. The Shaners purchased the company in 1985. They kept John's original rigid standards and secret recipes. The formula of the French dressing was challenged by U.S. standards at one time, but rather than change it, they chose to change the name to "imitation" to retain the quality. From left to right are Jeff, Roy, and Ann Shaner. (Jim Ellis, photographer.)

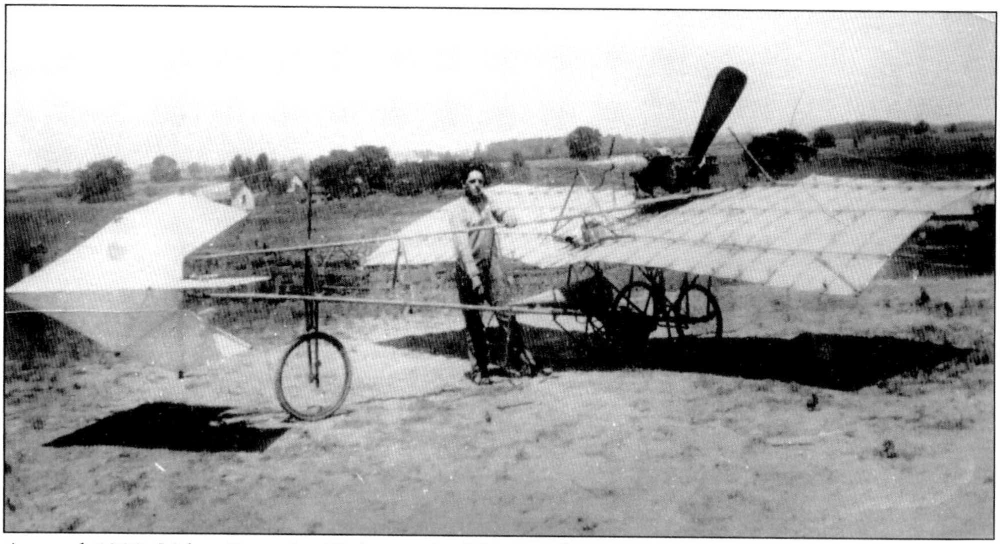

Around 1909, Usher Rousch, 17, began building and testing his first aircraft as a pioneer in aviation, even though he started quite a few years after the Wright brothers. At the time, the Rousches had not actually witnessed aircraft—flying or otherwise. Usher, Charles, and Berl all had a natural inclination for flying and had lots of success with their biplanes. Each met with tragedy, but Berl survived his plane crash and was left crippled. He never lost his interest in flying, however. (Emogene and Cheryl Mefford.)

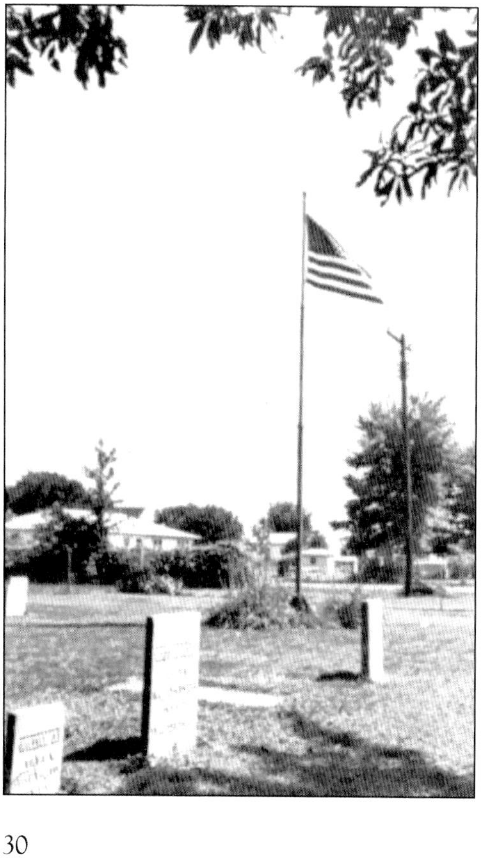

The old Kitchell cemetery's most famous occupant is Othniel Looker, who was a soldier in the Revolutionary War and the fifth governor of Ohio. Many people lovingly referred to him as "General." In 1844, he moved to Palestine to live with his daughter and her husband, Judge Joseph Kitchell. Many Kitchells are buried there, including Clarissa with baby John J. French. It is located in the southern residential part of Palestine. (JJ.)

Two

Robinson
Movers and Shakers

William C. Baker was responsible for surveying and platting what became the town square for Robinson late in the year of 1843. William C. Wilson of Palestine donated the 80 acres of land it required. At that time, it was prairie land with two homes, covered over with underbrush and very few trees.

Baker finished his labors on December 25, 1843, and the first lots were sold to Francis Waldrop. More sales followed suit, and a business hub was born. The county seat was then moved to Robinson in a small frame building north of the square as a temporary courthouse. A jailhouse made of logs was moved from Palestine. Later two brick structures were completed in 1845, and the courthouse north of the square and a brick jail replaced the old structures. Finally, a wonderful Gothic-style courthouse was placed in the middle of the town square as the permanent courthouse for Crawford County in 1896.

Out of the office of William C. (W. C.) Jones, Ethelbert Callahan, Alfred H. (A. H.) Jones, and J. C. Maxwell, improvements were made for which the city of Robinson can be eternally grateful. These men, along with several other prominent citizens, brought in the Big Four Railroad in 1871, built the beautiful Methodist Episcopal church, organized the First National Bank, and built the south side high school, the 1896 courthouse, the Carnegie Library, the post office (1916), and a telephone system. The city's first hospital was established by six of the best physicians in the city, namely Drs. T. N. Rafferty, C. E. Price, Isaac L. Firebaugh, Jonas W. and Betsy Carlisle, and LeRoy Newlin in 1908.

Ethelbert Callahan wrote a vision of the future of Robinson that rivaled that of Chicago's final achievement: "Twill be but a question of time until Robinson will spread over a vast area of our agricultural land . . . from chaos to a land of paradise—when we get gas." What they may not have achieved in size has been made up for in the quality of life.

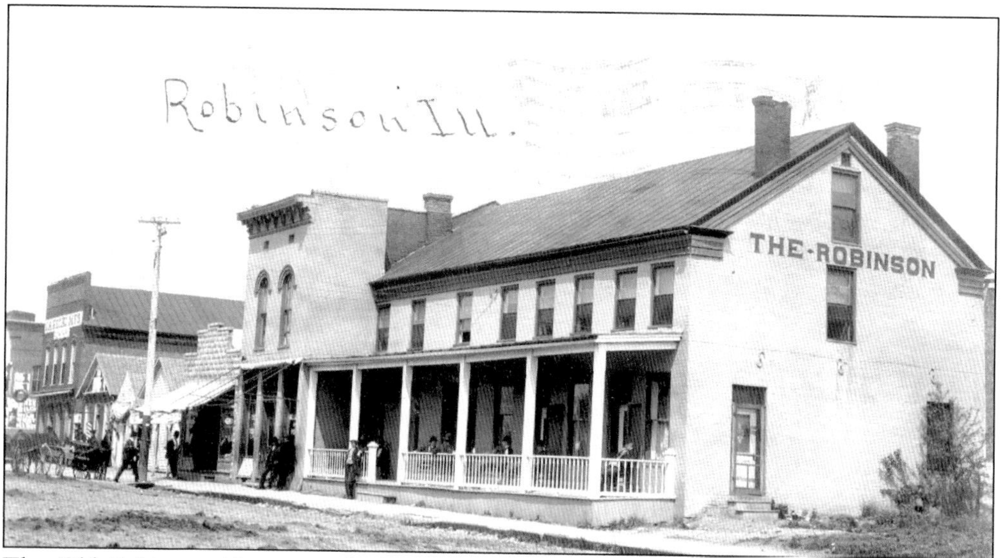

The Old Robinson House was built in 1800 by Thomas Barbee and was the best-known landmark on East Main Street. It had a wide porch and spacious rooms and was a competitor at that time to the Commercial Hotel, which was owned by Rose Biggs of Hutsonville. In the late 1800s, two managers of the Old Robinson House, A. B. Houston and Tom H. Griggs, went on to greater prominence. From left to right are Jimmy Sutfin, Harry Condit, Frank ?, M. M. Huston (manager), an unidentified youth, Paul Fisher, Tom Wilson, Dan ?, Nels Barley, and Frank Alexander. (SJ.)

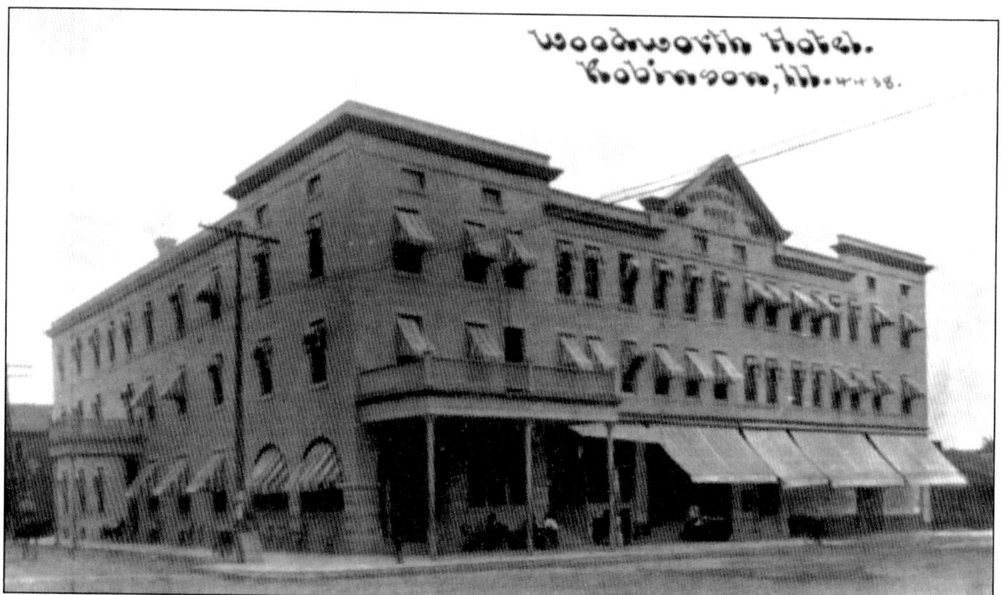

The Woodworth Hotel was one of the earliest hotels in Robinson, and its longevity was impressive. Built by Abner Palmer (A. P.) Woodworth, a pioneer banker, it housed such dignitaries as Eleanor Roosevelt. Woodworth had once clerked for John Lagow and went on to various business partnerships with him and enjoyed many successes. By 1902, he had become president of the Oil, Gas and Coke Company and owned one of the largest homes in the county. On January 28, 1979, the hotel was gutted by a fire. (SJ.)

A Victorian Gothic courthouse built in 1896 was the most elegant and capacious structure ever built in the county. In Ethelbert Callahan's words, "It was a monument to a wise and progressive county board and also shows the excellent taste of the citizens of the county." It definitely inspired some of the most progressive attorneys in the United States, not the least of which was Ethelbert Callahan himself, being revered by his peers for his honor and courtesy and setting a precedent for all. (SJ.)

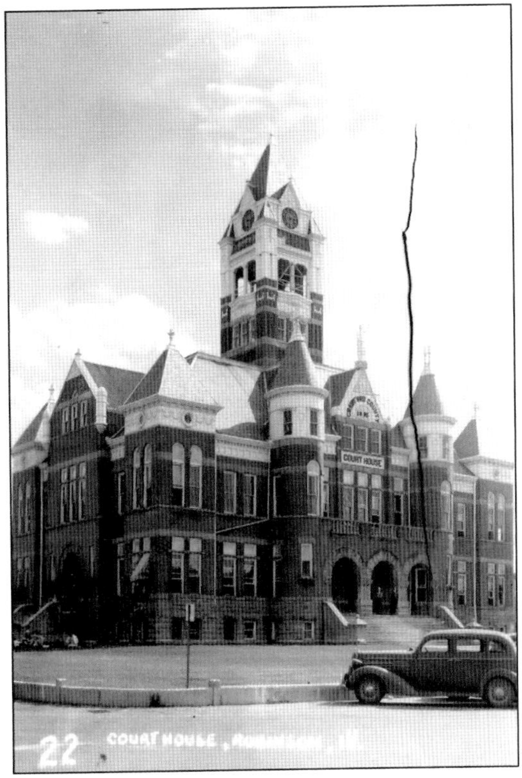

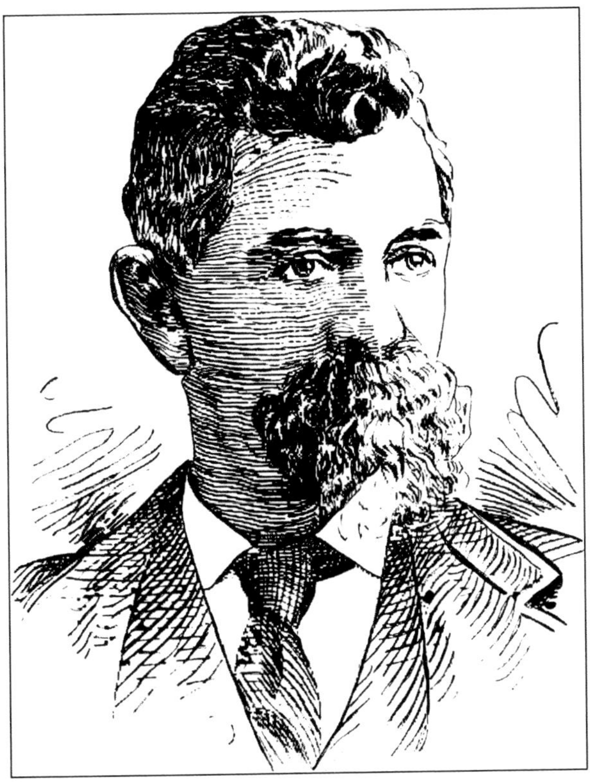

A. B. Houston moved to Robinson in 1866 after serving in the army during the Civil War. He ran Robinson House and then clerked in A. P. Woodworth's store for two years. In partnership with W. F. Hamilton, he again ran Robinson House as an owner and then gave it up to become sheriff. A restless businessman, he went into the livery business, then sold horses, farmed in Martin, and ran the Paris House in Edgar County. He returned to Robinson some years later and was reelected sheriff, showing that he merited the confidence people placed in him. (Benedict, artist.)

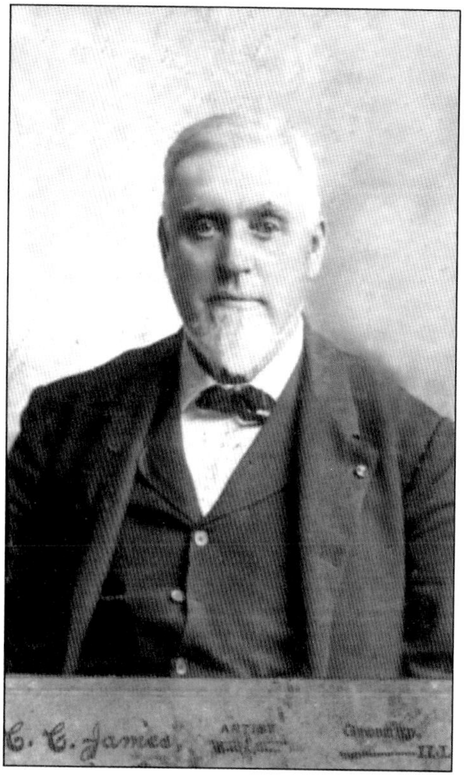

Gen. John T. Wilder was famous for his "Lightening Brigade," whose victory at Chickamauga on September 16, 1863, against the Confederate general Braxton Bragg has not been forgotten. He visited the Grand Army of the Republic Post No. 171 of Illinois on several occasions as several men from the Henry Longenecker Post had served and been killed at Chickamauga. Jacob C. Olwin was the first commander of the post. (SJ.)

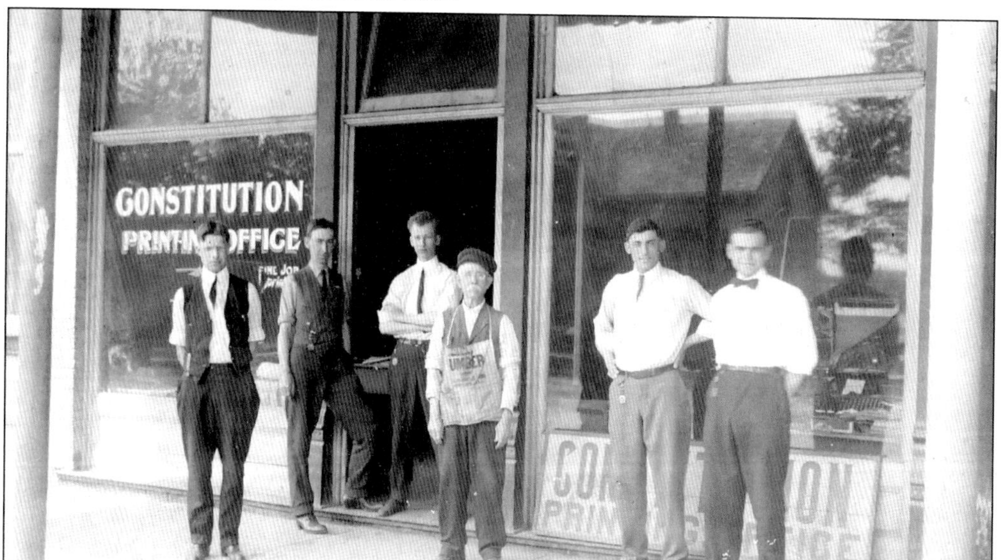

John Talbot started the *Robinson Constitution* in October 1863. Succeeding him were members of the Talbot family, Price, Smith, Fulton, and Hiser, through the years. John S. Abbot took over editorship on January 31, 1895, and became the owner. He sold it to F. W. Lewis in 1902 because he had been elected to become president of the Crawford County State Bank. The *Robinson Constitution* has been Democratic and had a long-running rival in George Washington Harper's *Robinson Argus*. Still owned by the Lewis family, it is one of the oldest running newspapers in the state of Illinois. (SJ.)

George Washington Harper was born near Richmond, Indiana, on September 17, 1837, and learned the printing trade as a young boy of 14. Harper moved to Illinois in December 1856 and worked at a Palestine newspaper. He married Hannah Goodwin the next year and published his own newspaper in Palestine two years later. He started the *Robinson Argus* in 1863. Harper served as postmaster, was a member of the First Christian Church for 40 years, and was equally responsible for bringing the Carnegie Library to Crawford County. (RP.)

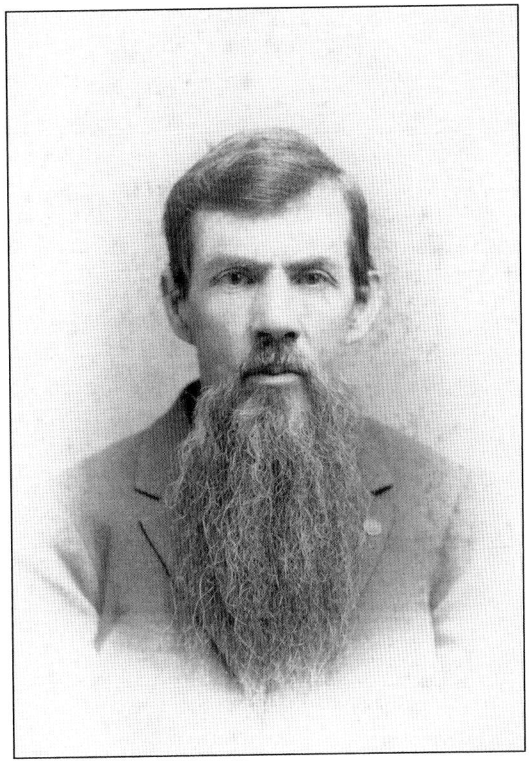

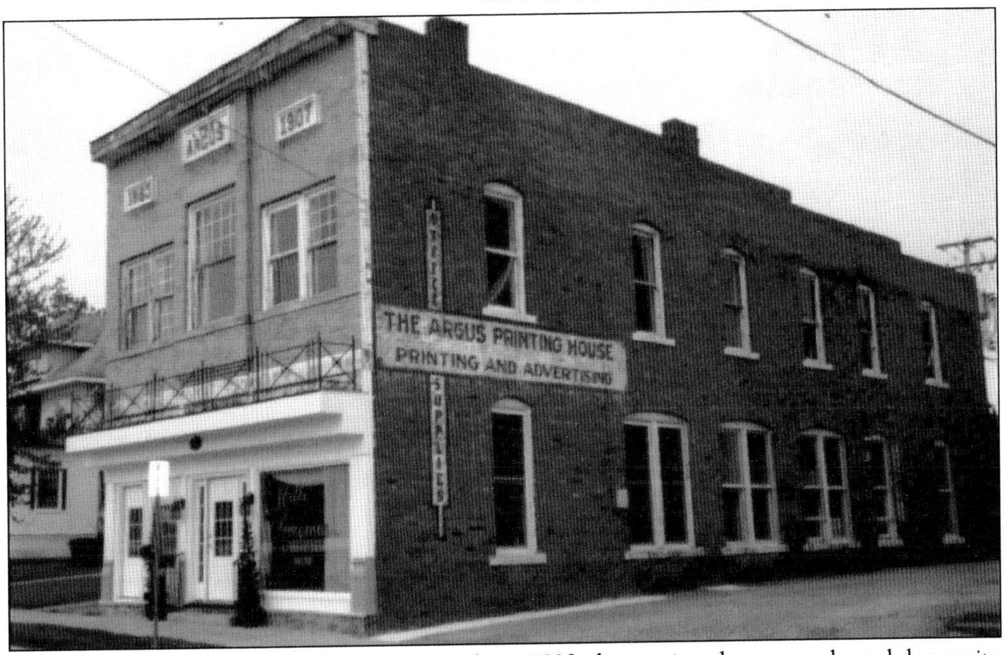

The home of the *Robinson Argus*, erected in 1893, has enjoyed unprecedented longevity considering the heavy use of the building. Some 100 years ago, it was equipped with a Campbell cylinder press and two job presses, a Fairbanks-Morse gasoline engine, cutting machines, and all the latest styles of type. The *Robinson Argus* was still in existence up to only a few years ago, but the home of the *Argus* still stands on South Franklin Street. (Evelyn M. Wallace.)

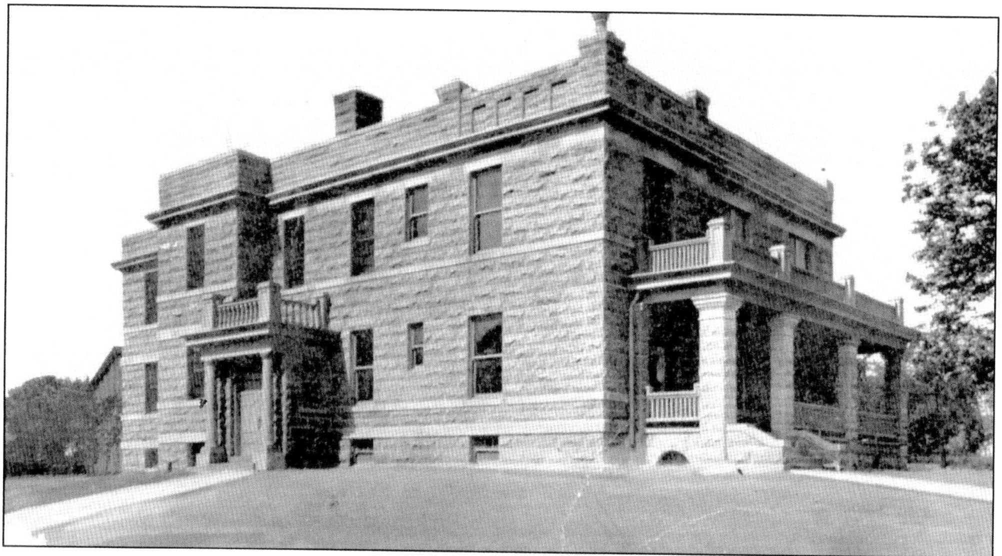

Robinson has had a long history of erecting and tearing down jailhouses. This one was no exception but was a rather attractive building for a jailhouse. This Richardsonian stone prison was erected between 1911 and 1912 on Walnut and Jefferson Streets. The current jail was erected in 1988, east of the post office, and the old stone building was replaced by a parking lot. (SJ.)

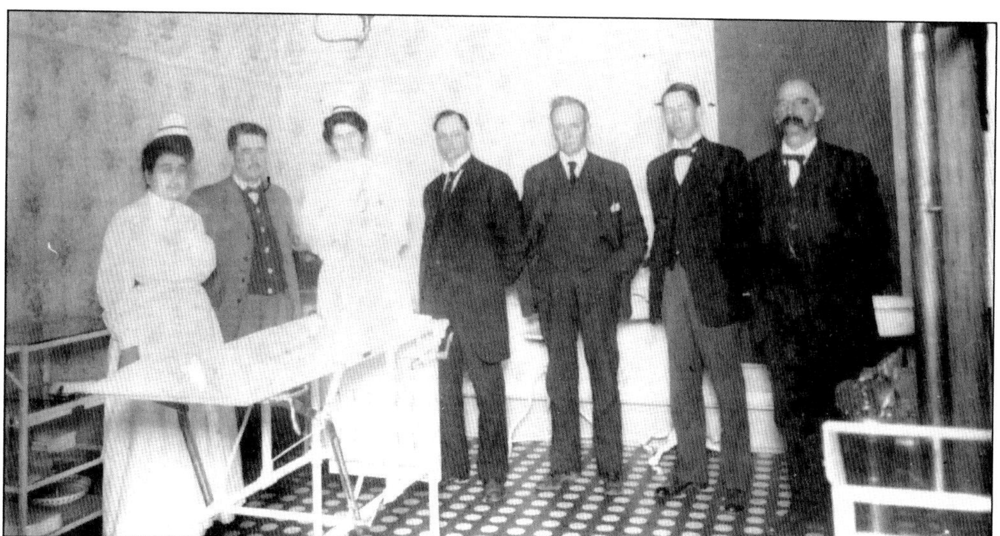

Instrumental in establishing the city's first hospital were six physicians: Dr. H. N. Rafferty, Dr. C. E. Price, Dr. Isaac L. Firebaugh, Dr. Jonas W. Carlisle, Dr. Betsy Carlisle, and Dr. LeRoy Newlin. The physicians purchased the building located at 205 North Cross Street in 1908 from Mrs. T. Gleeck for the sum of $4,000. The founding doctors served as the board of directors. It accommodated 16 patients on the second floor, and the operating room was located on the north side. (SJ.)

Jonas W. Carlisle, the son of James and Sallie Carlisle, was born in 1868 in Martin Township. He attended Merom College and Normal School in Valparaiso, Indiana, and taught school before entering Chicago Physio-Medical College with Betsy Ross, who married him and graduated with him in 1897. Along with five other doctors, he started the first hospital in Robinson. Betsy entered practice with her husband but resigned in 1900 to devote more time to the family. They had four daughters: Vera, Vivian, Iris, and Irma. (SJ.)

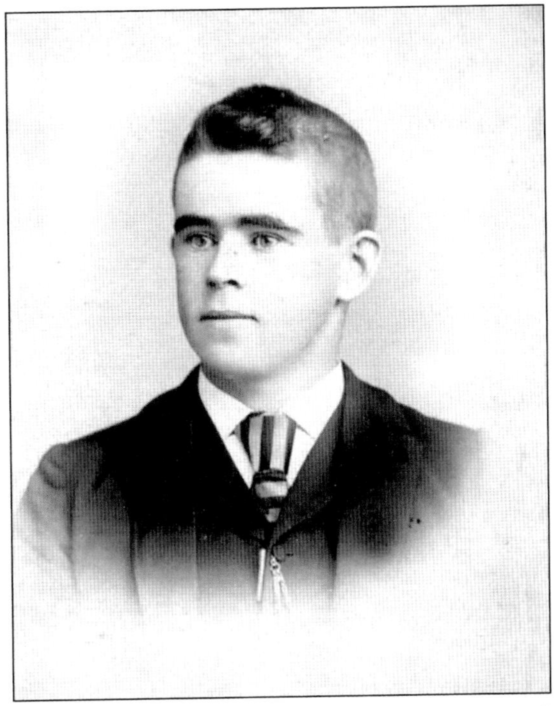

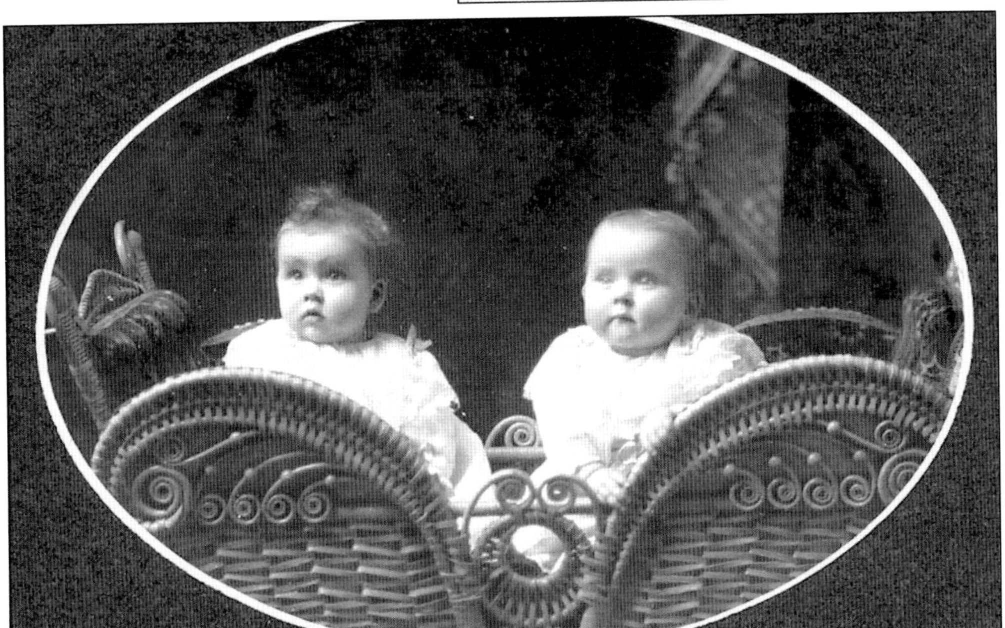

Vera and Vivian Carlisle, although born twins, experienced vastly different lives. Vivian (right) was killed in a flash flood in Boulder, Colorado, in 1909. Vera, who graduated from Lindenwood and the University of Wisconsin, taught school for a few years and then became the librarian in the Carnegie Library in Robinson. She married Harold Newlin, who had been a pilot in World War I, son of Dr. LeRoy Newlin. She knew James Jones as a young toddler when he started using the public library. In 1980, she received a Distinguished Citizens Award for service to the community. (SJ.)

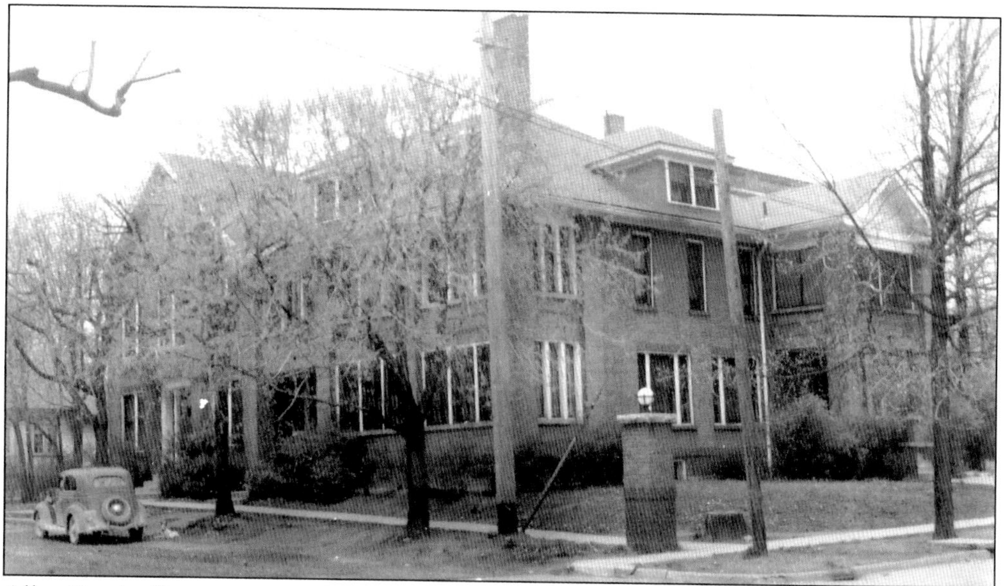

Allen Baptist Sanitarium was reconstructed continually to accommodate more patients from 1903 to 1919. It was named for Arthur W. Allen, the founder, chief surgeon, and chairman of the advisory board. It increased capacity to a total of 55 rooms, with 25 being private and some with outdoor sleeping porches. It also had a veranda on the two main floors extending along the south side of the building. (SJ.)

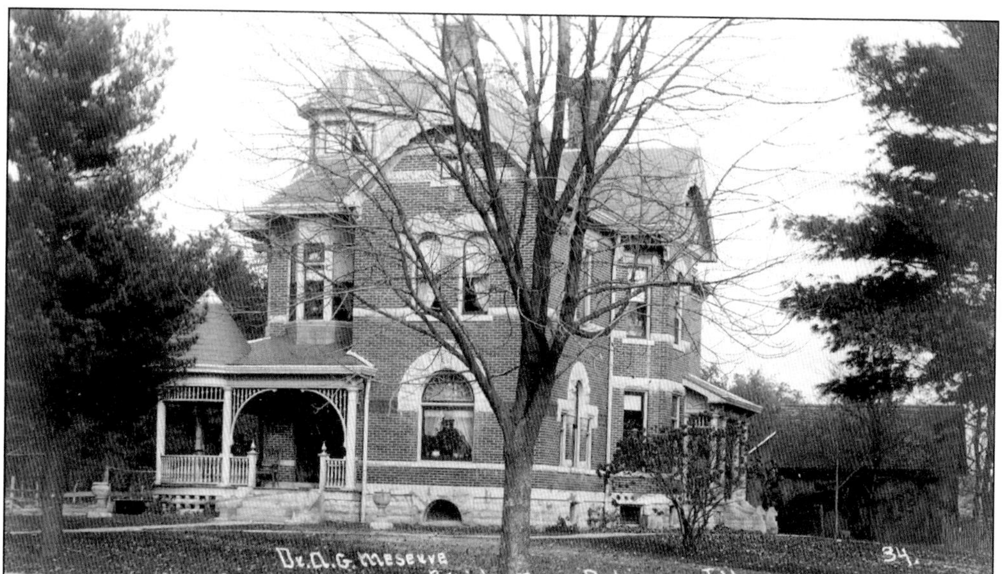

Situated on Locust Lane among other sumptuous homes is the Dr. Arthur Gray Meserve home. Born into the Stephen Meserve family in Hutsonville on May 6, 1854, Arthur moved to Robinson with his parents when he was three years old. His primary schooling was at the Crawford County Academy in Robinson, as his father was also a medical doctor, and he graduated from Miami Medical College in Cincinnati, Ohio, in 1874. Arthur and his father were instrumental in founding a county medical society, and he served as president for a term. On July 19, 1876, he married Theodocia Elizabeth Fitch. (SJ.)

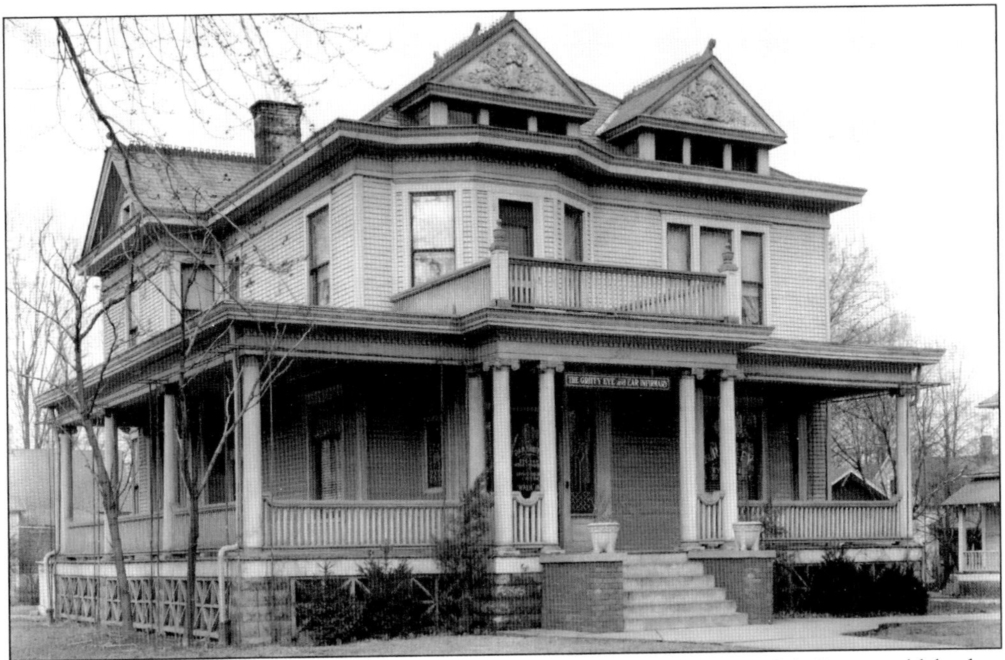

This beautiful home on 502 East Main Street was the home of Laura McCarty, sold by her on January 13, 1938. Originally it was erected by a Mr. Nichols during the oil boom in 1906. This photograph was taken in the spring of 1938. It was redecorated and equipped to become the Griffy Eye and Ear Infirmary shortly after on January 29. Laura McCarty passed away on June 2, 1939. (SJ.)

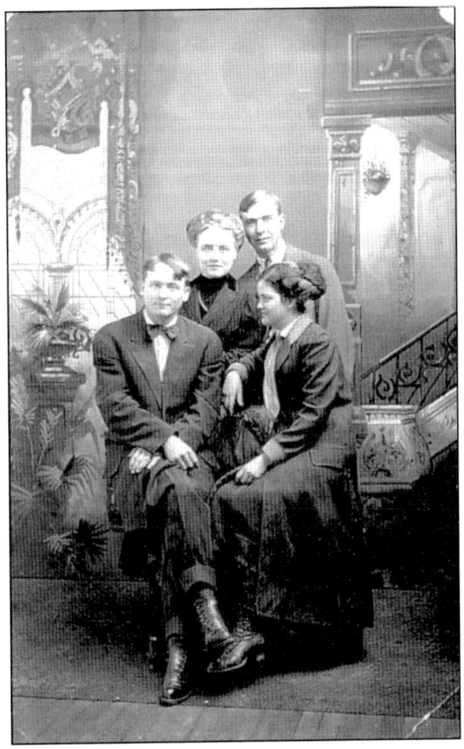

A portrait of Dr. Roy Griffy (far left) includes his wife, Nellie (seated), sister Valeria, and her husband, Mr. Collins. Dr. Griffy spent 57 years in practice, but he resided in Oblong and ran this hospital for 38 years. He passed away in 1971. (OL.)

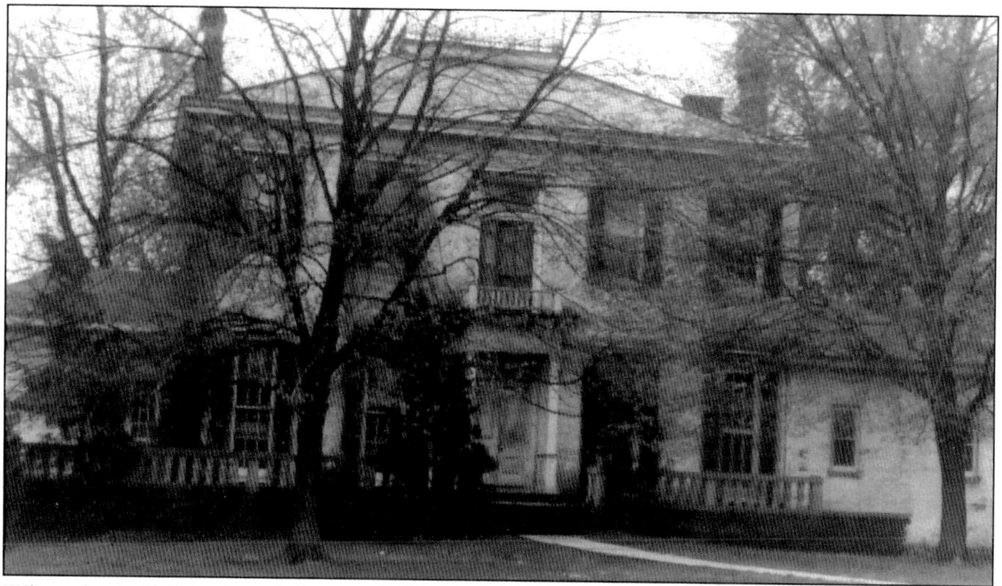

When the A. P. Woodworth home was built on East Main Street in 1867, it was the largest home built in the county, but when it was finished, there were 30,000 bricks left over and put up for sale. Dr. A. G. Brooks eventually purchased the home, adding wings and remodeling the facade, and it became Brooks Hospital. Dr. Greer, a medical doctor from Colorado, bought Brooks Hospital in April 1957 and ran it until he sold it to Kent Lewis of the *Robinson Daily News*, and it was converted into a nursing home. (SJ.)

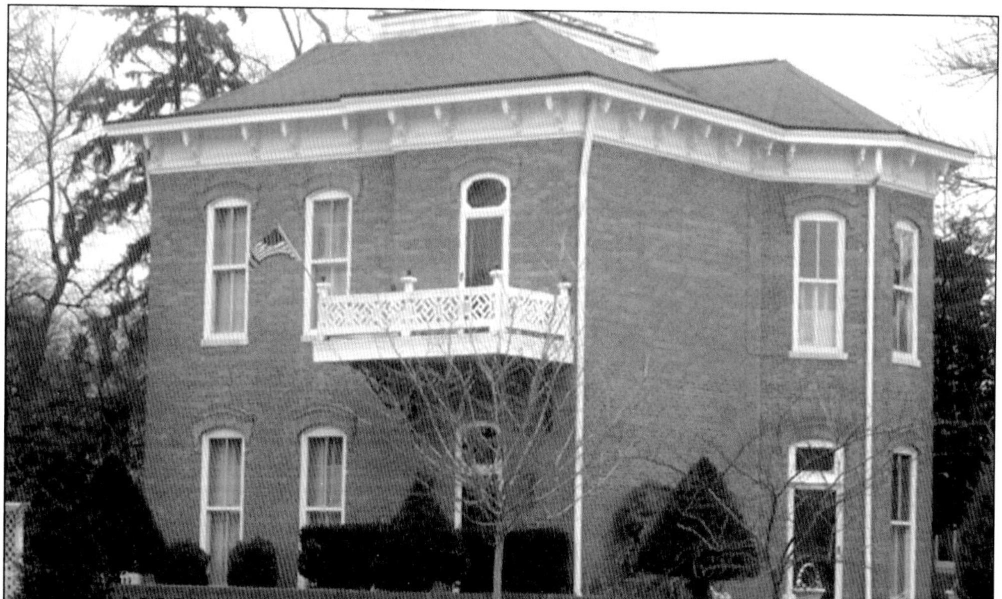

On the southwest corner of the Walnut and King Streets intersection, the former Ethelbert Callahan mansion, although not large, is still a unique vision compared to other grand homes in Robinson. It was erected some time before 1900 but is currently in very good condition thanks to Mrs. McNutt and her son Louis, who bought the mansion in the 1960s and completely restored it. (SJ.)

Ethelbert Callahan's grandfather was a soldier in the Revolution and a Methodist preacher in Ohio. By 1849, Crawford County was Ethelbert's home, and he became a teacher. He edited the *Wabash Sentinel* for a year, moved to Marshall and worked for the *Telegraph*, and then moved back to Crawford County and married Mary Barlow Jones and had a daughter, Mary Callahan Mercer. A short while after marrying, he was elected justice of the peace and finally pursued a law career. He was admitted to the bar in 1859. He retired in 1911. (RP.)

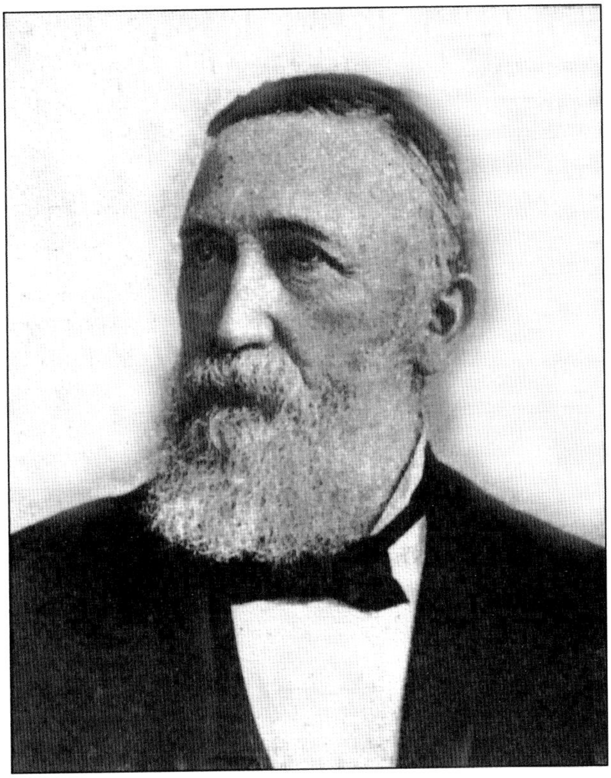

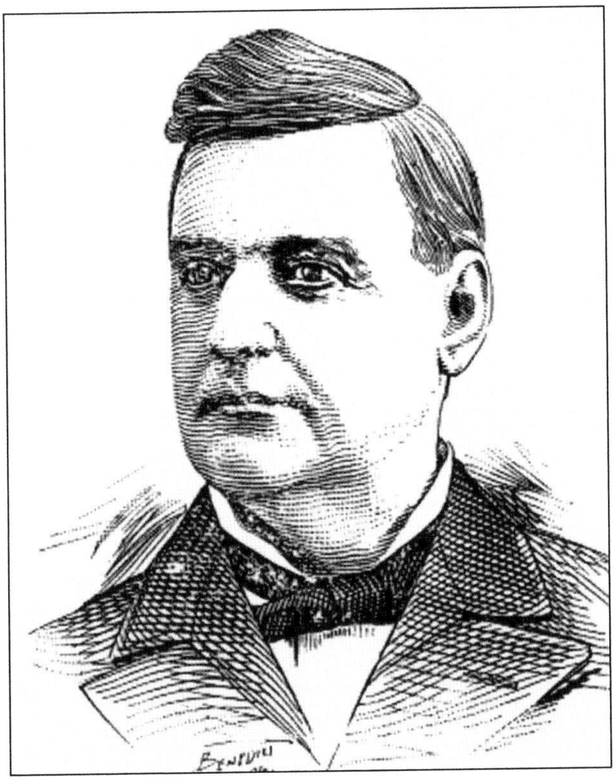

Judge William C. Jones was elected the county judge in December 1877. He was among the most respected lawyers in the area and was an accomplished poet and large landowner. His most famous book, *Birch Rod Days*, displayed a true talent with words. He was in partnership with Ethelbert Callahan for 19 years and together with other prodigious lawyers, such as A. H. Jones and J. C. Maxwell, exerted great influence for improvements to Robinson and Crawford County. He married Mary H. Steel in 1869 and had three children: Caswell, William, and Dorothy. (Benedict, artist.)

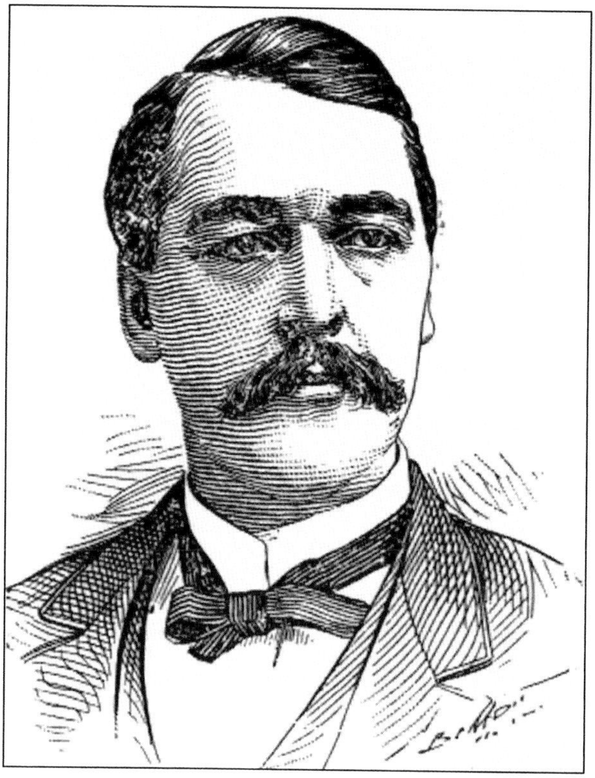

Alfred Hanby Jones was born in Flat Rock on July 4, 1850, on the same farm as his father, John Miller Jones. After graduating from Westfield College and Normal School in Lebanon, Ohio, Alfred taught school for three years. From 1873 to 1874, he studied law in the office of Callahan and Jones and was admitted to the bar in 1875. His first wife, M. Ellen, bore him his only surviving child, Gus. M. Ellen died young in 1874. Four years later, he married Catherine Beals. Their son Roscoe only lived three years. Despite personal tragedy, his career was successful, gaining honor for championing pure food laws, and he was equally involved in local improvements. (Benedict, artist.)

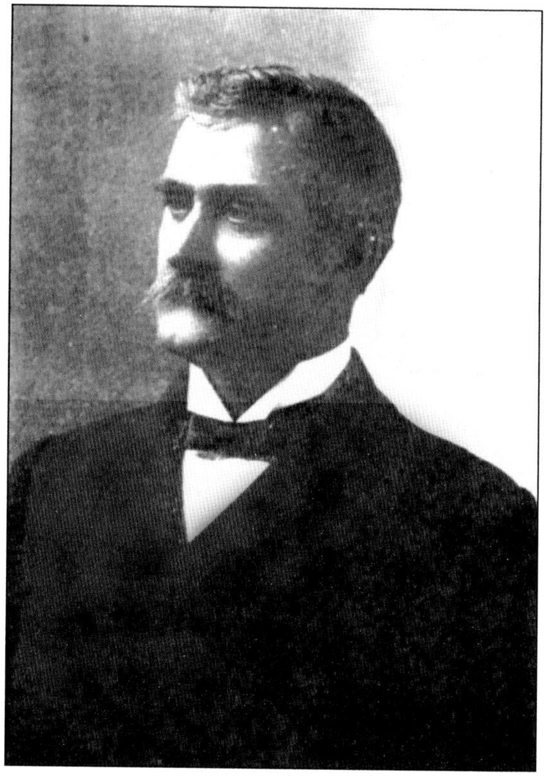

Presley G. Bradbury originally came from York and taught school in Crawford County for seven years. Bradbury became superintendent of schools in 1873. During this time, he read law with Franklin Robb, who was a giant in the field, and was admitted to the bar a few years later and became Judge Robb's partner. He married Jennie Kelley, who came from Sullivan County, Indiana, in 1879, and they had five children, two of whom also became lawyers, J. Stanley and William E. (RP.)

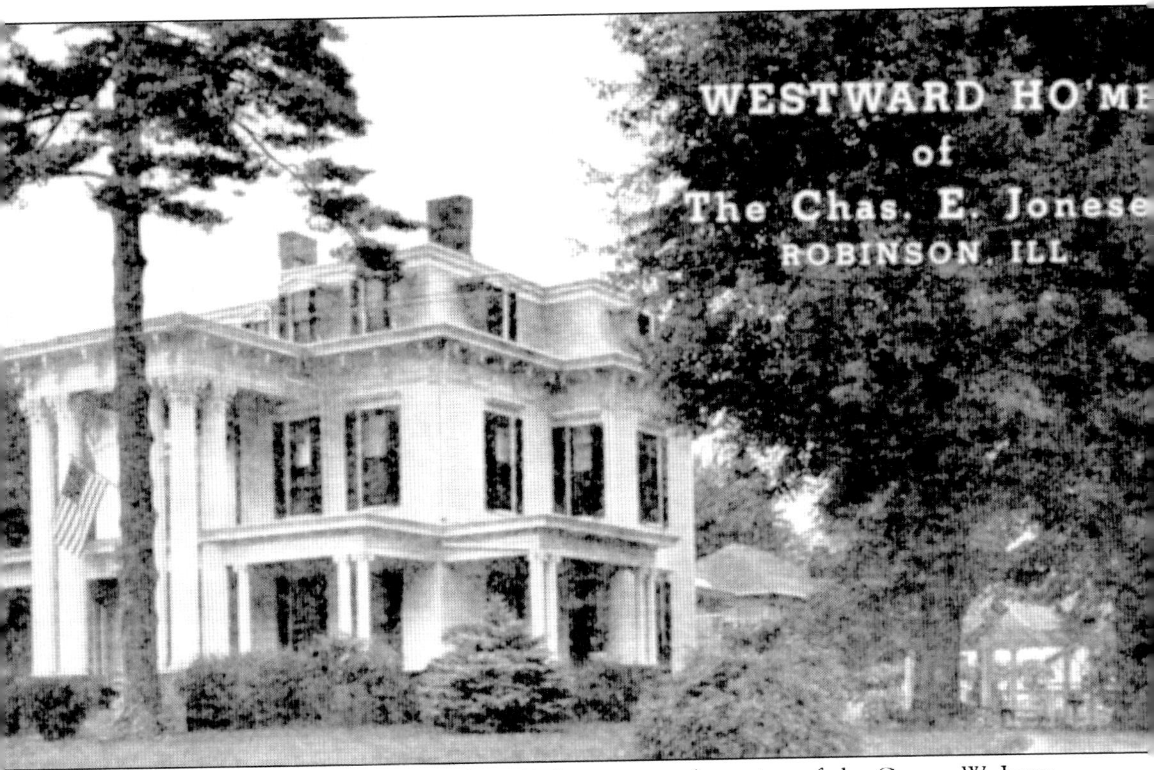

Perhaps the worst architectural tragedy in Robinson was the razing of the George W. Jones mansion in 1967. Ira B. King built it in 1881, and it passed through several hands until George purchased it from F. L. Dewey in 1920. Dewey had rebuilt it by adding 22-foot Corinthian pillars and the covered porch. Inside the mansion were frescoed walls that had been done by a prominent artist who also decorated the Carnegie Library, the Elks home, and E. E. Lindsay's home. George W. Jones was the son of John Jones, born in 1860. He attended Westfield College, read law with W. C. Jones and E. E. Newlin, was admitted to the bar in 1891, and had a partnership with J. C. Maxwell. Politically he vacillated between the two parties and was a prominent member of the Methodist Episcopal Church. At the time of its razing, the last owner in the Jones family to have possession was Charles "Chas" E. Jones, who was James Jones's uncle. The Argus headlines read, "Old Jones Mansion Dies Hard." (SJ.)

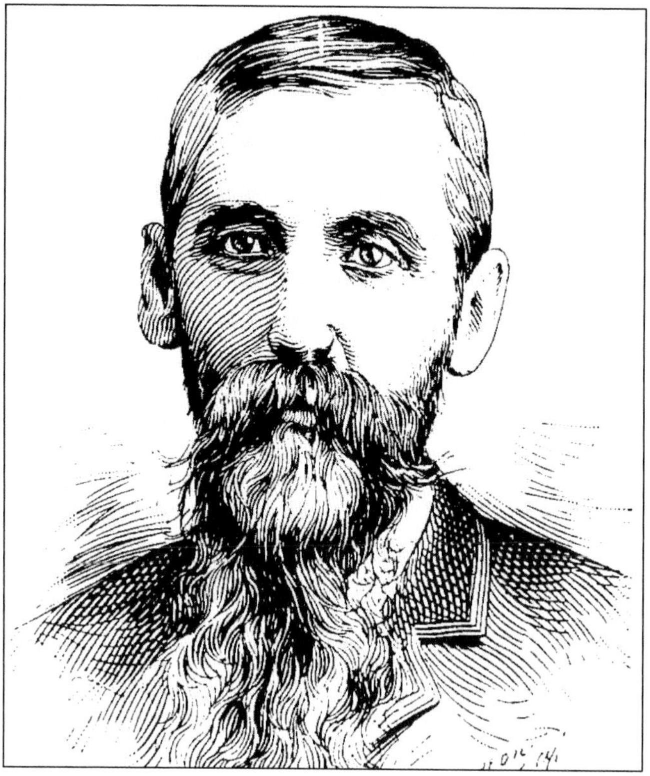

Charles O. Harper, born in Palestine to John B. Harper in 1848, took courses at Terre Haute Commercial College and then enlisted in company H in 1865. He served six months with the 152nd Illinois Infantry. Back in Palestine, he married Catherine Lisman and worked on his father's farm until 1884, when he decided to enter the grocery business in Oblong. He was elected justice of the peace in Oblong and was appointed postmaster five years later. He served both offices until 1893, when he was elected to be county clerk of Crawford County. (Benedict, artist.)

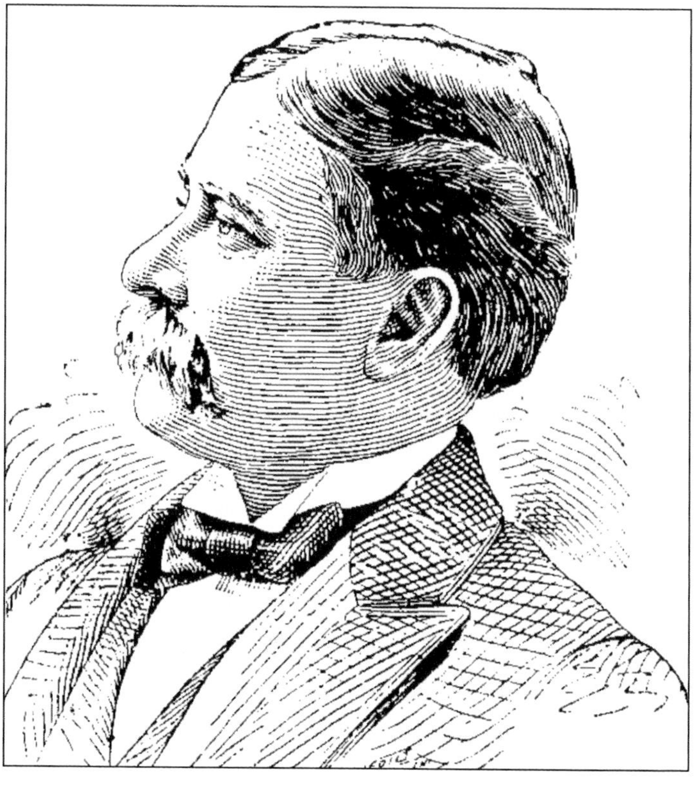

Joseph B. Crowley's humble beginnings were an indication of the tough spirit he housed. Crowley worked hard jobs and tried to better himself through education. He was admitted to the bar in 1883. He formed a partnership with George N. Parker and three years later was elected county judge. After several reelections, he resigned to accept the nomination to Congress. His committee work centered on invalid pensions and the militia. (Benedict, artist.)

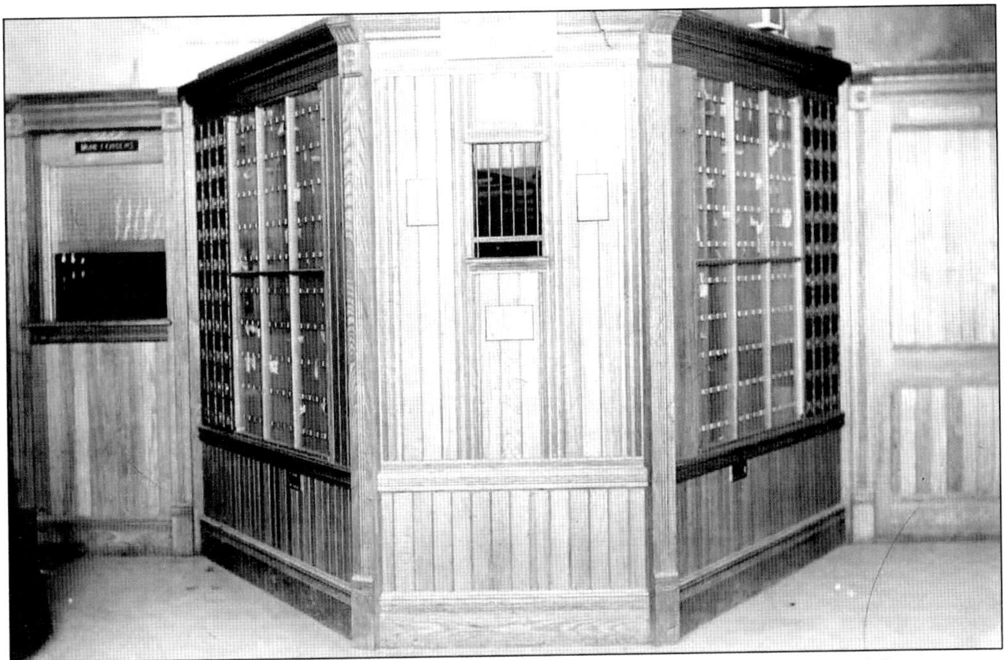

Interiors of the post offices varied from utilitarian to palatial. This was the interior of the new post office in Robinson, built on the south side of the public square. A. H. Jones and John S. Abbot, who was also a member of the chamber of commerce, made a special trip to Washington, D.C., to take the matter of needing a bigger and better post office before Congress. Senator Cullom secured the appropriation for the building and the grounds. It was dedicated in June 1916. (SJ.)

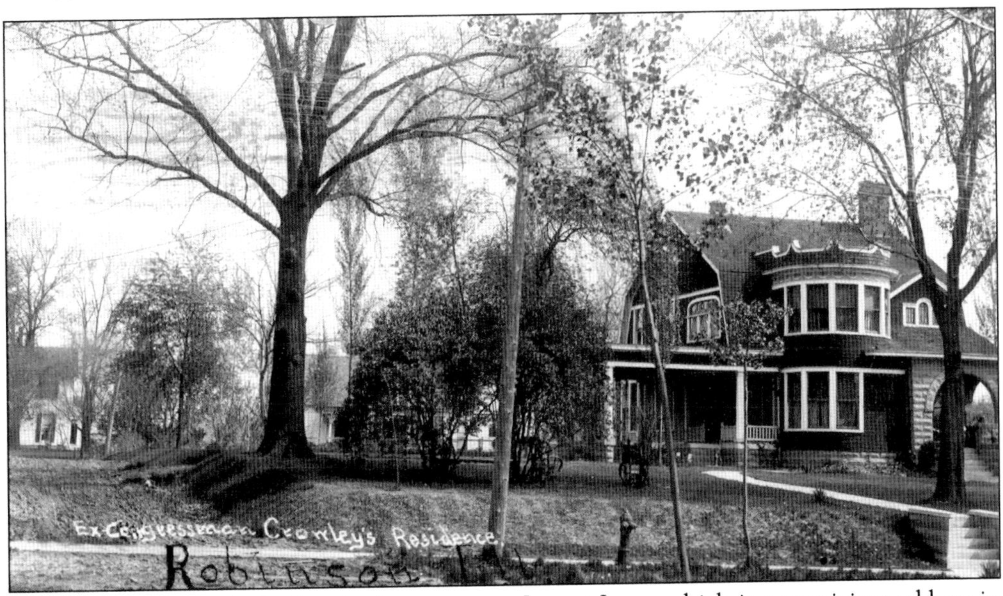

The Honorable Joseph B. Crowley home was on Locust Lane, which is a prestigious address in Robinson even today. This was a true sign of prosperity for the lad who was born in Coshocton, Ohio, in 1858 and moved with his family first to Jasper County and then in 1872 relocated to Robinson. He grew up on a farm, attended country schools, and began working by carrying mail on horseback from Robinson to Lancaster—a 40-mile trip. (SJ.)

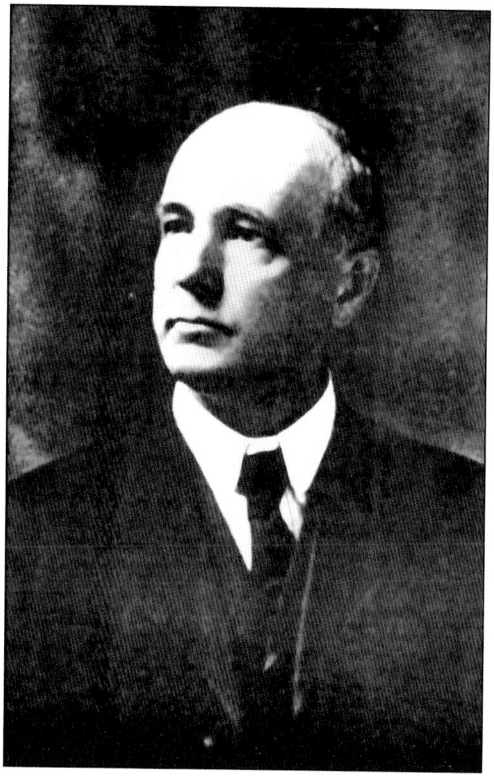

E. E. Newlin had the good fortune to enter the law office of Callahan and Jones in 1880. Two years later, he was admitted to the bar and worked his way up, starting with nothing but a burning desire to succeed. In less than a year, he was appointed city attorney and was grateful for the experience, saying, "There is no office so valuable to . . . a lawyer as that of [being] state's attorney." (SJ.)

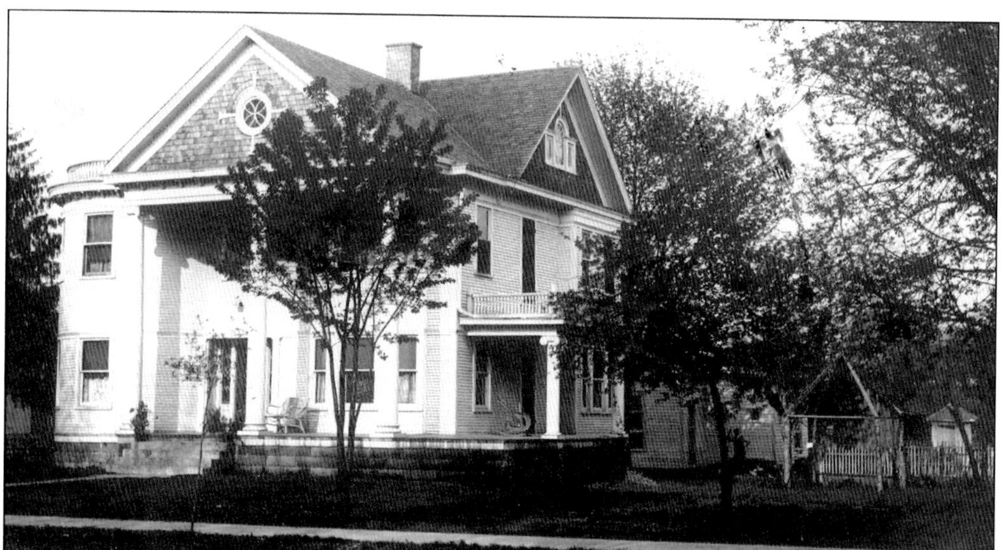

Located on the east side of Pine and Cross Streets, across from the Otey mansion, is the John S. Abbot home. The homes were equally impressive in architecture and are still showcase homes. Abbot started out in newspapers in Elizabethtown, which was also the hometown of his wife, Martha. He became editor and owner of the *Robinson Constitution* in 1895. Abbot decided to sell out to F. W. Lewis in 1902, when he was named president of the new Crawford County State Bank. He remained there until he passed away in 1934. (SJ.)

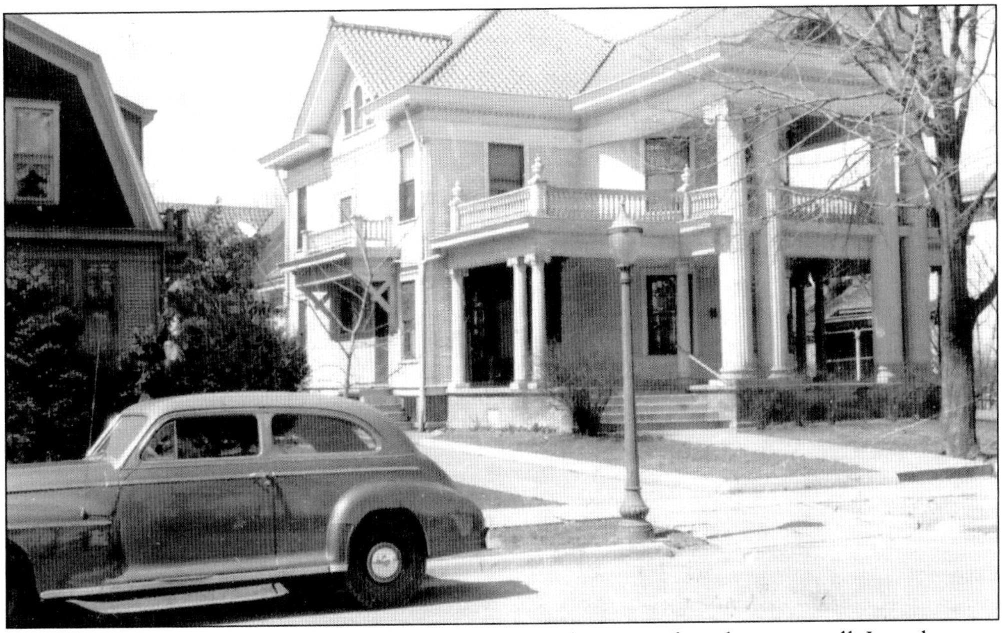

Harry E. Otey's home was built almost entirely of oak that came from his own mill. It took a year to build and is still in wonderful condition. In 1863, he moved to Robinson with his parents and went into business with his father as Otey and Son. He was responsible for the extensive system of paved streets and for securing electric lights and water service for the city. As a real estate developer, he opened new additions and erected business structures, including the Otey Block on South Cross Street. (SJ.)

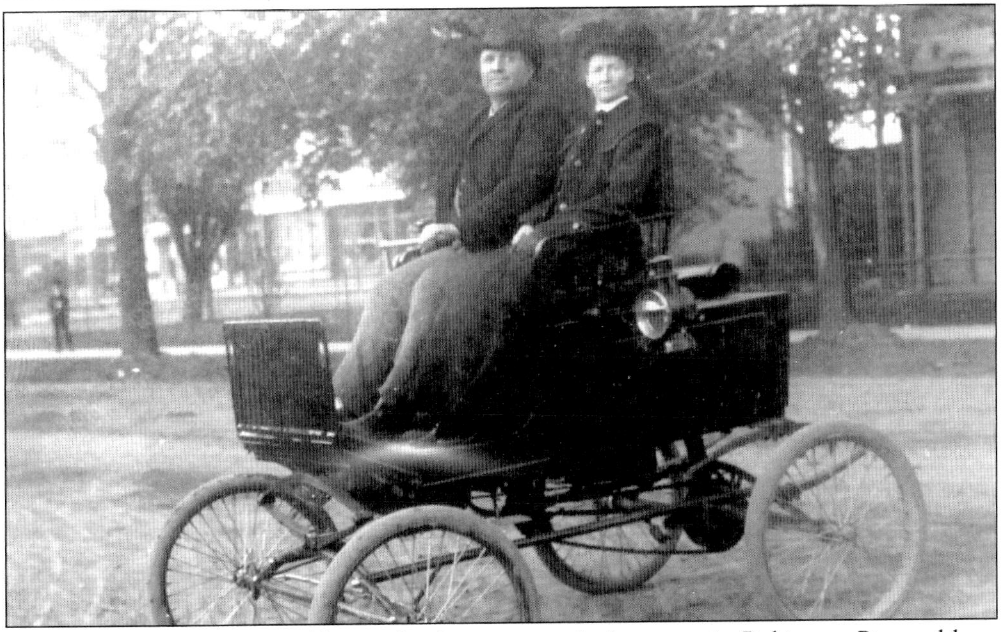

Harry had the distinction of being the first motor vehicle owner in Robinson. Pictured here with his wife, Alice, they loved showing it off and giving people rides in their horseless carriage. Harry was known to Robinson as a great civic and social affairs leader and because of that he was destined to become mayor of Robinson and president of the First National Bank. (SJ.)

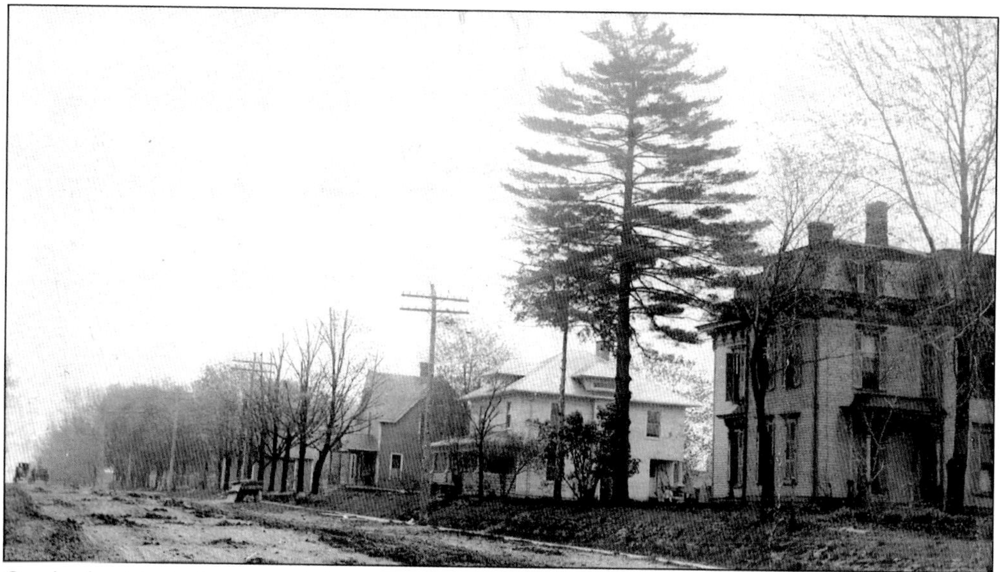

On the far right is the original chateau-style George W. Jones home. The date of this photograph was some time before 1907, when Sarah Wilkin, Henry Wilkin's daughter, had inherited it and taken possession. Henry Wilkin had been a county circuit clerk. From right to left, the second home is the Guthrie Eaton home, and the third home was Dr. Jonas W. Carlisle's home. (SJ.)

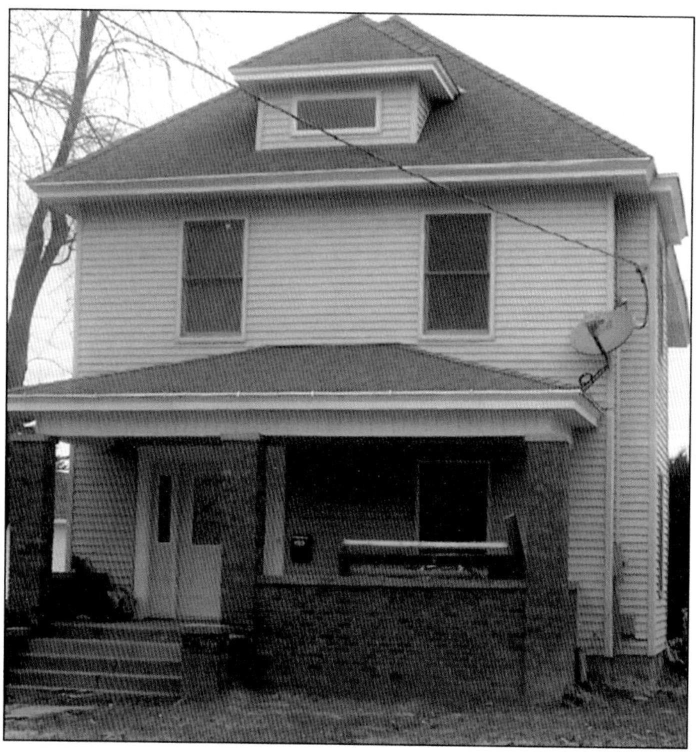

James Jones's boyhood home stands at 400 East Walnut Street and is still within walking distance, through a parking lot, from the old Carnegie Library building. Jones's home has been in various stages of restoration since 1990 and is currently under the protection of a private owner. This was his home through his high school years, but when he returned from the war, his mother, father, and oldest brother were dead and the home was sold. (SJ.)

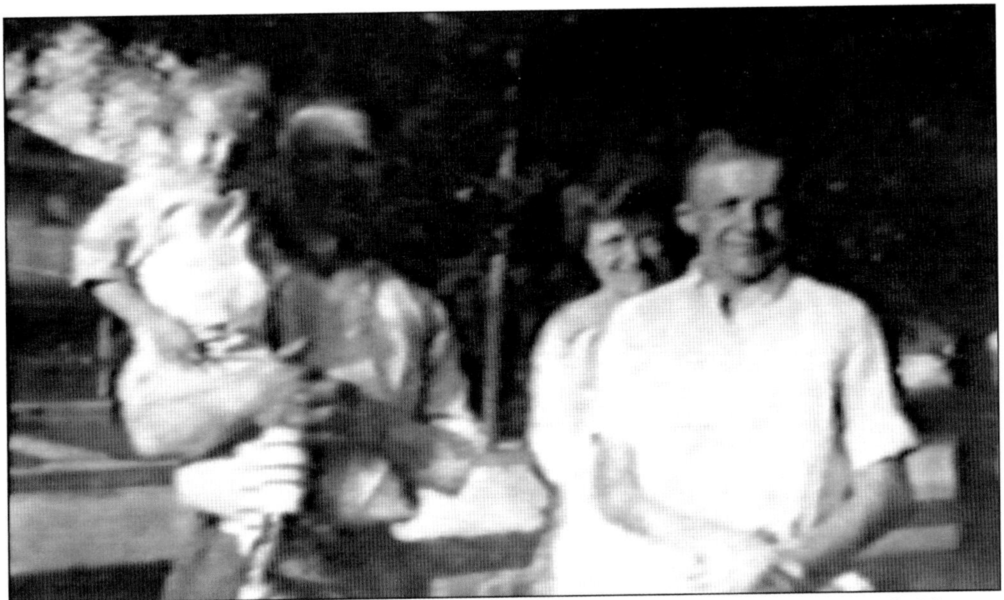

Born in Robinson on November 6, 1921, James was the second son of Ramon and Ada Blessing Jones. This photograph was taken when James was over a year old; his brother, Jeff, was a teenager. From left to right are Ramon (holding James), Ada, and Jeff. James's tribute reads, "There was a Carnegie Library in my home town in Illinois and looking back on it now . . . I am sure that building and its contents and the people who ran it had a great deal more to do with my becoming a writer than I had any concept of at the time." (Jones family collection.)

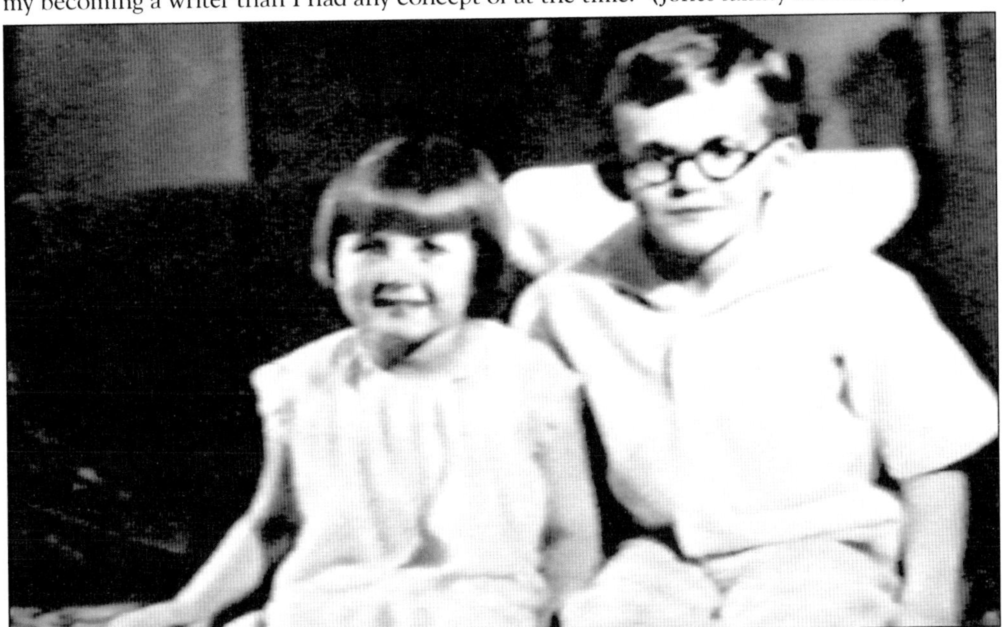

James and his younger sister, Mary Ann, had a close relationship growing up. James grew up "his way" because his mother had unknown ailments and his father was a drinker. In spite of little discipline, he seemed to be able to restrain himself—to a point. When he was not reading, he liked to pick fights around town just for boxing practice, and he had a tough time getting his collections as a newsboy. (Jones family collection.)

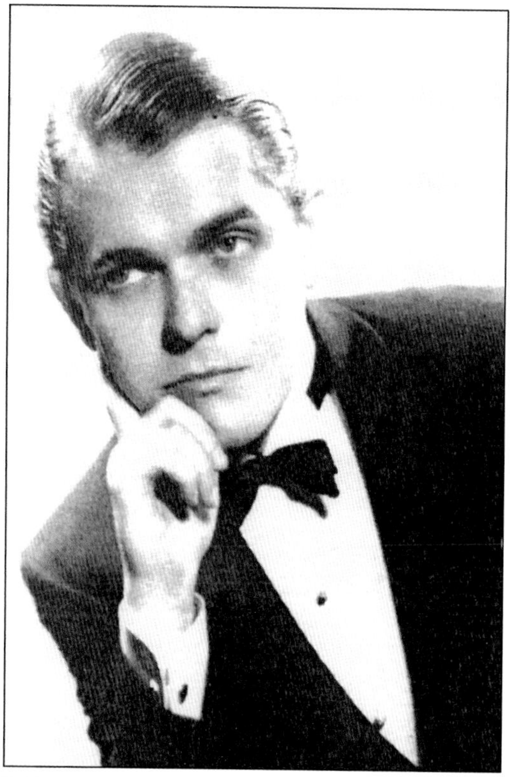

Born in St. Mary's, West Virginia, in 1904, Frankie Masters (née Masterman) spent his boyhood in Robinson and attended Indiana University, where he joined a small band on campus. On summer vacation, Masters played strings with the orchestra on the S.S. *Madison*, traveling through the Far East. He had a succession of stints in major hotels in the United States until he landed a hit with "Scatterbrain," which was on the Hit Parade for 13 weeks in 1939. He married Phyllis Miles, his lead singer, and they had a television show called *Lucky Letters* on WBKB-TV in Chicago. (SJ.)

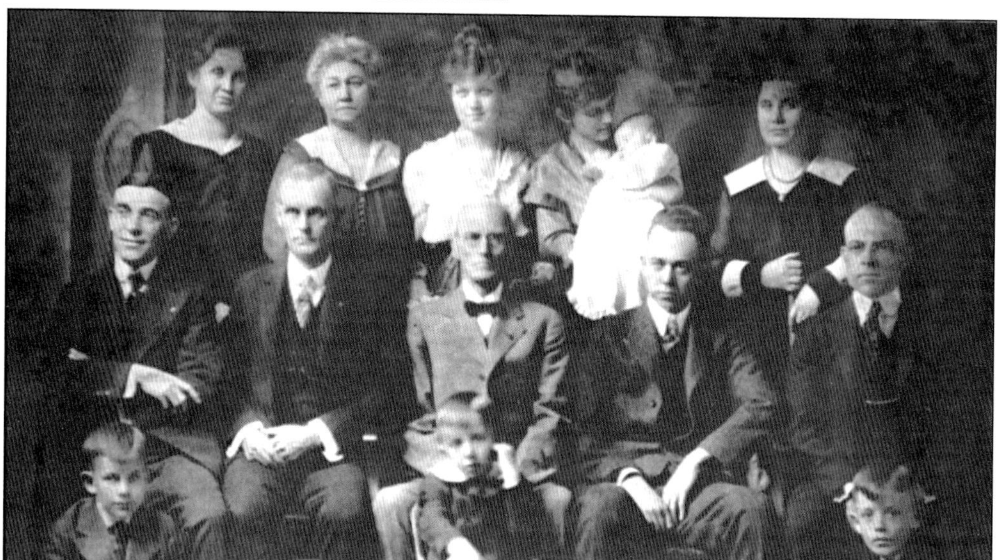

The Brubakers in 1917 were major lumber suppliers for over 35 years. Robert Brubaker had many parts in movies and television, his most notable being that of playing the bartender in *Gunsmoke*. From left to right are (first row) Harold Newlin, Lindsay Newlin, and Walter Newlin Jr.; (second row) Walter V. Newlin, C. C. Brubaker, Elisha Brubaker, George A. Brubaker, and Fred Bradley; (third row) Kate Newlin (née Brubaker), Belle Brubaker (née Titus), Mary Brubaker (later Mary Fife), Carrie Lee Brubaker (with baby son Robert in her arms), and Nellie Bradley (née Brubaker). (SJ.)

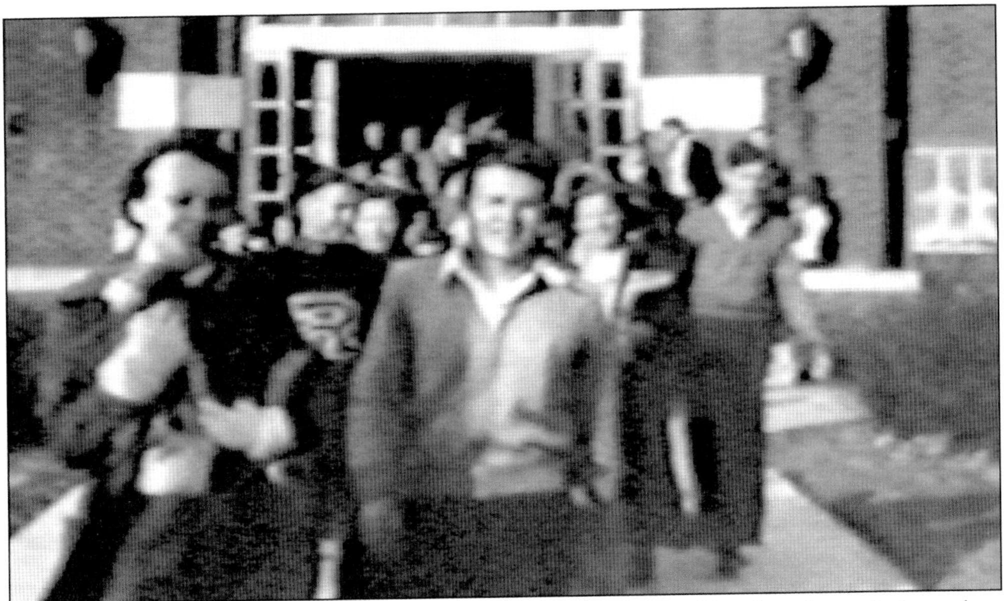

James Jones and March Grandy were caught in a rare moment of laughter by an independent filmmaker in the late 1930s. Teachers reported that he was often bored in class and given to clownish behavior. One day it was reported that he climbed onto the high school roof, fell through the glass skylight, and landed in the auditorium in one of the center seats. "We thought he'd killed himself," his father was later told. (Jones family collection.)

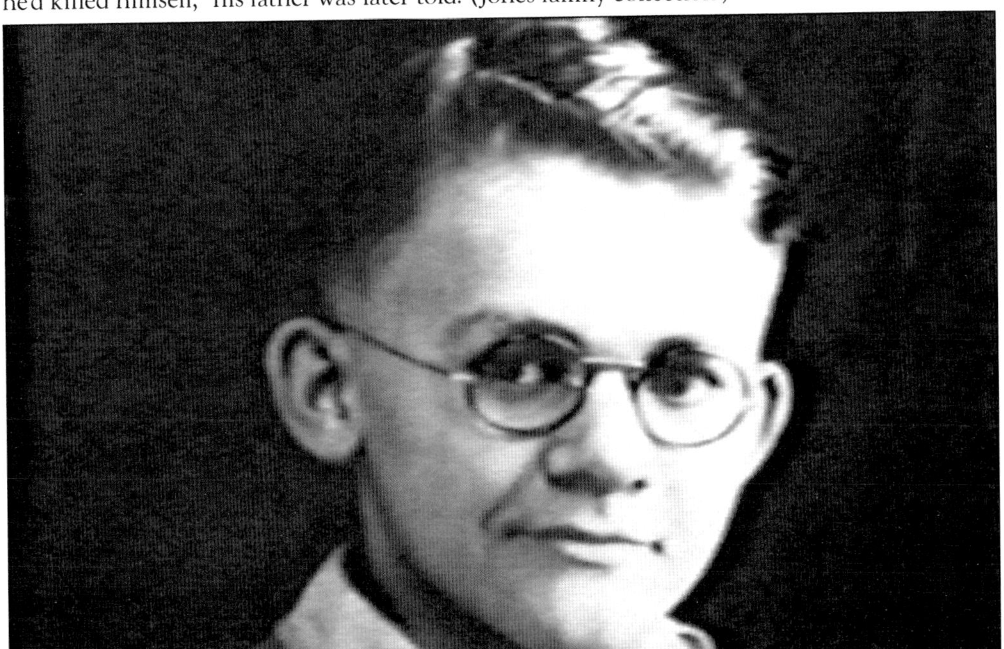

In November 1939, Jones enlisted, trained at Chanute Field, and eventually wound up at Schofield Barracks. He came out of the Pearl Harbor attack unscathed physically but was wounded in action in 1943 at Guadalcanal. When Jones went back to Robinson, he floundered for a while until he met Lowney Handy, who, with her husband, housed him at their home on Mulberry Street while he wrote *From Here to Eternity*. (Jones family collection.)

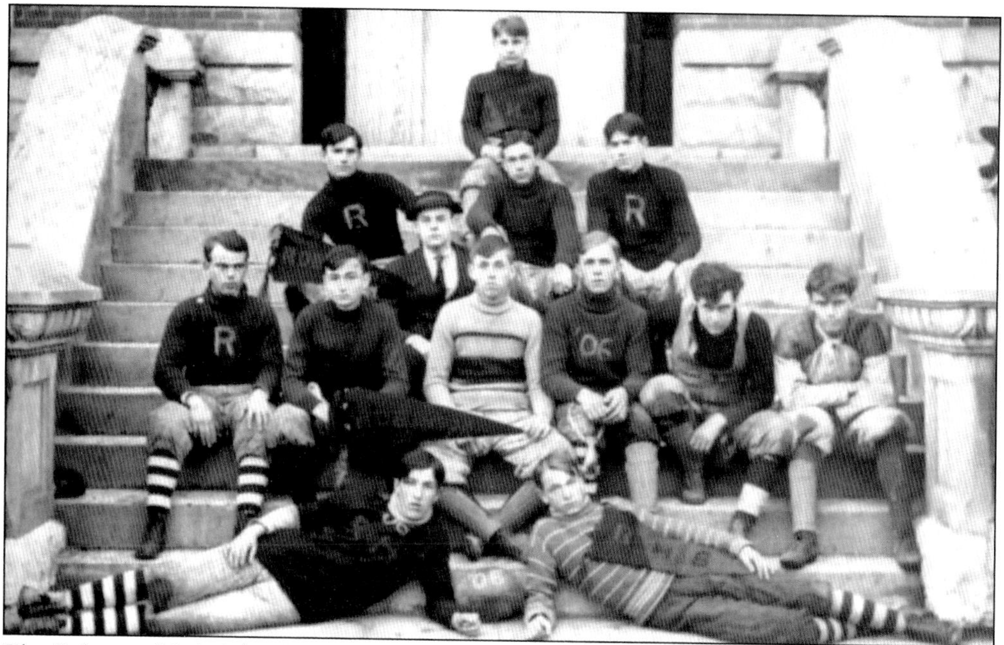

The Robinson High School football team in 1906 comprised, from left to right, (first row, lying down) Bill Shipman and Fred Kessler; (second row) Mark Joseph, unidentified, Charles Van Treese (trainer, wearing hat), Eugene Mail, Sam Springer, unidentified, and Kelso Westerman; (third row) Jonas Springer, Charles Everingham, and Harry Springer; (fourth row) Charles Jones. (SJ.)

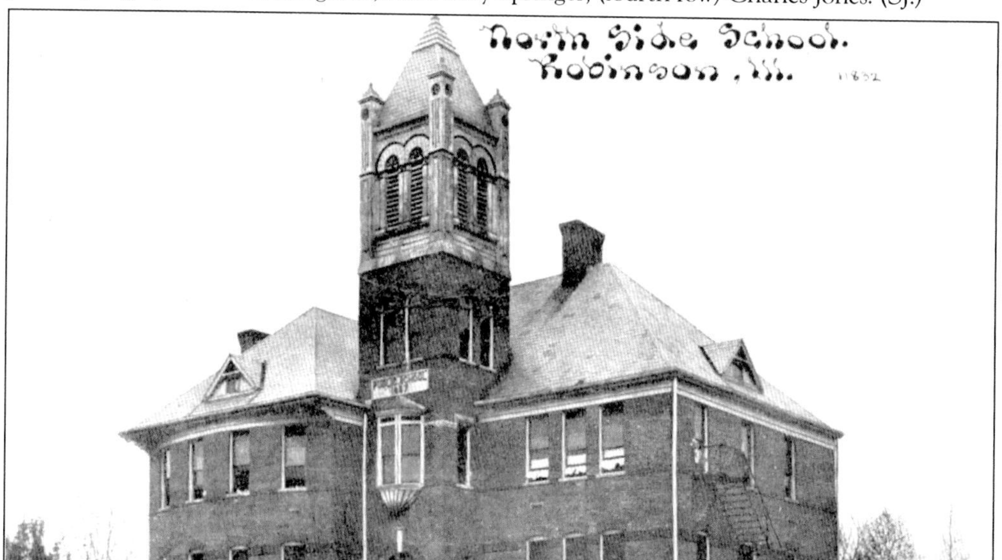

Jefferson High School was erected in 1897 at the location where Robinson's public library now stands at 606 North Jefferson Street. It was built to take the overflow of pupils, some of whom were still attending the top floor of the 1885 south side school, now known as the Lincoln Grade School, which was on the south side of Robinson. Prior to 1927, kindergarten children attended school in the basement of the Carnegie Library. (SJ.)

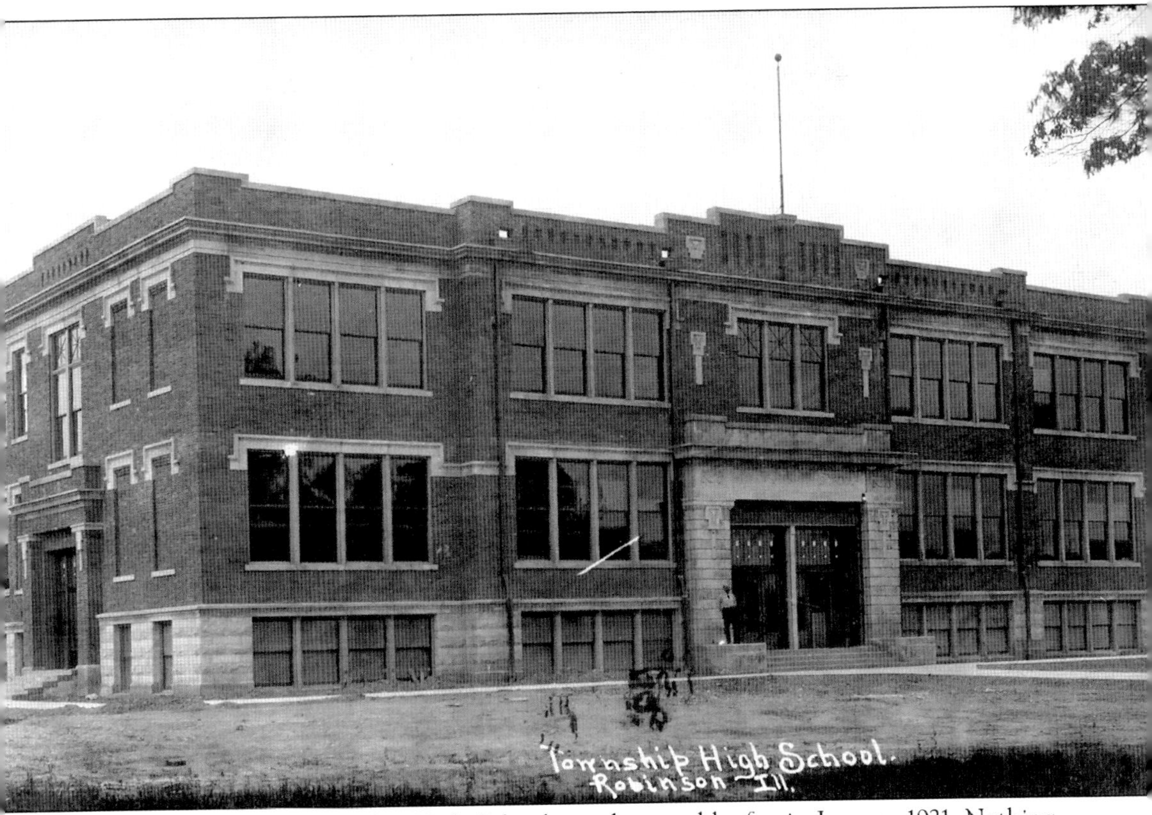

The second Robinson Township High School was destroyed by fire in January 1921. Nothing but the east, south, and west outer walls were left. While waiting for it to be rebuilt, the entire community united in an effort to get the pupils back in classrooms. Local churches, the Elks Club, and other facilities were converted for temporary use, and school assemblies were held in the Strand Theatre. (SJ.)

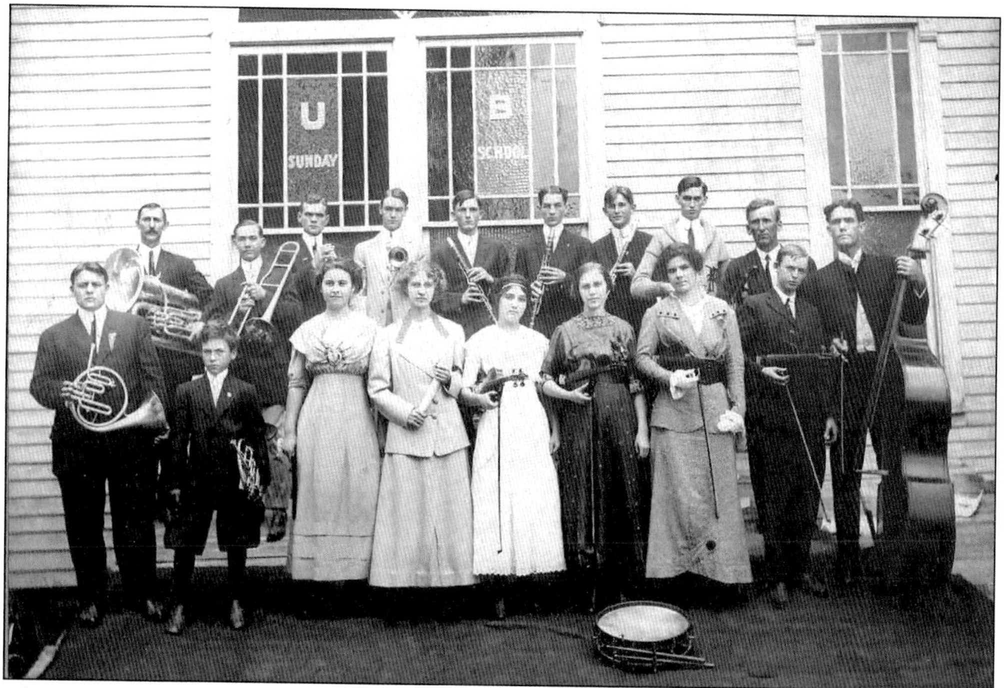

The United Brethren Church Band was comprised of, from left to right, (first row) Leo Venette, Wamer Seall, Ola McColpin (Monahan), Dale Dennis, Jessie Broadstone, Bessie Klingler, Sina Springer, and Andrew Sharard, preacher; (second row) Tom Laurence, Lourance Kefir, Cecil Martin, Harold Norveil, Roy Laurence, Paul Connett, Carl Laurence, Earl Allen, S. H. Seall, and unidentified. (SJ.)

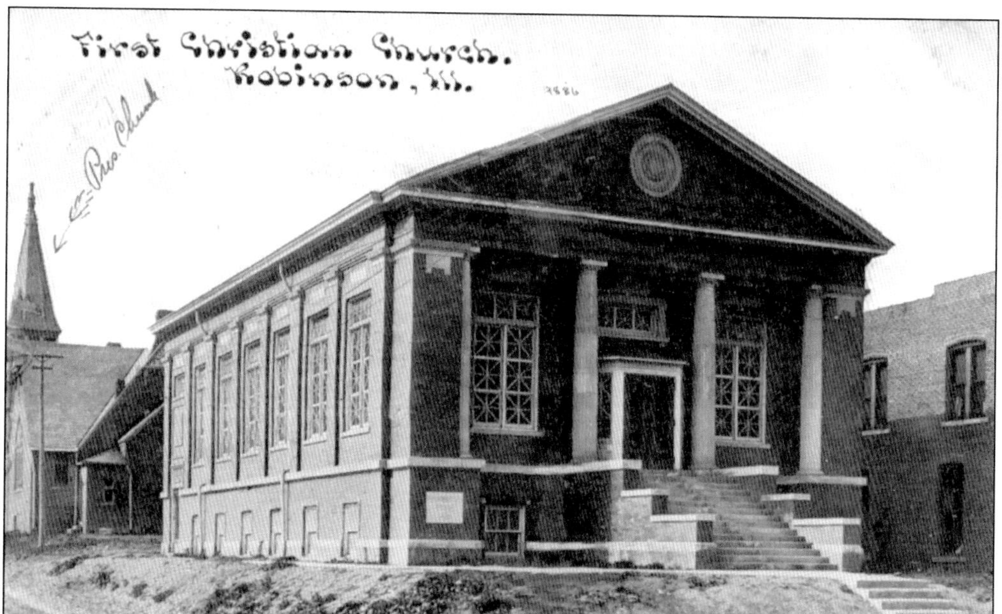

The First Christian Church in Robinson was located on the southeast side, close by the Presbyterian church and the Catholic church. Some members were J. C. Eagleton, E. E. Stiles, Harry C. Brown, A. D. Foreman, and J. C. Olwin. (SJ.)

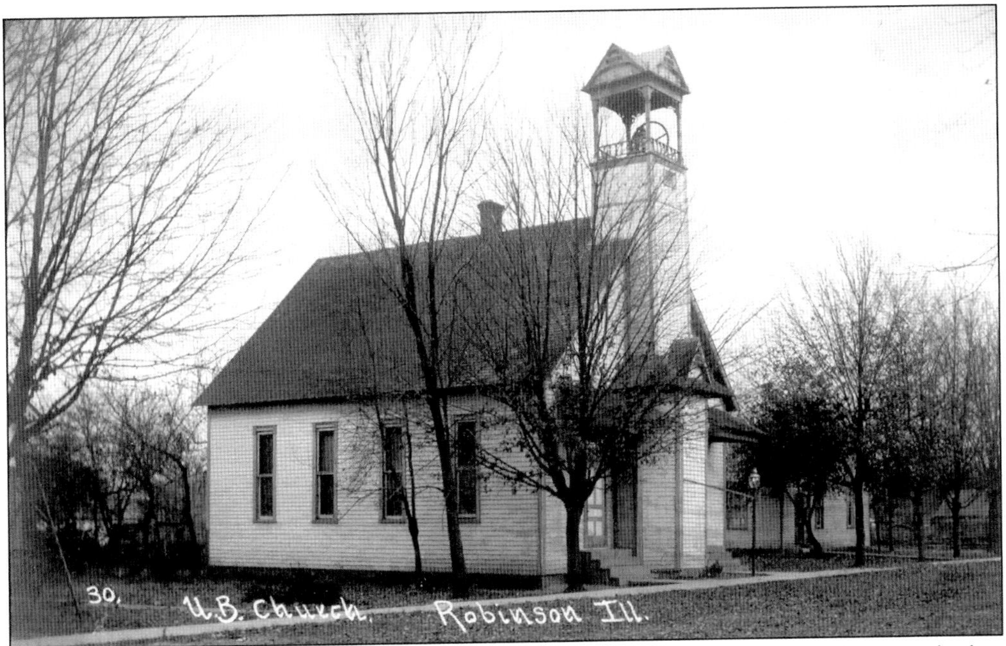

The Lower Wabash Conference of the United Brethren for Christ reported a class attached to the New Hebron circuit around 1887. In 1892, a Robinson class was organized, and in 1895, a wooden building was erected on the corner of East Pine and South Jones Streets (pictured here) on ground donated by Christian Shire. Later, as the church grew, it became the Evangelical United Brethren Church and, most recently, Otterbein United Methodist Church in a new spacious church building. (SJ.)

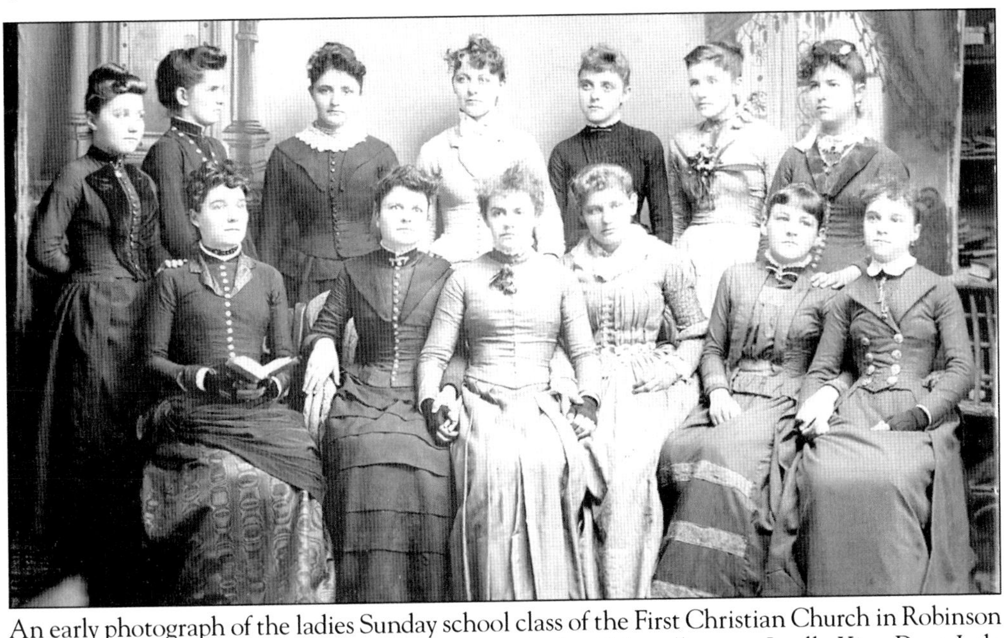

An early photograph of the ladies Sunday school class of the First Christian Church in Robinson shows teacher Mrs. Skidmore, Nell Zermerman, Amber Schmalhausen, Luella King Dyer, Lola Ritchie Eagleton, Amy Turner, Estella Harper, Meca Bashears Shires, Lue Hummel, Catherine Hill Beeman, Lillie Bashears, Dora Surrel, and Lizzie Cawood (center back). (SJ.)

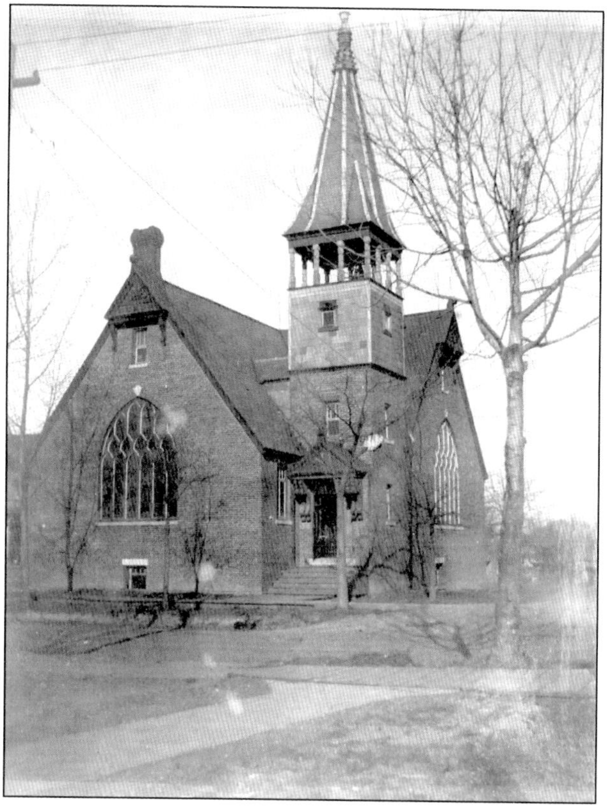

In 1902, Rev. S. A. Caldwell was pastor of the Presbyterian church. Franklin Robb and the Woodworths were among the parishioners. (SJ.)

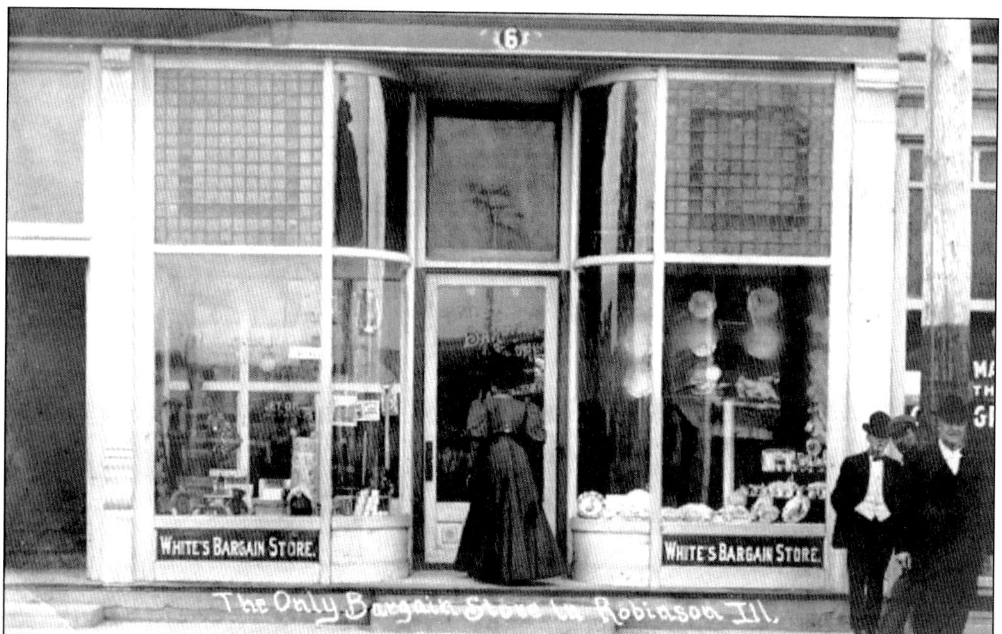

P. C. White's bargain store on the southwest corner of the public square was the only bargain store in Robinson in 1909. It sold notions, tinware, fine china, jewelry, hardware, glassware, wooden ware, and cutlery. (SJ.)

Rev. J. W. McNeill was pastor of the Methodist Episcopal Church and was supported by Ethelbert Callahan, A. H. Jones (who served as chairman of the building committee when the new church was erected in 1899), W. W. Arnold, George W. Jones, E. E. Newlin, A. B. Houston, S. T. Lindsay, C. C. Brubaker, H. M. Lewis, Arthur Hill, and Zalmon Ruddell. (SJ.)

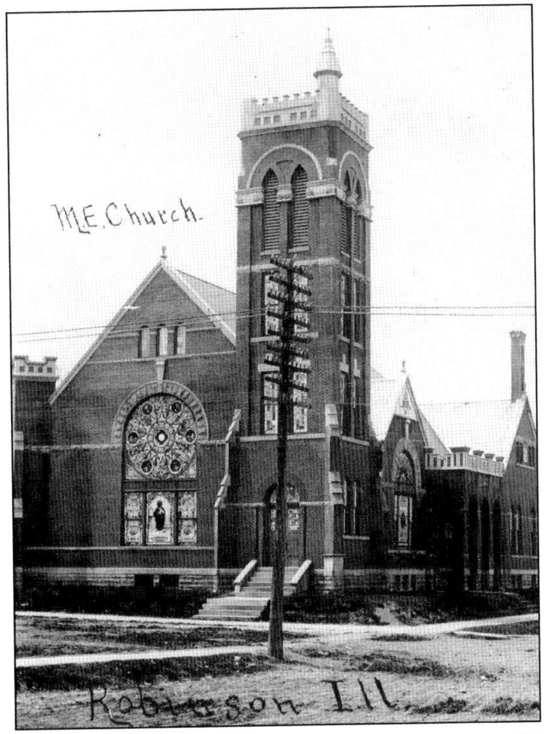

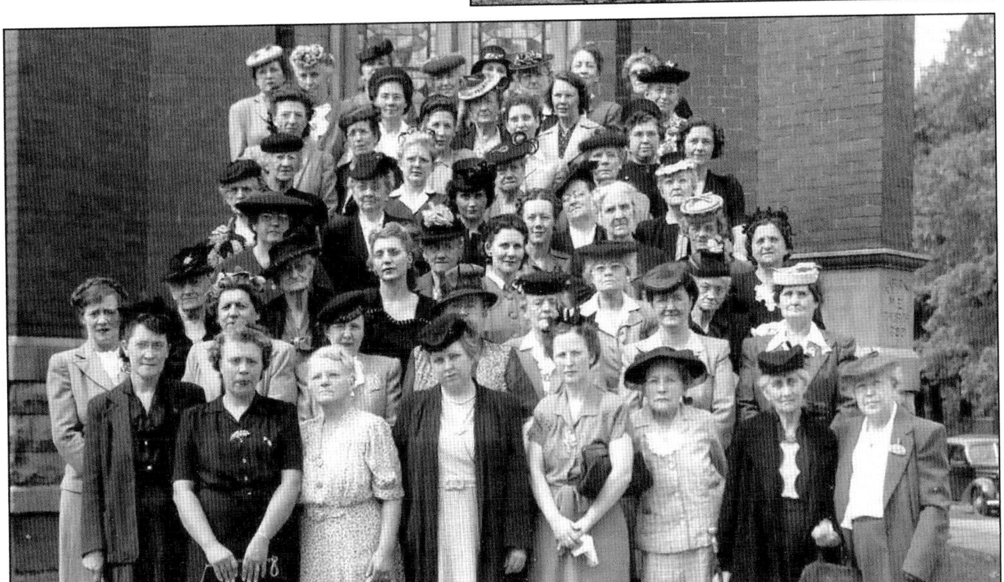

The Methodist Episcopal Church women are, from left to right, (first row) ? Simmons, ? Williams, ? Hurley, E. Brown, ? Faucett, ? Cawood, and ? Gordon; (second row) ? McFadden, ? Haskell, ? Woodard, J. W. McColpin, ? Green, ? Hazelton, and ? Musgrave; (third row) ? Griffy, ? McQueen, L. Keith, ? Sebastian, E. Lindsay, R. Lindsay, and J. Jones; (fourth row) ? Akers, E. K. Halberstadt, L. Sparks, ? Hedden, and ? Jared; (fifth row) S. Martin, ? Clark, K. Boyd, ? Allison, and A. Haskin; (sixth row) ? Estes, M. Smith, ? Frankes, ? Davis, ? Forte, ? Sutton, unidentified, ? Shafer, and ? Martin; (seventh row) ? Albert, ? Plank, E. Snider, F. Turnipseed, and ? Martin; (eighth row) ? Ellison, N. Bradley, ? Brown, ? Wilkins, ? Stover, ? Royd, A. Smith, and ? Orcutt. (SJ.)

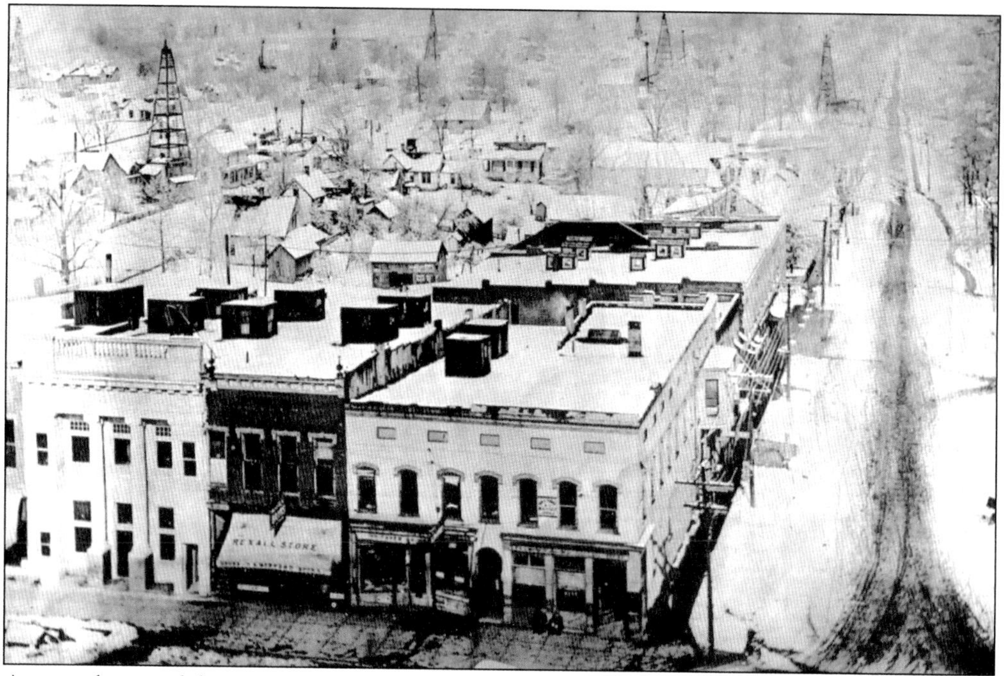

An aerial view of the north side of the public square around 1915 reveals the Crawford County State Bank on the far left. Rembrandt's Photography Studio was a walk-up just to the left of it, and Rexall's was right next door. It is purported that Walt Disney's parents stayed in the building and that he was born there on December 5, 1901. Oil derricks dot the background because people were willing to drill in their yards for oil at that time. (RP.)

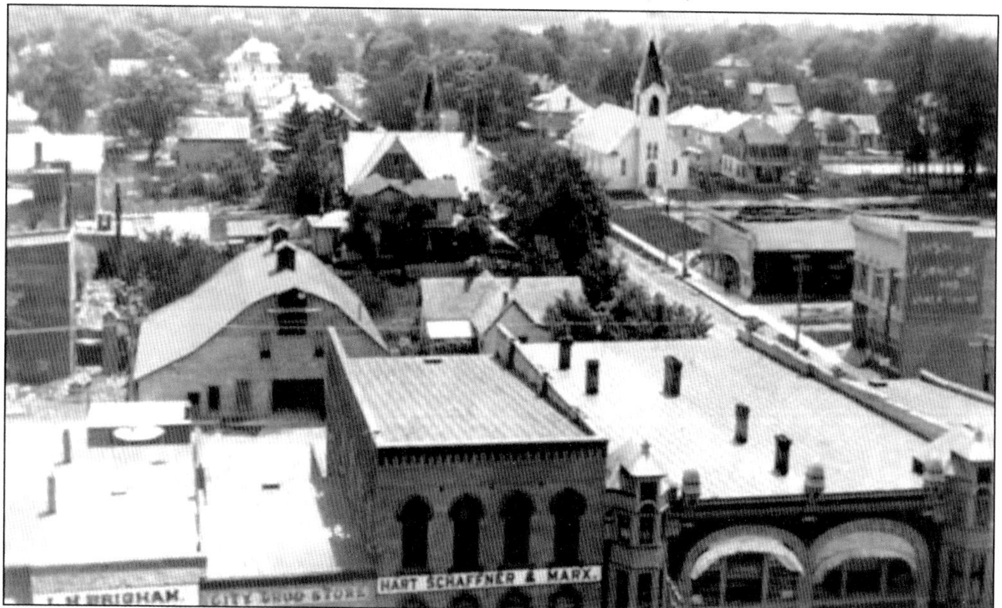

Robinson's southeast side is shown from the courthouse. In the distance, St. Elizabeth Catholic Church, with its looming square tower, can be seen along with the tower from the Presbyterian church, which was just west of it, in close proximity to James Jones's home. Luther H. Brigham and J. P. Eagleton's meat market and grocery is shown in the foreground. (SJ.)

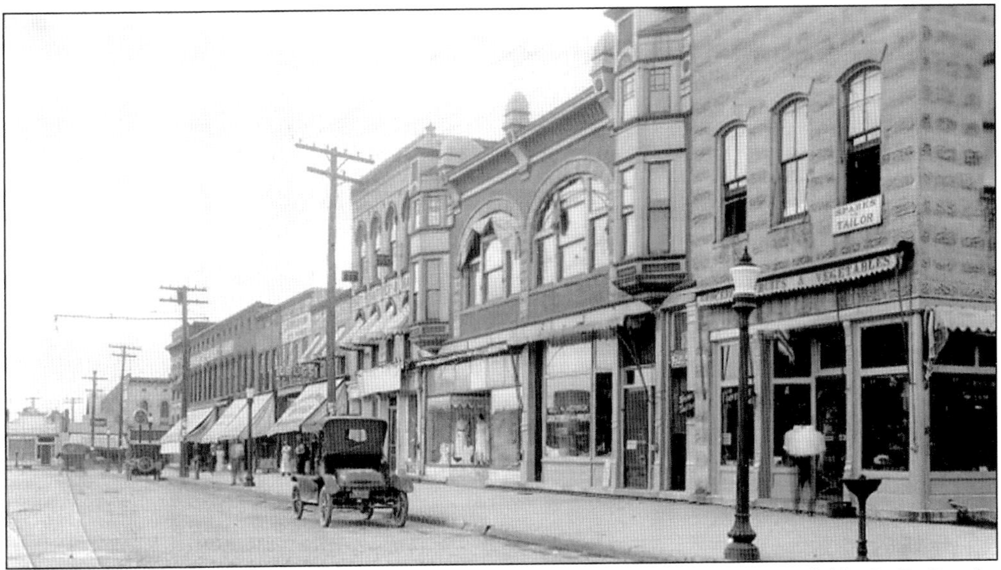

The west side of the square about 1910 had many merchants and services available. L. D. Sparks was the tailor located on the northernmost corner; Boofter's Grocery was directly beneath at the corner storefront. Will Jones (son of W. C. Jones) started a clothing store on September 7, 1901, and was very successful. F. L. Dewey's store, the Boom, offered dry goods, clothing, shoes, and furnishings. (SJ.)

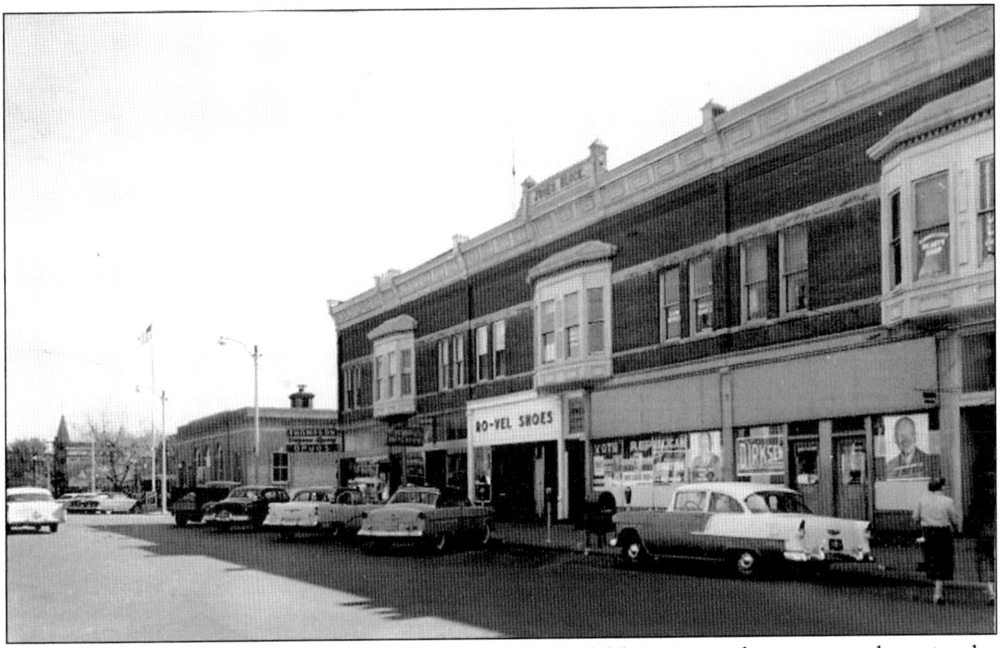

During the 1950s, the south side of the square looked like a typical town anywhere in the United States. The storefronts have an updated look even with the older structures still intact. Thompson Drugs and Bo-Vel Shoes were the established merchants, and the Ike posters are apparent. In the background is the original post office. (SJ.)

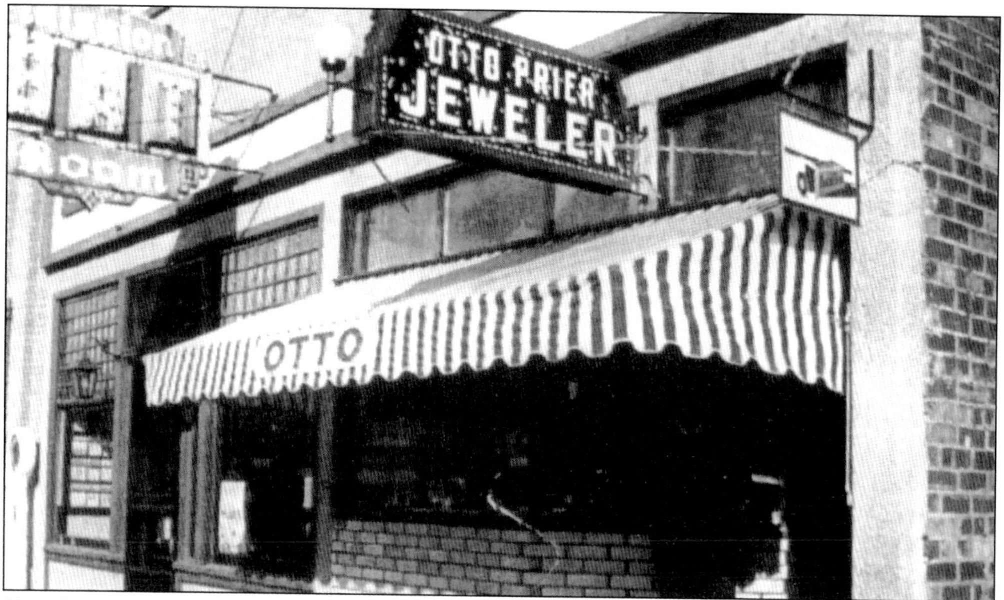

Otto Prier Sr. opened his store on the north side of the square on June 13, 1931. It sat next to the notorious Mission Tea Room (where James Jones used to involve himself in fistfights for money) at 106 East Main Street. Prier offered jewelry, American-made watches, and silverware and was watch inspector for the Big Four Railroad. His store also offered shoe shines for 10¢. Prier operated the store until his death in 1943, when his widow, Eva, continued running it and sold it in 1955. (Otto Prier Jr.)

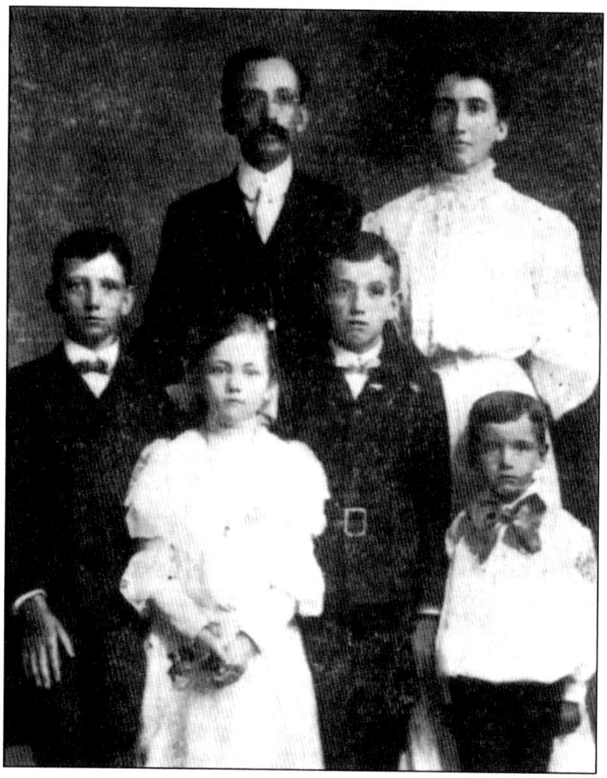

In 1902, the Heath family resided in Effingham, where L. S. Heath was a Greek professor at Austin College. Pictured from left to right are Bayard, L. S., Ruby, Everett, L. S.'s wife, and Virgil. On January 7, 1914, L. S. Heath purchased Byrd G. Olwin's Ice Cream and Candy Store. The Heaths became pioneers in offering ice cream for sale in winter months. In 1927, Bayard developed Heath English Toffee, and sales expanded so quickly that he formed a partnership with George Connett and expanded the business to start a candy factory in 1934 on Jackson Street. (RP.)

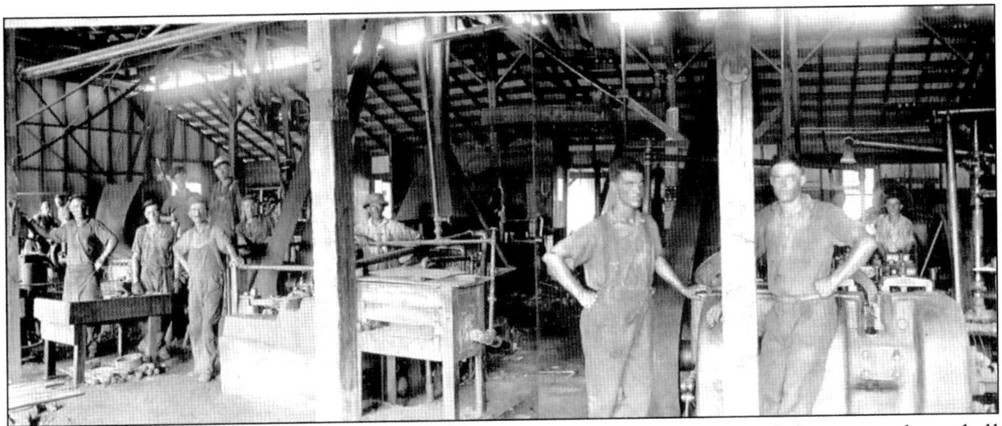

Norris Brothers built oil field equipment, and iron pieces for mechanical devices such as drill bits, forging steel for oil derricks, and making engine parts such as sucker rods were the largest part of the business. (BM.)

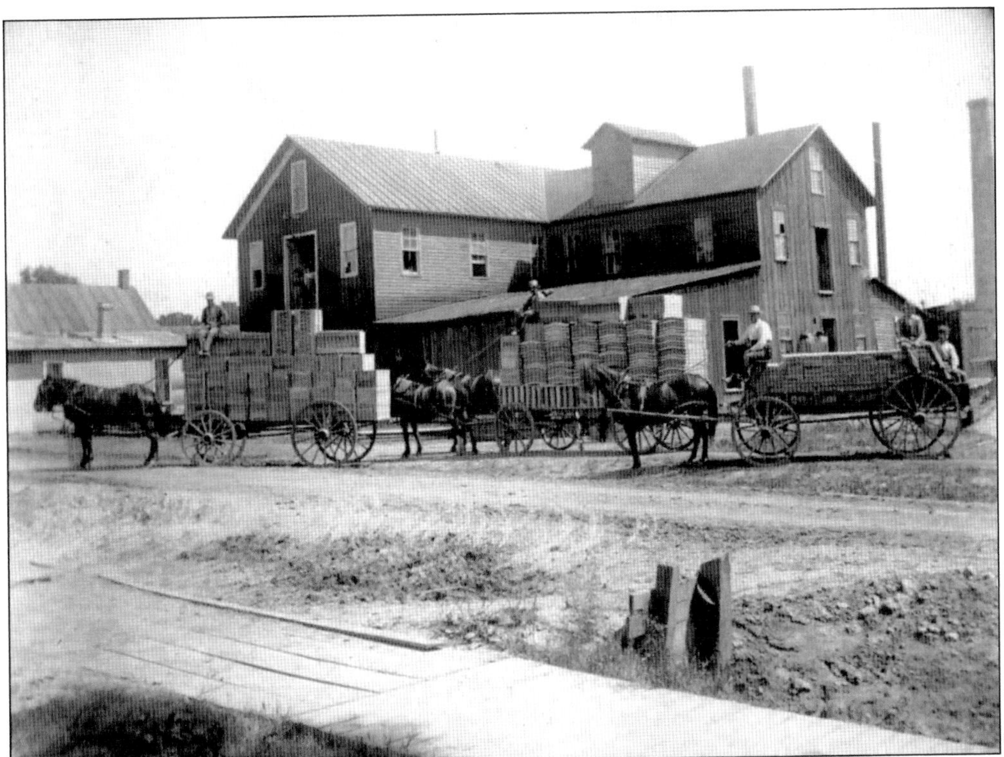

Harry E. Otey's planing mill and lumberyard was located on South Cross Street near the Illinois Central Railroad. He went into business with his father and then took it over in 1899. They sold the finest wood in the country. All the woodwork that went into the 1896 courthouse was his own, as was the south side of the square and other residences besides his own on Cross. (SJ.)

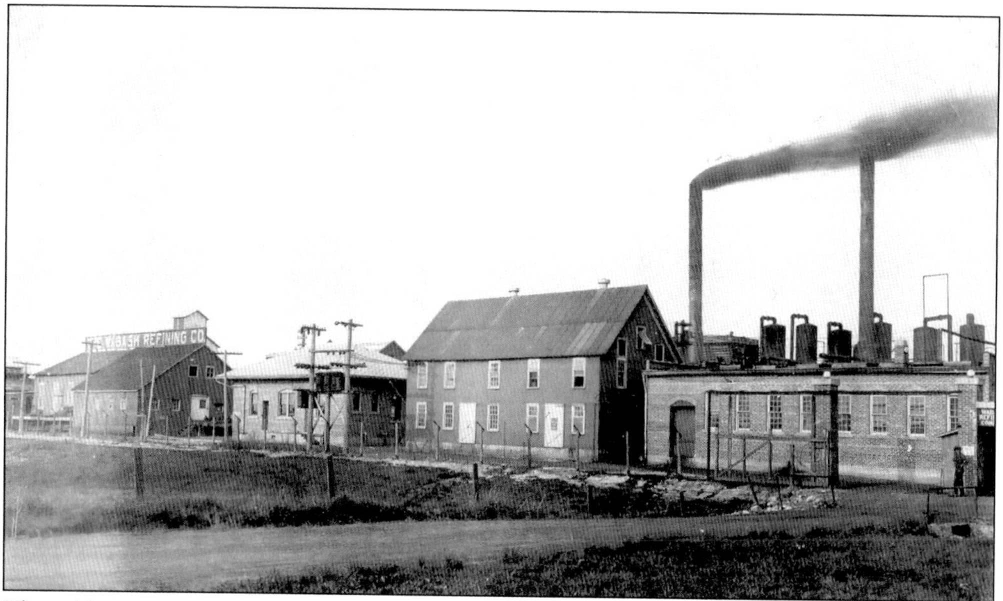

The oil boom in Crawford County was anticipated by those who regarded the early boom that started near Westfield in 1866, farther north in Clark County, Illinois. Wabash Oil Refinery, pictured here, thrived on the "oil rush" started in 1906 with Shire No. 1, and several more refineries have existed in Crawford County ever since, including the current Marathon Ashland Petroleum. The prominent men of Robinson supported and benefited from these oil rights, among them, A. P. Woodworth, W. C. Jones, and F. L. Dewey. (SJ.)

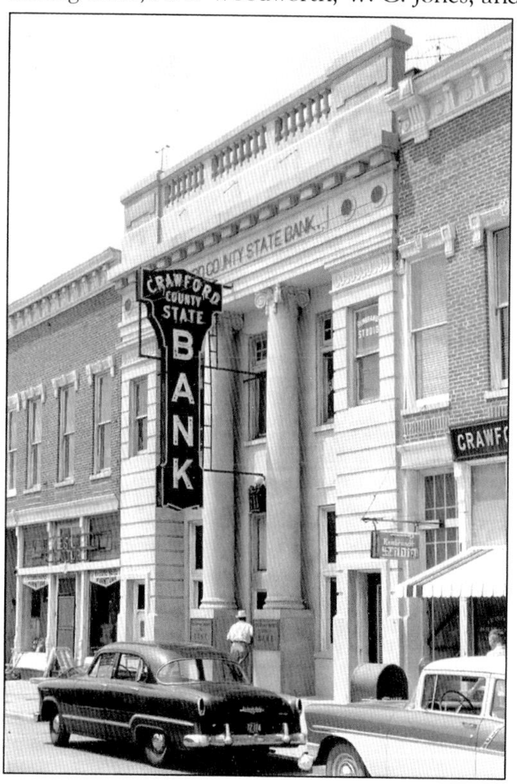

The organization of Crawford County State Bank started with Valmore Parker, John S. Abbot, and W. G. Eaton in 1902. In a meeting it was decided that Abbot would be the president and Parker would serve as vice president and legal advisor, his primary profession being law. Abbot kept the position of bank president to the end of his life in January 1934. On behalf of the organization, Abbot worked actively to promote and back a number of local manufacturing plants and farming communities. (SJ.)

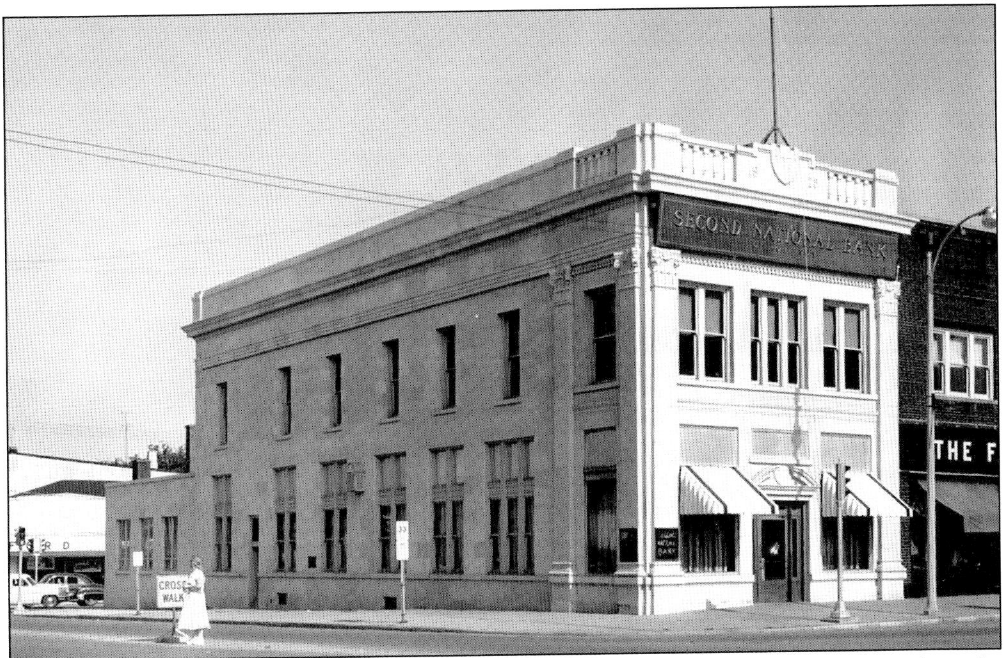

The Second National Bank, located on the northeast corner of the square, came about by several transformations from earlier establishments, originating from Woodworth Brothers and Company in 1875, the oldest financial institution in Robinson. When it was reorganized as First National Bank, the capital stock was $50,000, and A. P. Woodworth was president, W. C. Jones vice president, and the directors were M. B. and J. L. Woodworth, C. S. Jones, A. H. Jones, S. L. Bennett, and Z. Wirt. (SJ.)

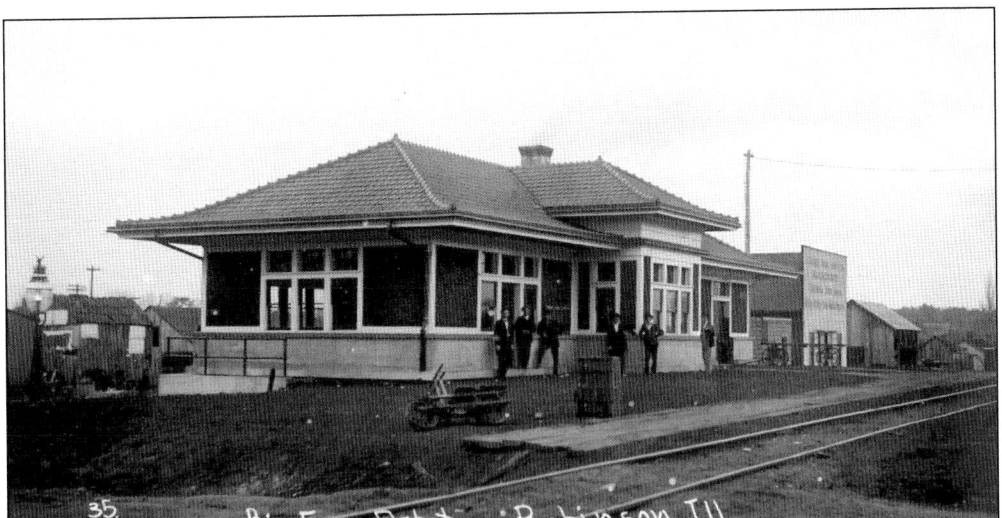

The Big Four station was heavily used by salesmen and Chicago businessmen. In 1913, the building of the railroads and the almost concurrent oil boom vied with each other in the promotion of the population and economy. L. W. Singleton, an Illinois Central Railroad employee, telegrapher, and cashier, recalled that passenger trains often carried all sorts of produce and merchandise in the baggage car. This building is now the VFW Memorial. (BM.)

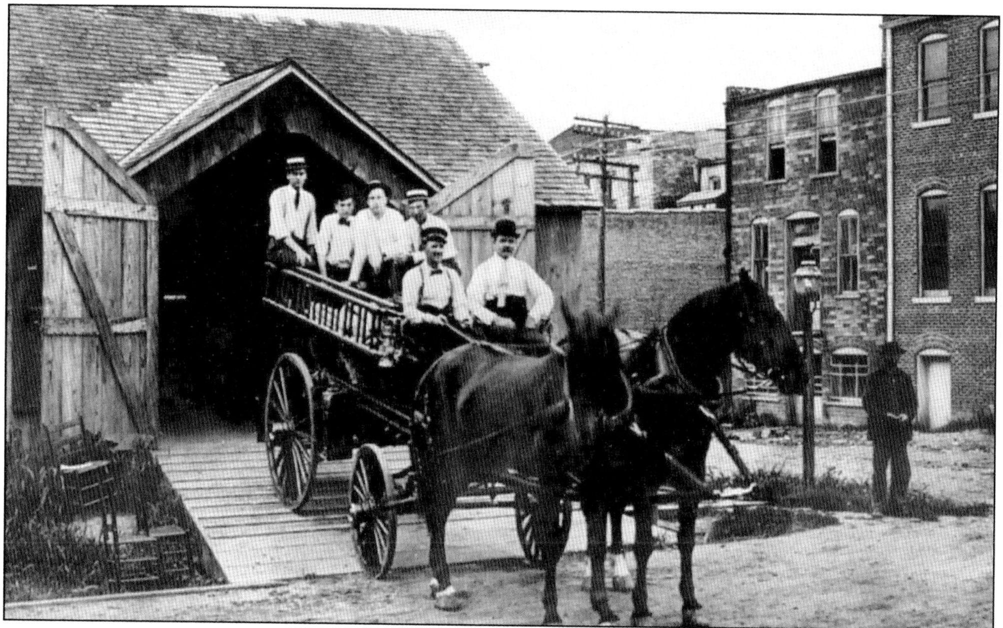

The first Robinson Fire Department started in 1881. It was a hook and ladder apparatus, and rubber pails were added. The next year, a fire engine was purchased from Vincennes and was put to use. An official fire station was established in August 1893. In 1911, this station was responsible for saving the lives of the people in Flat Rock from a disastrous business section fire that nearly burned down the entire district. (SJ.)

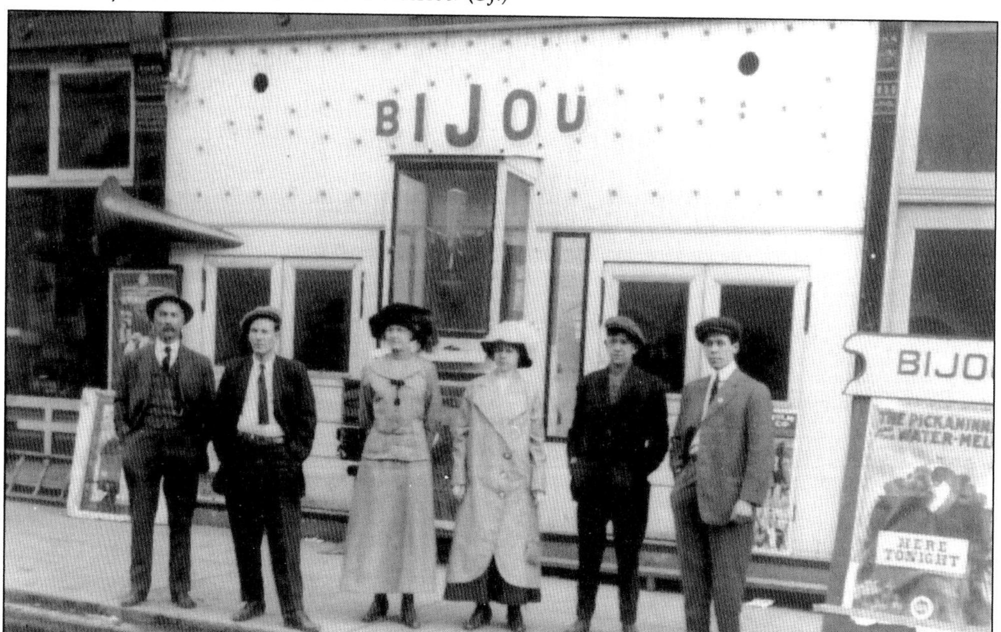

Publicity for the Bijou Theatre surfaced in a Robinson newspaper on May 9, 1907. Originally located on Jefferson and Walnut Streets, it was relocated to the west side of the square on March 12, 1914. M. C. Stewart, the original owner, sold out to R. B. Roberts. These people are in typical dress for movie theatergoing for the time. (SJ.)

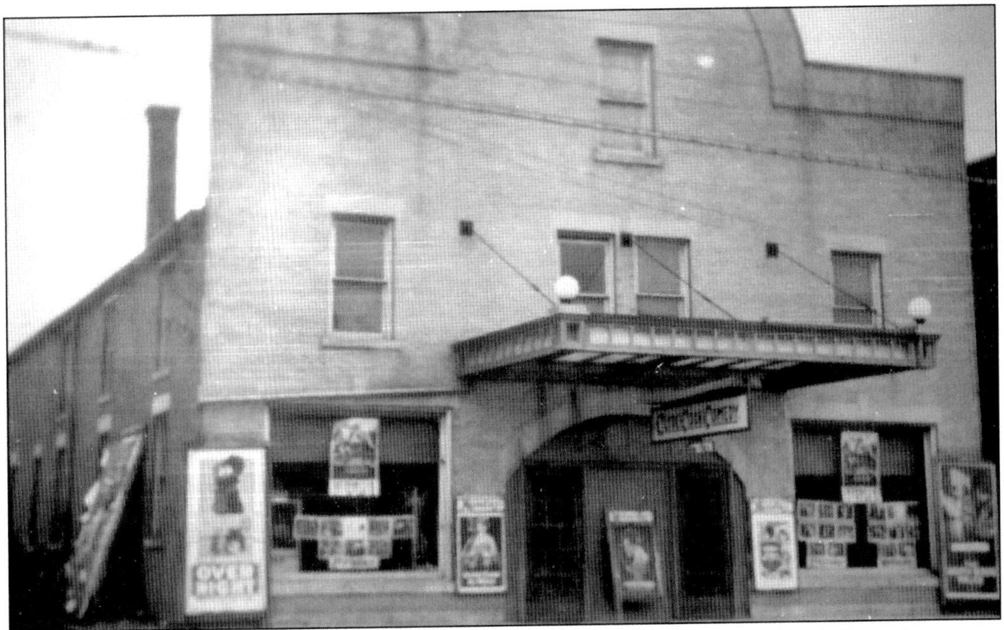

The Strand Theatre was built on the west side of Main Street about one block from the square where the former Garrard Livery Stable had been located. The theater opened in October 1916 to much fanfare created by Stewart Crebs, the original owner. It enjoyed longevity until it burned down in 1929, was rebuilt, and then burned down again in 1939, costing $25,000 in damages. (BM.)

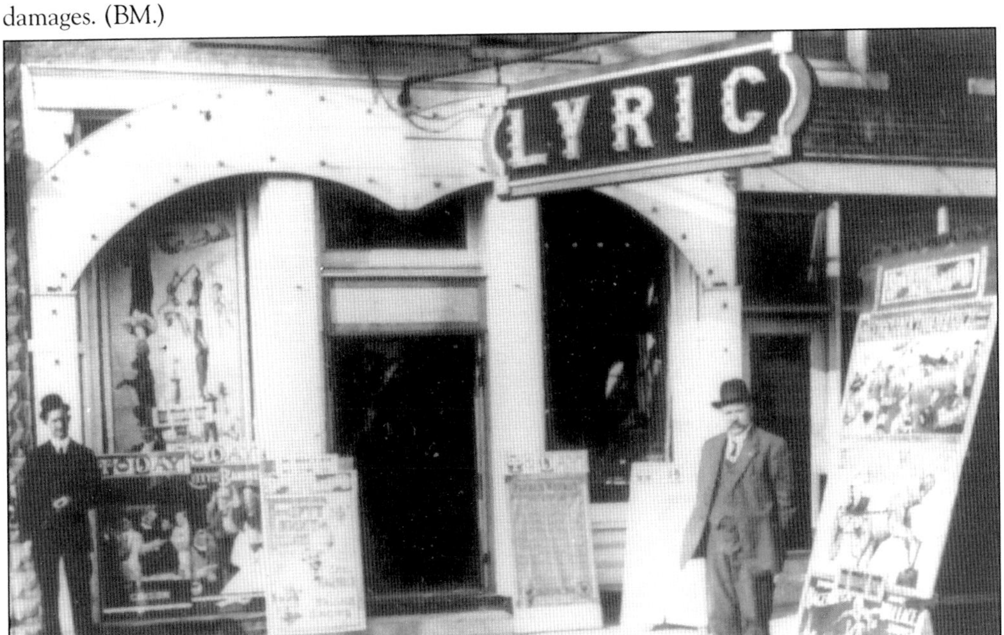

M. C. Stewart also owned the Lyric Theatre, which was located on East Walnut Street, but sold out first to L. W. Gleeck, who in turn sold it to Mrs. Charles Wilson. The news coverage of the fire that swept through this theater on July 19, 1911, described a fast spreading and dangerous fire, which cost $2,000 in damages. Wilson's insurance covered $1,500. Fires were a common risk to theater owners at that time. (SJ.)

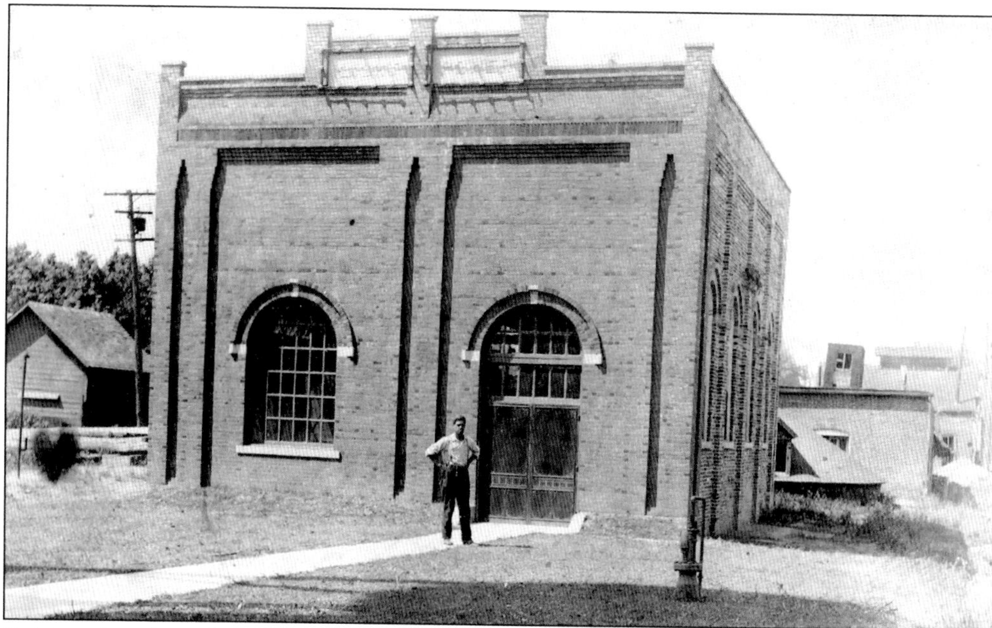

Robinson's earliest electric power plant was planned by the city board and was built around 1895. Located near South Cross Street near the Illinois Central Railroad, it had four compartments: the engine and dynamo room, the boiler room, the coal bin, and the pumping room. The dynamo had a capacity of 75 lights. Ross Smiley was the first electrician to manage the plant. It blew up in the 1930s. (BM.)

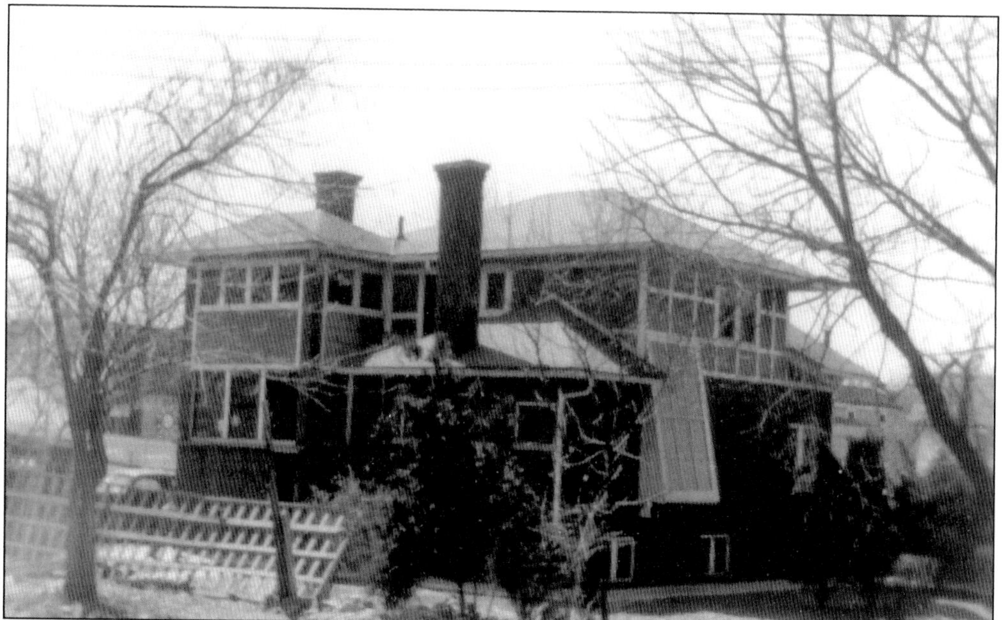

Daugherty Studio, built in 1902, was located at 206 North Cross Street, a short distance from the public square. William E. Daugherty, who was born to Jefferson and Selena Daugherty at Palestine in 1872, moved to Robinson with his parents in 1885 and went to Robinson schools. He studied photography in Marshall, Terre Haute, and St. Louis before he returned to Robinson and ran a successful gallery. The large window on the north side was to provide natural light. (SJ.)

Three

HUTSONVILLE
PEARL BY THE WABASH

Hutsonville has retained a more rural atmosphere than many of the comparatively large towns of Crawford County. It hugs the west side of the Wabash River, where sizable pearls were found in the mussel beds in the early 1900s. The larger natural pearls made their way to Tiffany's and even royal crowns.

Among the earliest settlers was the Hutson family, which was well known because of the massacre that took place in the early part of the 1800s when the fort dwellers started to build homes on the open prairie land. According to an interview published in the *Saturday Evening Herald* on June 19, 1886, by a young eyewitness,

> Major Hutson lived right across the prairie from us. Father and Major Hutson went to the mill one day. The Indians went to a man who was making rails in the timber. His name was Dickson, and they killed him, cut off his head, and stuck it up on a stick. Us children looked out upon the prairie toward Major Hutson's house and we saw a beautiful fire from what we thought was a haystack but it was Major Hutson's house and in it were Mrs. Hutson and their seven children . . . all being burned by the Indians.

A reenactment of the Hutson massacre is played out each August at the Hutson Memorial Village, which began in 1967 to honor the Hutson family. The memorial cabins were reconstructed about 1,000 feet directly east of the actual site of the massacre.

The ferry, which went into heavy use by 1854, was the only route across the Wabash River for the county and carried mostly farm equipment and horses. A bridge was built in 1939 with a lot of celebration, which made the use of the ferry obsolete.

Back when William Fife was busy readying his farmland north of Palestine around 1866, large mounds of unknown origin came to his attention and the inhabitants'. Geological surveys have been conducted over the years on the mounds, and each one tested has served up specimens of extraordinary texture and content. In 1882, W. B. Hurst and Jacob Holderman used some of the material for pottery, and the Hutsonville Brick and Tile Company came into existence by 1893. It was said at the time that it was the most durable material ever used for tile, brick, and building blocks.

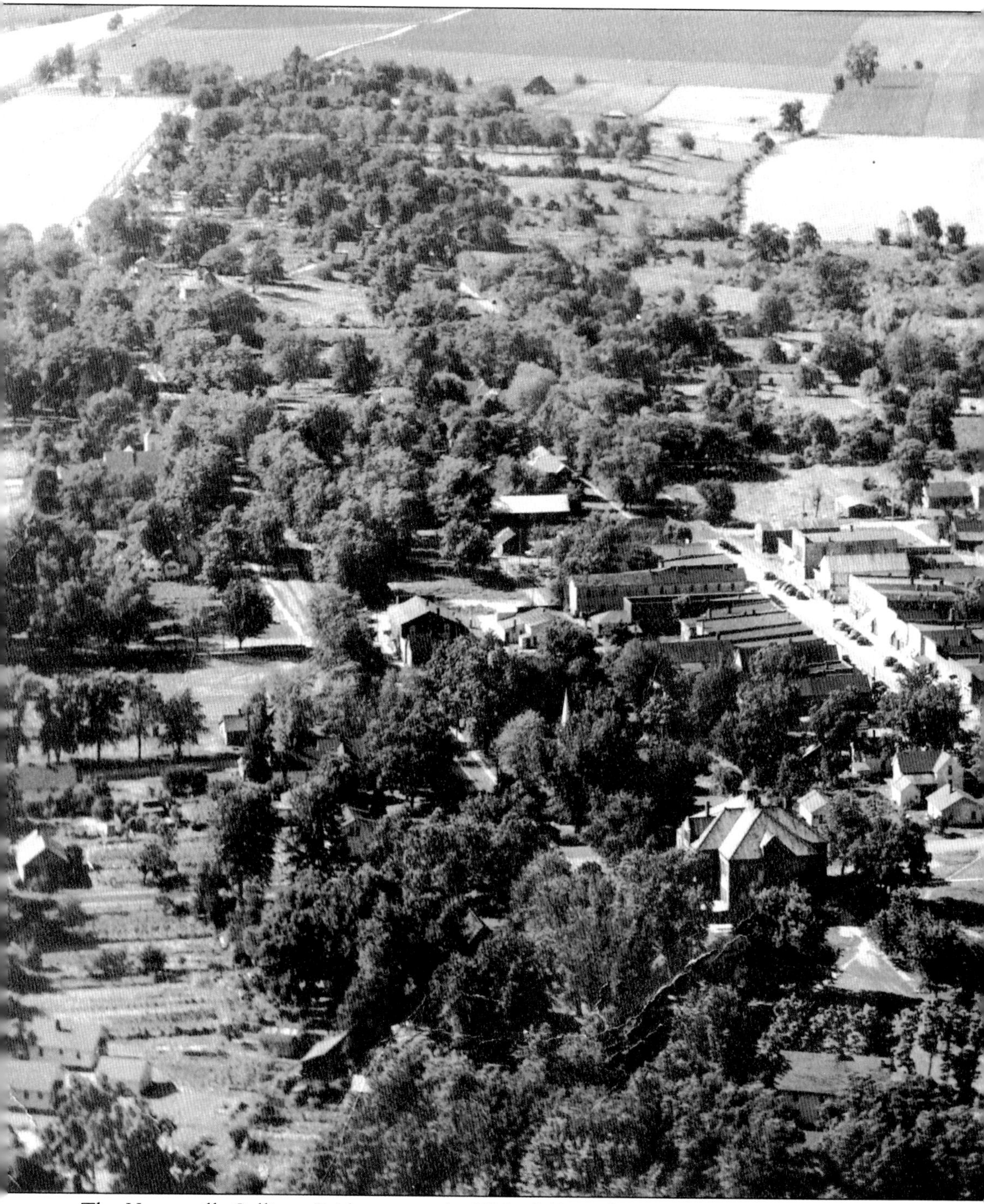

The Hutsonville-Sullivan Bridge across the Wabash River between Sullivan County, Indiana, and Hutsonville, Illinois, was the fifth of six self-supporting bridges to be built in the western hemisphere. The Wisconsin Bridge and Iron Company of Milwaukee was the contractor, with Robinson and Steinman of New York City as consulting engineers, and R. V. Milbank was the resident engineer. Set up to be a toll bridge, it connected highways in the two states leading to

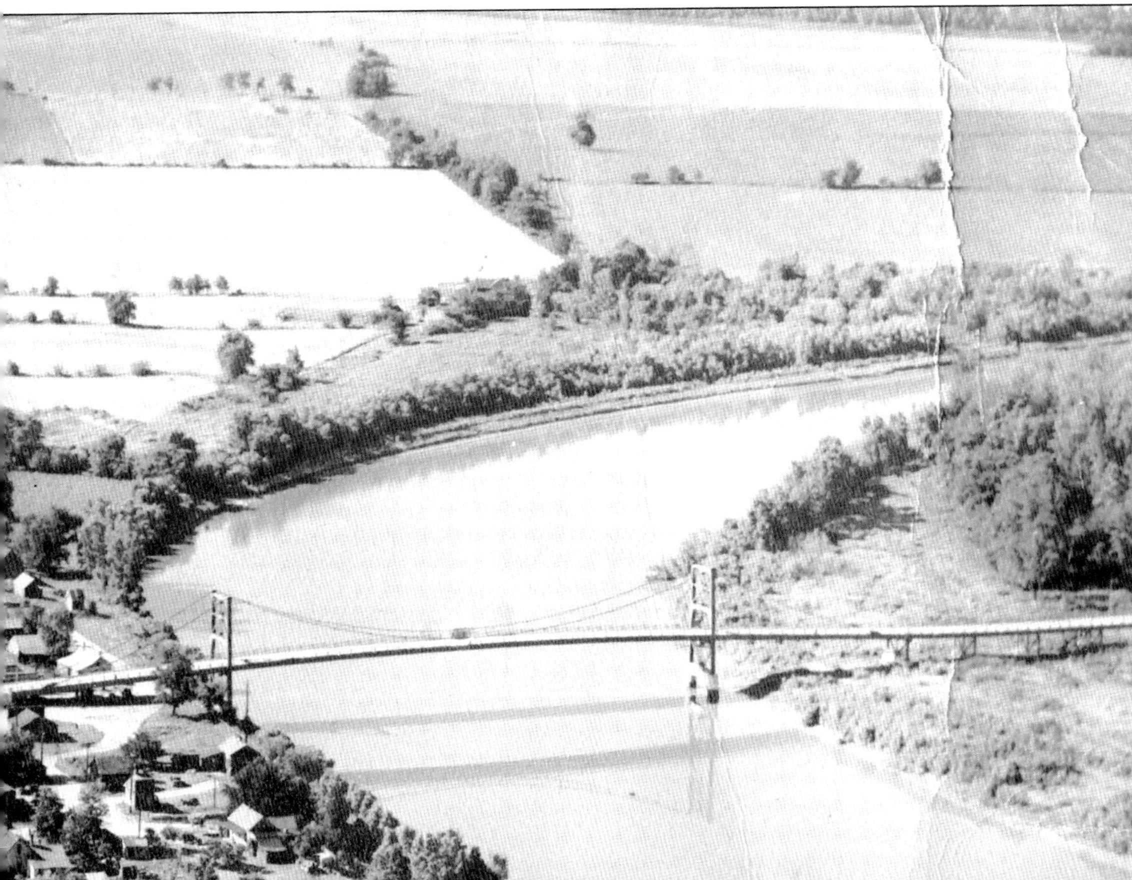

Route 1 in Illinois and Routes 154 and 41 in Indiana. Mr. Robinson was 90 years of age and walked the girders and towers of the new bridge before it opened. He was famous for designing the 1,000 Island Bridge across the Great Lakes. The day of opening the temperatures soared into the 90s, and he suffered a heat stroke and recuperated at the McNutt house. (SW.)

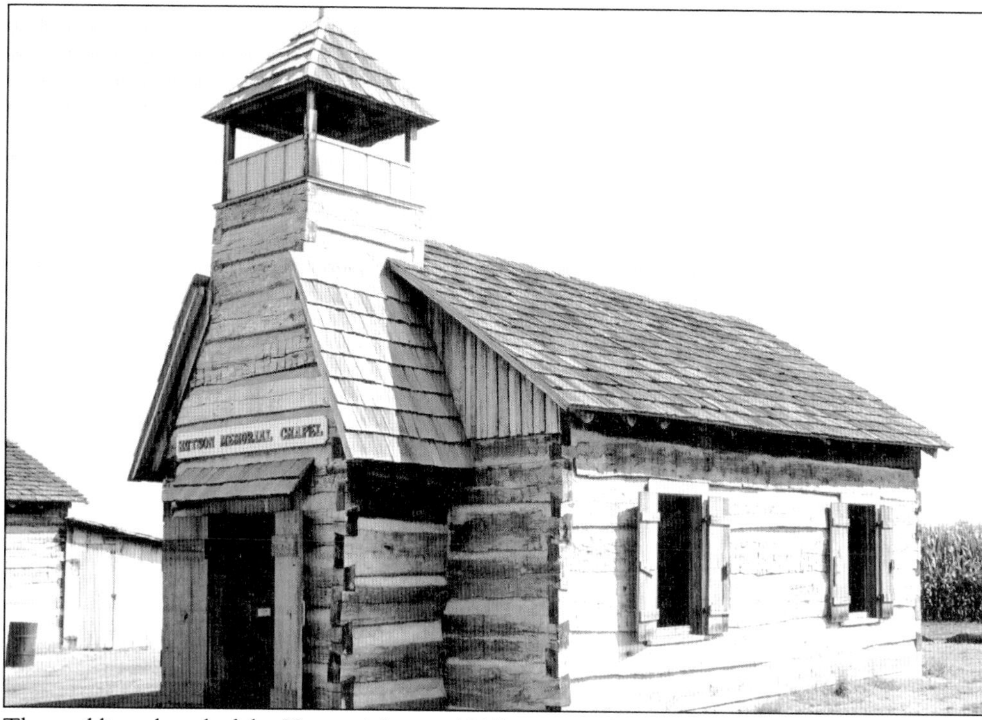

The wedding chapel of the Hutson Memorial Village is used regularly for Sunday services and for weddings. In all, there are seven cabins, including a store, barn, home, Brashear Inn, museum, and weaver's cabin, which have been reconstructed from materials of older cabins. All are fully functioning, including the weaver's cabin, which has looms still used by local craftswomen. (SW.)

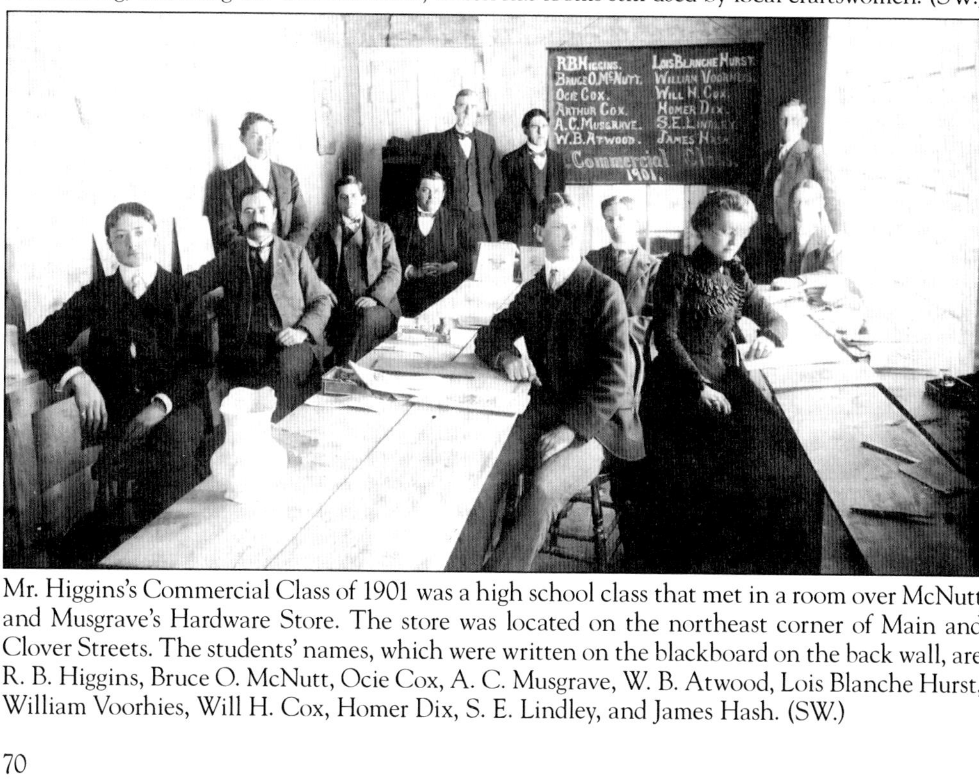

Mr. Higgins's Commercial Class of 1901 was a high school class that met in a room over McNutt and Musgrave's Hardware Store. The store was located on the northeast corner of Main and Clover Streets. The students' names, which were written on the blackboard on the back wall, are R. B. Higgins, Bruce O. McNutt, Ocie Cox, A. C. Musgrave, W. B. Atwood, Lois Blanche Hurst, William Voorhies, Will H. Cox, Homer Dix, S. E. Lindley, and James Hash. (SW.)

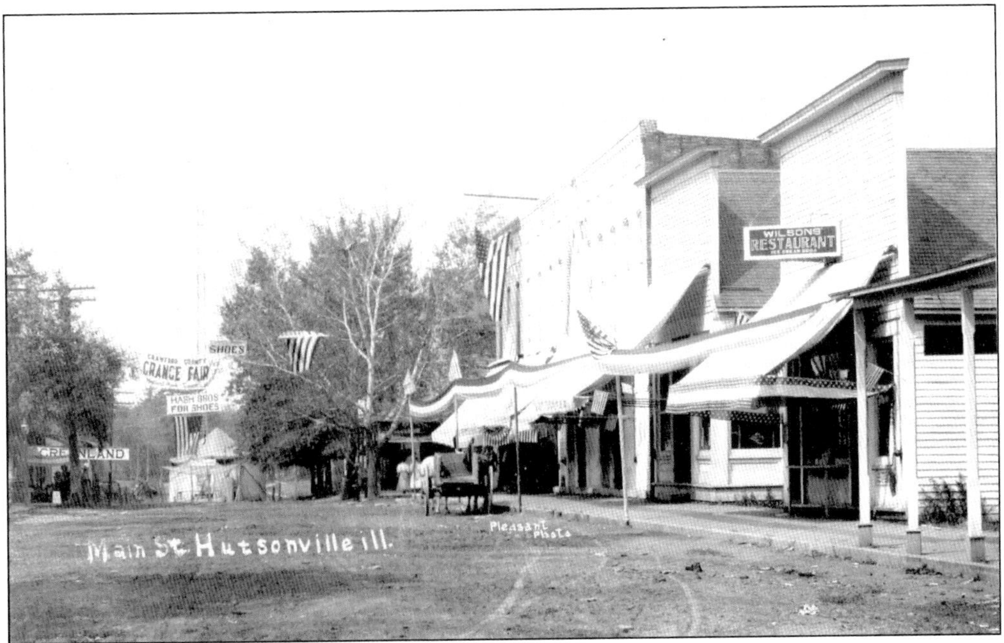

Looking north on Main Street in Hutsonville in 1902, 18 merchants offered medicine, groceries, hardware, household furnishings, clothing, and two millineries, even though the population was only 582 at the time. The original plat contained 48 lots, as it was surveyed and platted in 1832. The William Cox home was the first building, and William Hurst's was the second. They were the first merchants. (SW.)

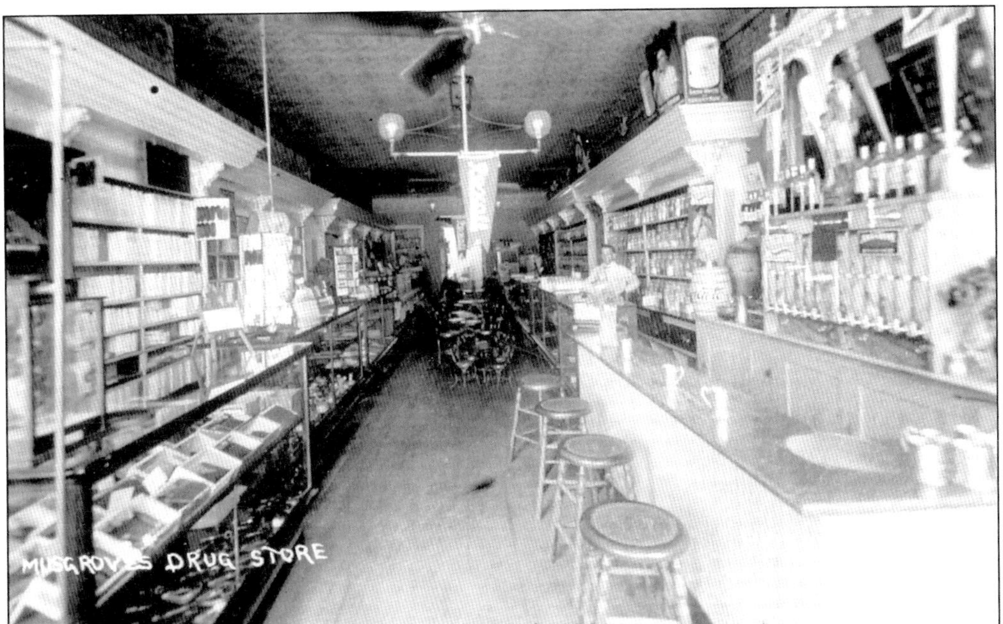

Musgrave's Drug Store was featured on this postcard, which advertised "Rexall's Remedies." Andrew C. Musgrave owned and operated this drugstore over 50 years. On his passing on October 13, 1952, he was mayor of Hutsonville and the oldest businessman in town. (SW.)

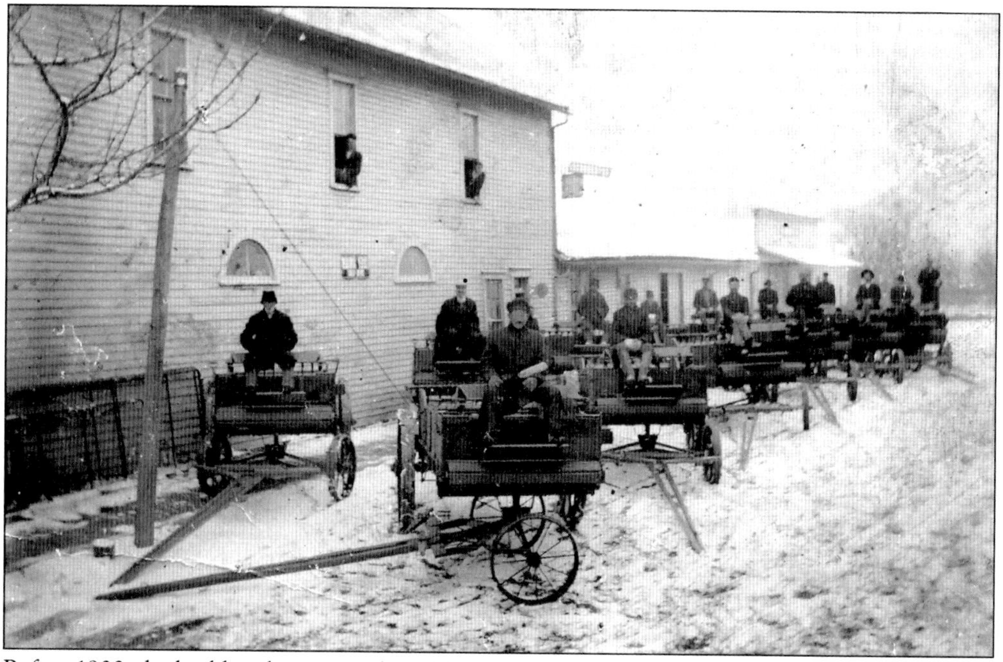

Before 1900, the building known as the Old Hardware Store did brisk business from both sides of the river. It was established in 1837 and changed hands several times. In 1885, John M. McNutt took it over and continued its operation, eventually including Mahlon Musgrave as his partner, until his death in April 1900. Bruce O. McNutt, John's son, gave up his schooling at DePauw University to run the business and did so until his death in 1937. (SW.)

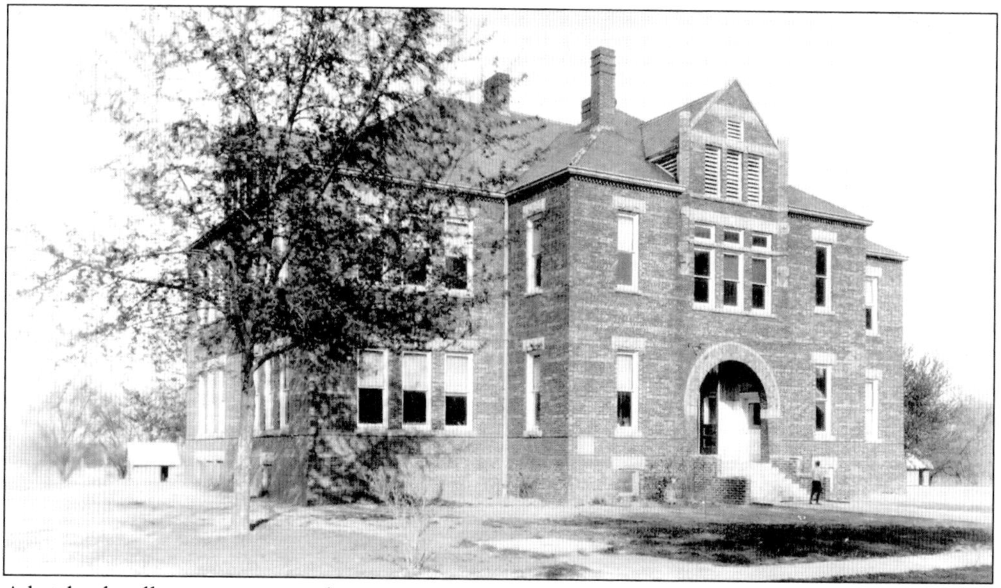

A brick schoolhouse was erected in 1900 on South Pleasant Street and had four rooms downstairs for the grade school. There was one large room and two classrooms on the upper floor. Beulah Holderman taught her first year in the grade school in 1903 and taught there for 40 years. In 1911, it officially became the township high school because of an enlarged enrollment and increased to a faculty of four. (SW.)

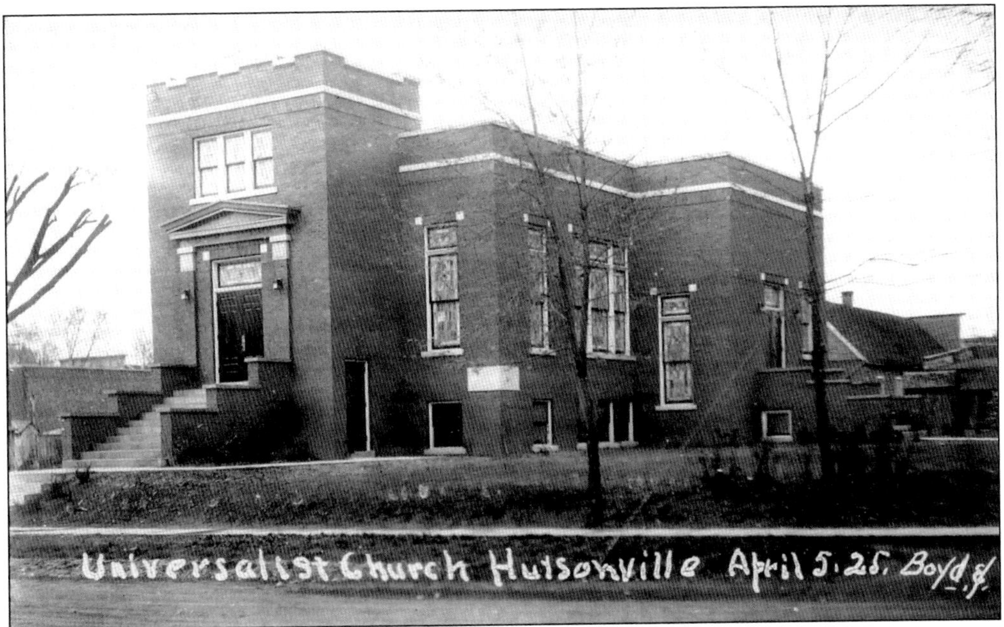

A formal organization of the Universalist Church was created on April 5, 1870, northwest of Hutsonville to build a church. With the assistance of Rev. R. G. Harris, a donated acre of land in a wooded area was consecrated on January 2, 1871. Ezekiel and Rebecca Bishop provided the land. By 1918, a new church was proposed. The church depicted in this photograph was built in Hutsonville and dedicated on April 5, 1925, at a cost of $25,000. (SW.)

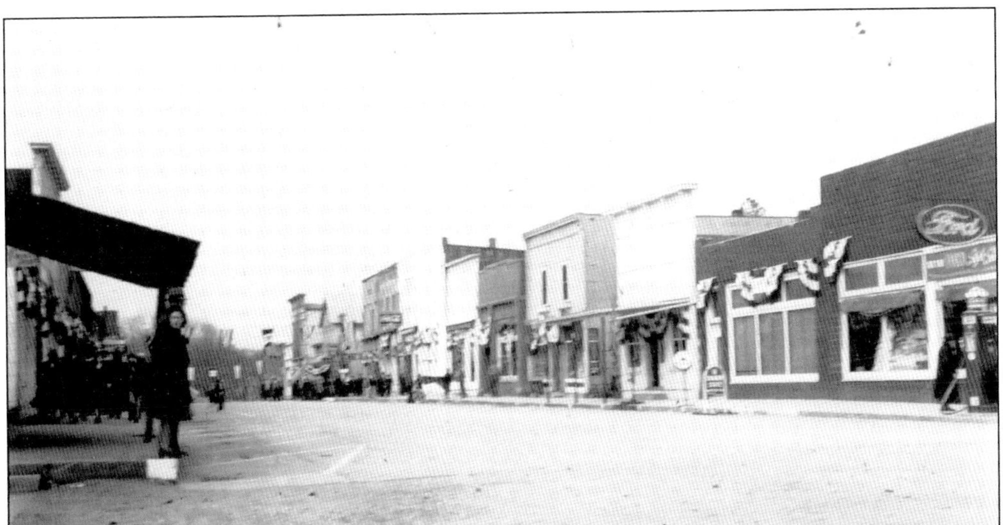

Main Street's east side during the special celebration of the opening of the Hutsonville-Sullivan Bridge looked barren at this moment but had a large turnout on the bridge that day. It was November 18, 1939, at about 7:30 in the morning. The day's activities consisted of concerts by three bands, a parade, contests, a chorus composed of grade and high school pupils, the speaking program, and fireworks at night. The master of ceremonies was Sen. Charles H. Bedwell of Indiana. (SW.)

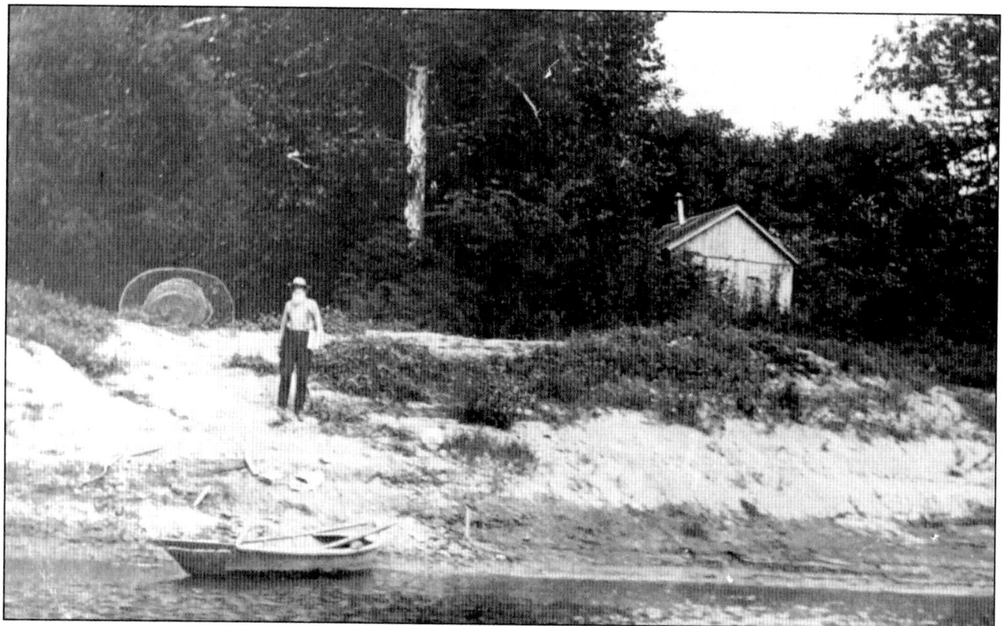

A small houseboat wound its way up the Wabash River in 1885 and shored up at Turman Creek. The owner of the boat was a man who called himself Capt. Roland B. Smythe. He built a cabin for himself on land owned by Dr. J. L. Durham. He exchanged river and wild game he caught with Durham for use of the land, and when he would talk to people, they found him extremely intelligent and educated. He lived this way for 26 years, shrouded in mystery as to his origins. (SW.)

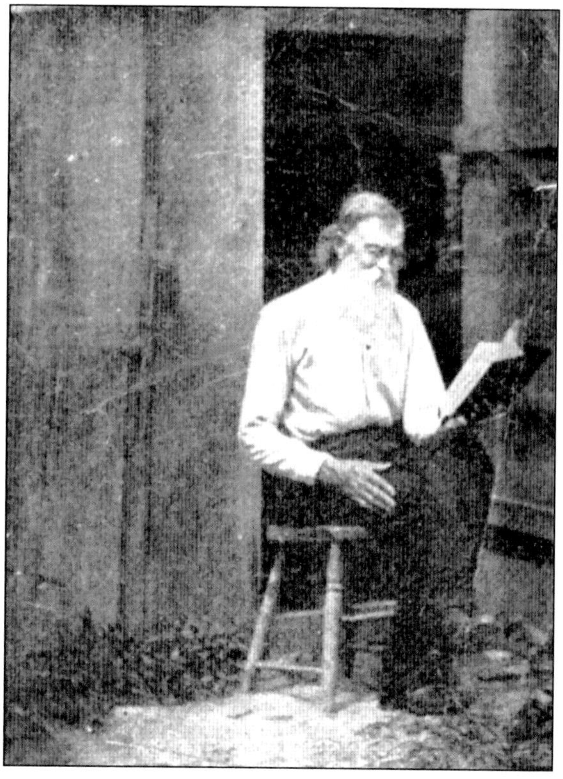

The "Hermit on the Wabash," as people had come to know him, found a pearl the size of a hazelnut and many Terre Haute jewelers tried to bargain with him for it. Eventually, he was discovered by an insurance company that traced him for his family to Hutsonville, and he was thereafter known as Robert A. Caskie, who had been a lieutenant colonel for Gen. Robert E. Lee. He had been the biggest wholesale distributor of tobacco in Virginia but lost his fortune and refused to live off his well-to-do wife's money. Eventually, he went to live with his children and never returned to his cabin. (SW.)

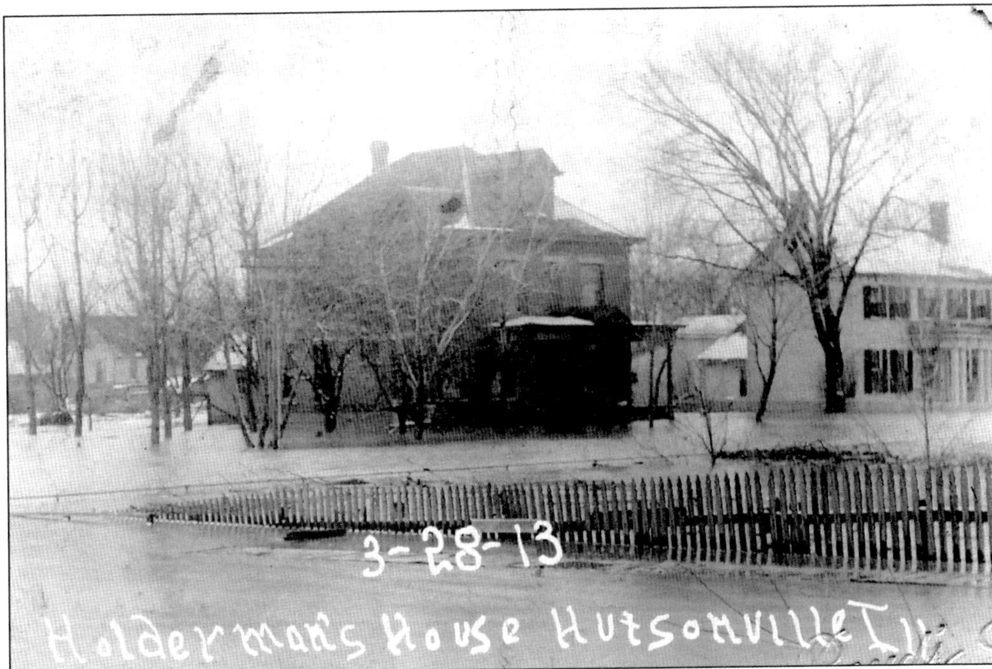

Ham Holderman's house in the winter of 1913 sits square in the middle of the Hutsonville residential district. He ran Holderman Exchange and had other financial interests on the board of directors at Hutsonville Brick and Tile, a company founded by Richard Canaday. (SW.)

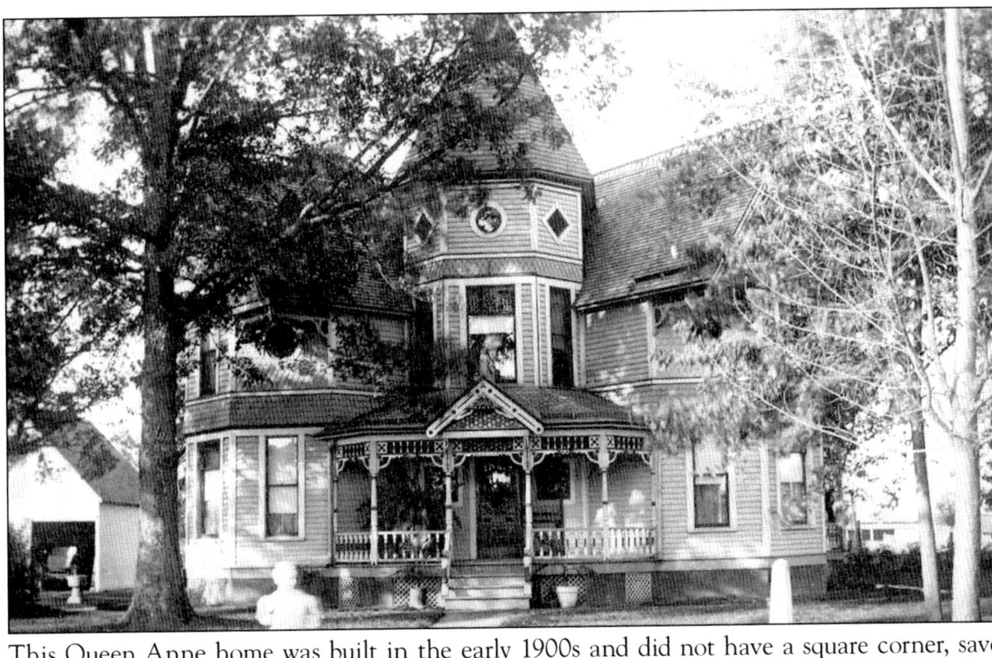
This Queen Anne home was built in the early 1900s and did not have a square corner, save one. The windows on the second floor were all given diamond, octagon, or clover-shaped panes. It was the residence of Steven D. Newlin. The architect, Clyde Kinney, was a well-known and excellent carpenter for the county. Newlin owned the Hutsonville and West York lumberyards, so only the finest wood was used. (SW.)

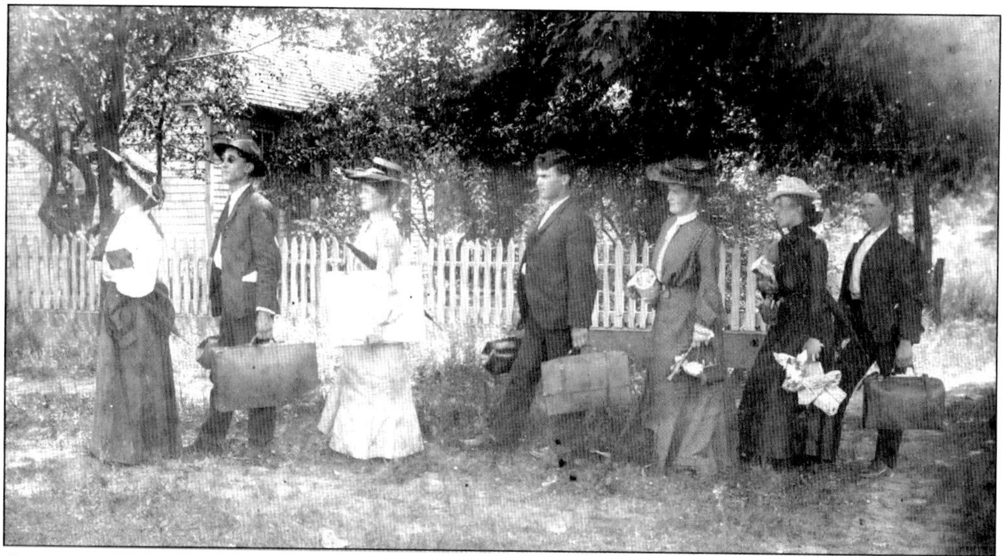

A tongue-in-cheek photograph was taken before the Musgraves went off to the St. Louis World's Fair in 1904. From left to right are Bertha Rains, Elmer Musgrave, Nellie Musgrave, John T. Musgrave, Estella Musgrave, Edna Everingham, and Dee Rains. (SW.)

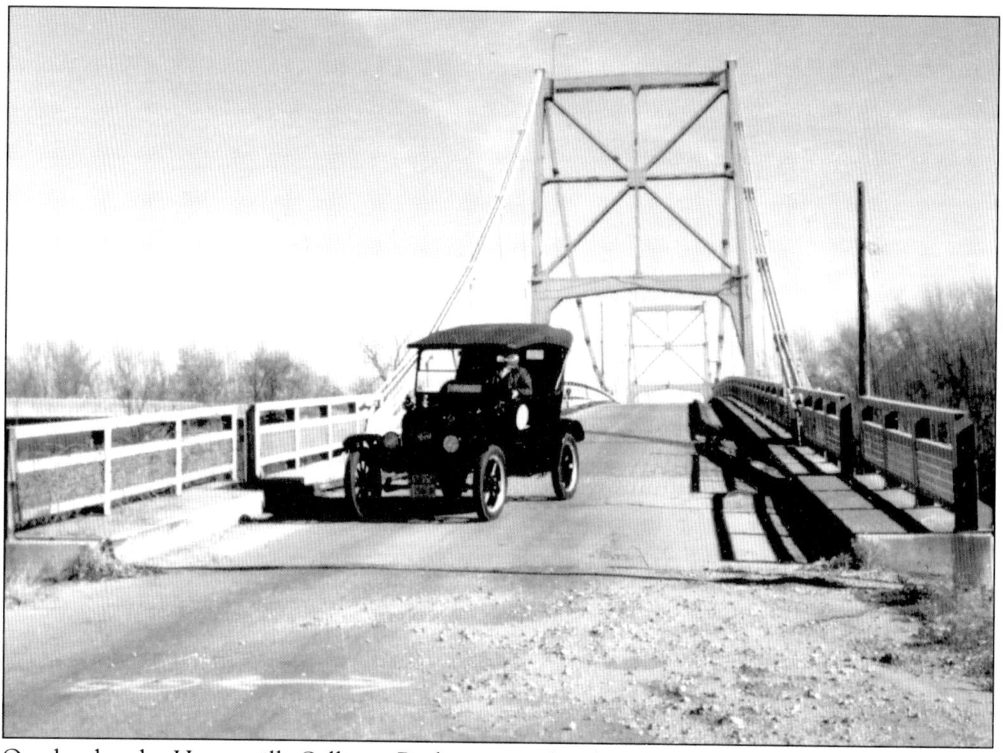

On the day the Hutsonville-Sullivan Bridge was to be closed down in October 1988, Morgan Newlin drove into town in his 1923 Model T touring car and by chance was drinking coffee with the engineers of the bridge project. He learned that the old suspension bridge was being closed to the public, so he asked if he could be the last to drive over it. His wish was granted since he was also the first person to officially cross over it in 1939. (SW.)

Four

OBLONG
THE GEM CITY

Oblong is now the only town in the world by that name, and for its size it certainly deserves the distinction of being unique. It may also be the only town in the world back in 1906 which grew, literally overnight, from a population of 795 people to over 2,000. The oil fields that developed in the county after the discovery well on John Shire's farm sustained the economy of Oblong, Robinson, and Palestine for well over a half century. Oil wells still dot the landscape of the western edge of Crawford County, and Marathon Oil employed over 600 highly skilled people by 2004.

Early in the 1800s, Lot Watts, a native of Tennessee, entered the area south of Oblong and built a cabin not far from the present site of the cemetery on the east edge of town. Lot Watts's name was the first registered at the U.S. Land Office, for section 6. The first mill went up in 1832. It was a combination gristmill and sawmill run by George Miller. Two other industries, a distillery and a blacksmith shop, were operated by Jesse Barlow in 1849.

The Vandalia Trail ran through the village and followed the road that is now Route 33. This was the only road in the area until 1852 when Range Road, which runs north and south, was laid out.

Another well-known pioneer who settled in Oblong was Joseph E. Wood, who went through Indiana in 1809, lived in Vincennes, and went to Fort LaMotte as a ranger hired by Pierce Andrews. Wood served throughout the War of 1812. Eventually, he settled east of Oblong along Big Creek and became the owner of 2,000 acres of land.

Oblong was laid out in 1872, about the same time that a spotted fever epidemic hit and over 100 people died. The town was incorporated in 1883, and the first village trustees were elected in the office of D. W. Odell Sr., the first village president and postmaster. Joe Barker was the first clerk, James Hopper the town treasury, and Hiram McCrillis, J. G. Bloom, and David Spencer became members of the board.

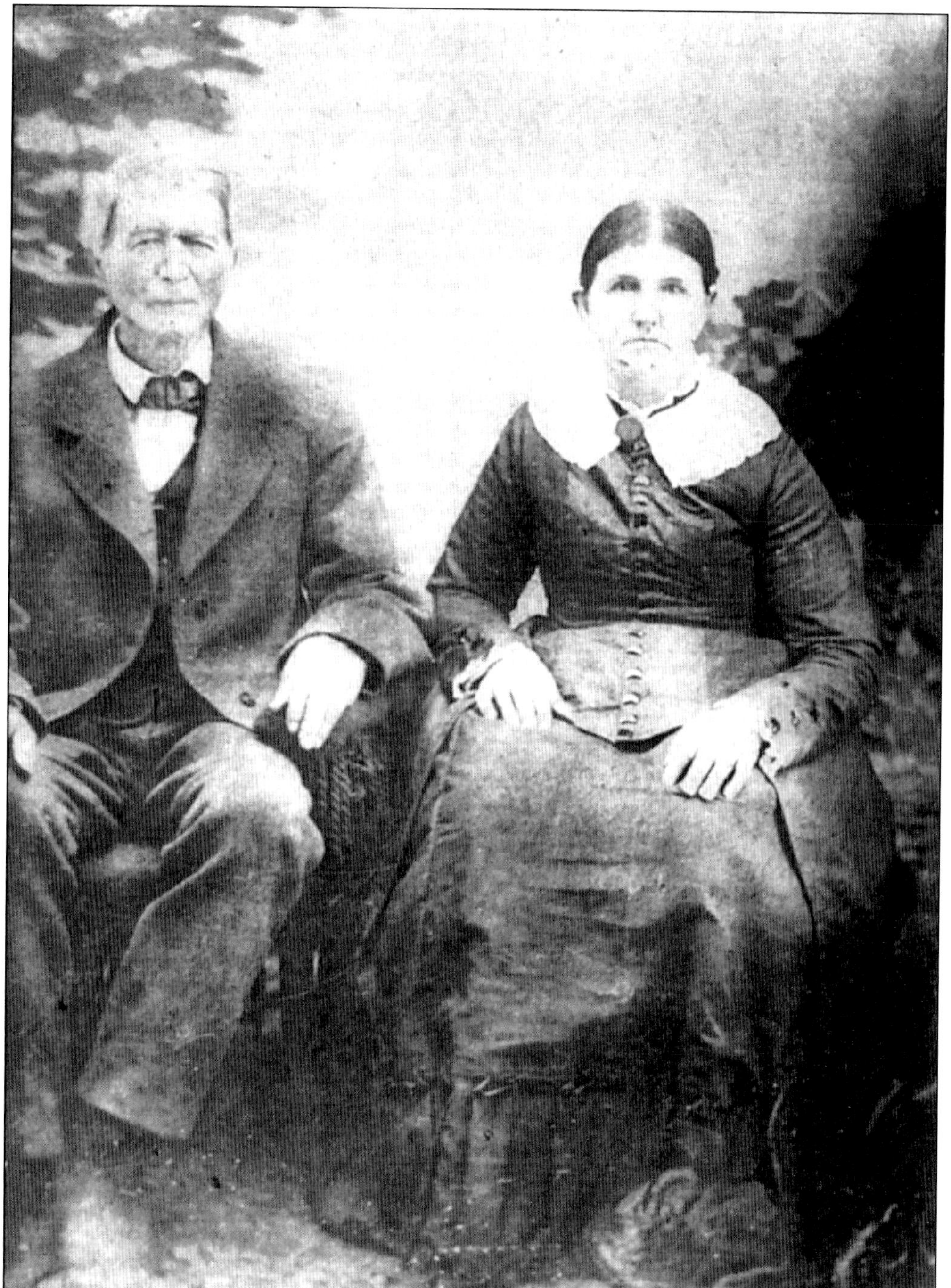

Henpeck was the very first store in Oblong and was established by a man named Henry Peck. He is pictured here with his second wife. Their children were Suzie, Frances, Clara, and son Laban. It is speculated that the location was in a cabin near Watts cemetery on the western edge of town. (OL.)

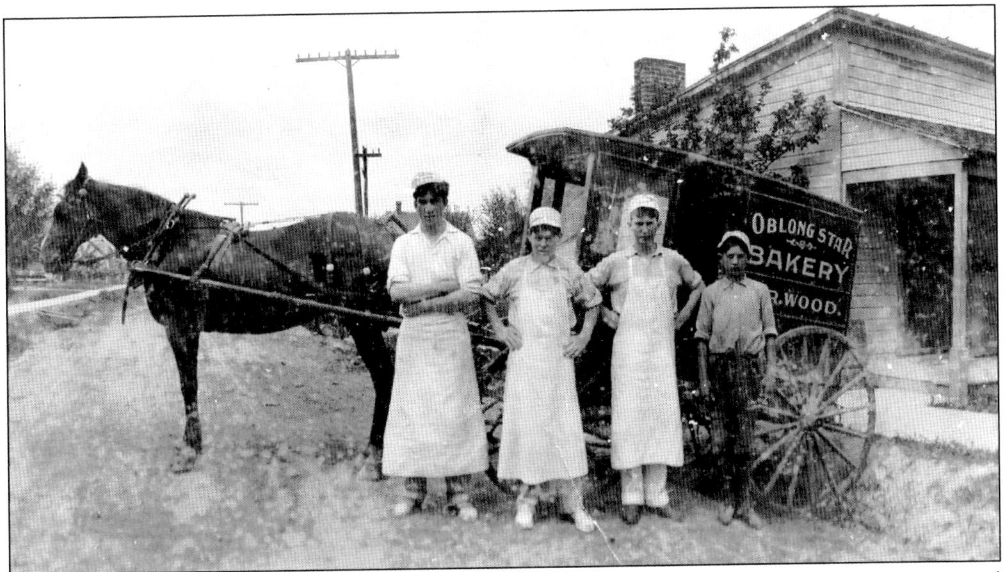

The Oblong Star Bakery was owned by Reuben Wood. He started this business in 1903 and continued to serve the Oblong community for over 50 years. The first shop was built in the back of the Robert Wood home. The first oven was a Dutch brick, built by Frank Moody. From left to right are Roy Henry, Adam Cooper, Reuben Wood, and Wylie Dennis. (JF.)

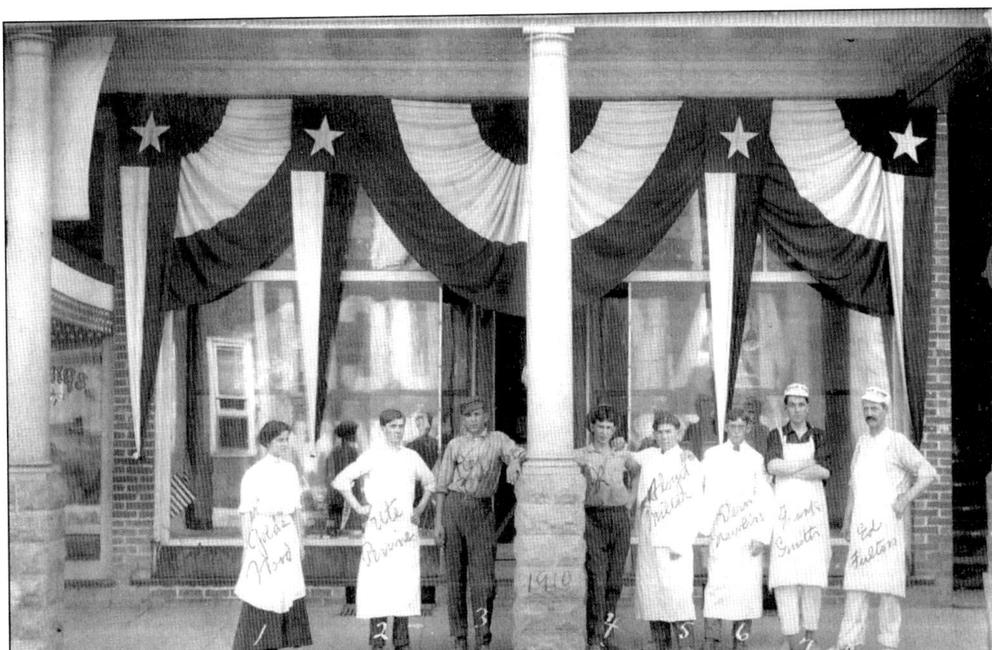

This photograph was taken before Reuben Wood entered the service during World War I. He became a lieutenant and a training instructor in an army baking school until 1919. After the oil boom, the bakery grew quickly, the building was expanded, and new equipment was added. In 1941, the bakery was completely destroyed by fire and was rebuilt with newer and more modern equipment in 1942. From left to right are Golda Wood (wife), Ute Perrins, Roy ?, Reuben Wood, Floyd Miller, Vern Newlin, ? Smith, and Ed Fulton. (RP.)

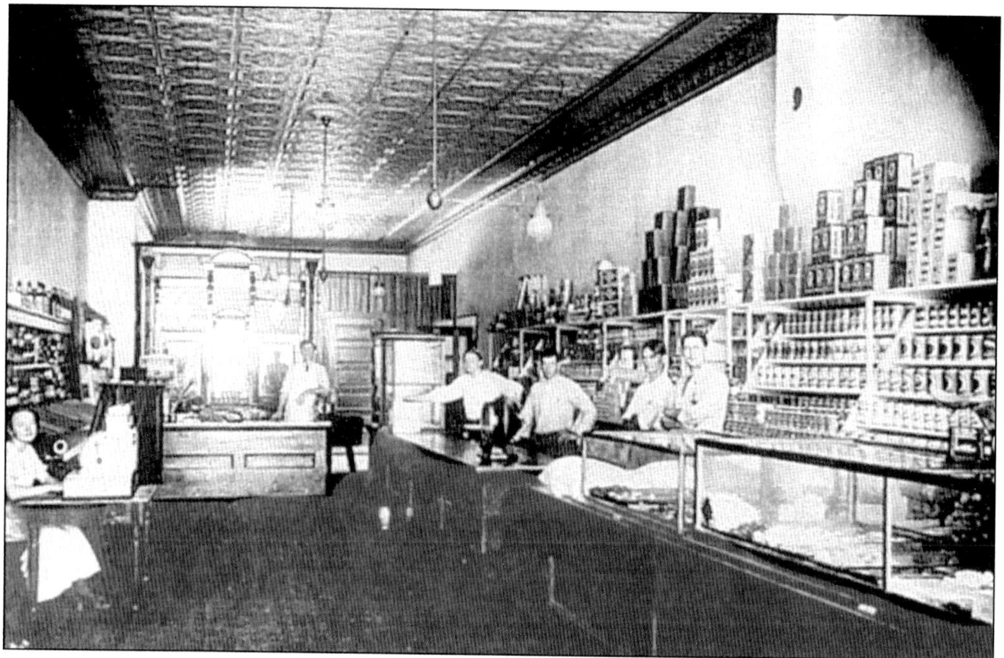

This photograph reveals the interior of the McClain general store around 1917. Wylie Dennis, who worked for Reuben Wood at Oblong Bakery, is pictured third from right. (SJ.)

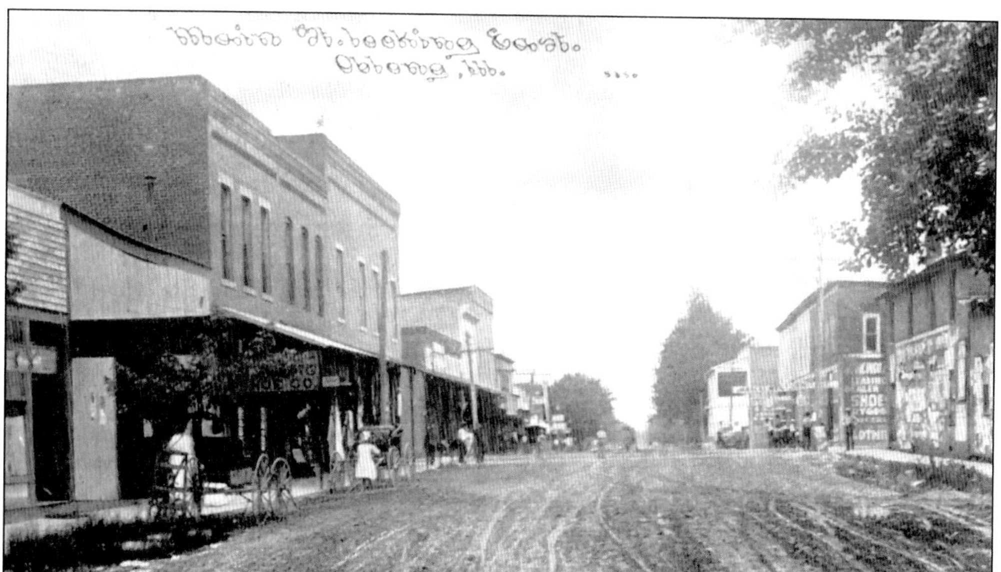

Before 1900, Oblong had a full roster of merchants lining Main Street and South Range Road. These included Bottenfield's carriages and furniture, Condrey's grocery store, the Fitt's Livery, Peter Frank's drugstore, and Pearl Sheets's printing shop. This view looks east on Main Street one half block west from the corner of Main Street and Range Road. (JF.)

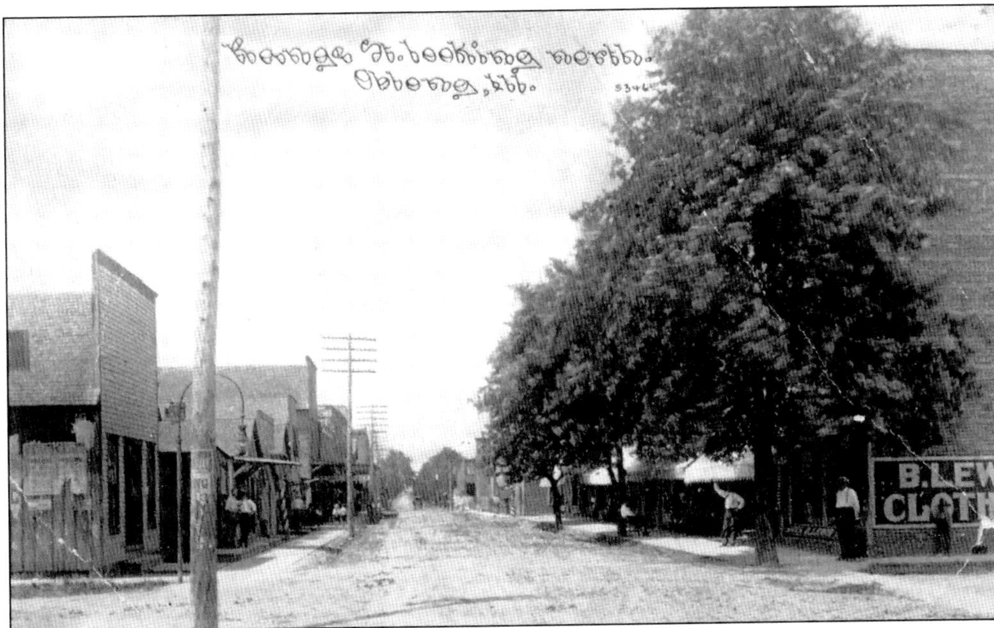

The Odell and the Wood families were largely responsible for the development of Oblong, particularly in administration and business. Many descendants of these pioneers are still residents of the community. The Odells owned a jewelry store, and the Muchmore brothers went into the general store business adjacent to this corner with Robert Wood (William Wood's father), continuing the same line of merchandise until 1919, when the building was razed. (SJ.)

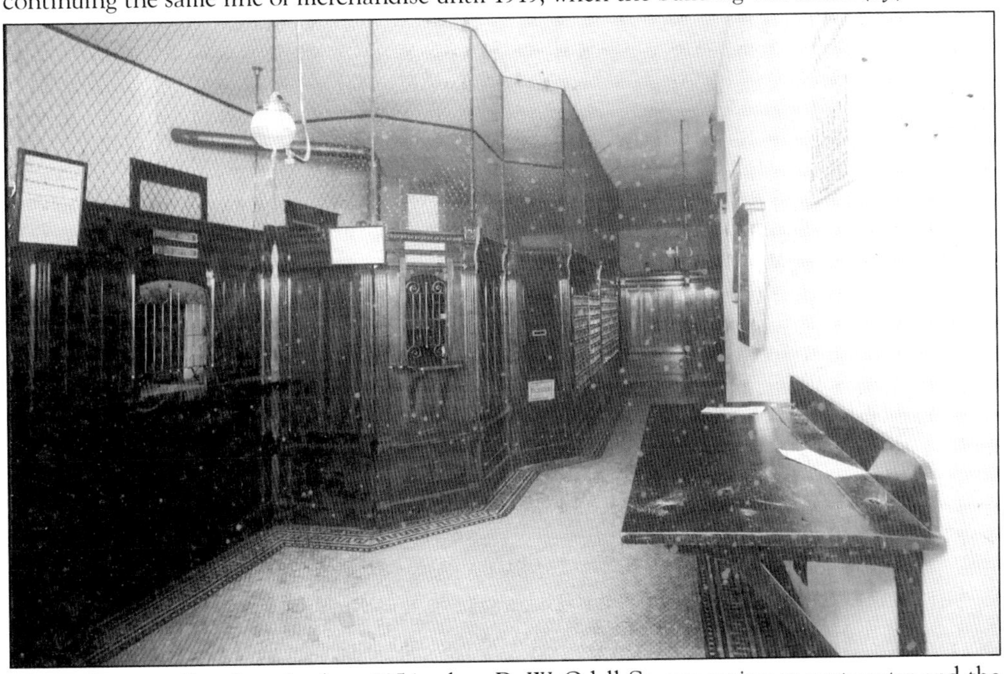

The early post office dates back to 1854, when D. W. Odell Sr. was acting as postmaster and the post office was in his store. He took on the position at that time, but two years later, Joel Ziegler was officially appointed by the U.S. government to fill the post when the town officially became Oblong. By 1906, when this photograph was taken, William Robert Wall was the postmaster. (SJ.)

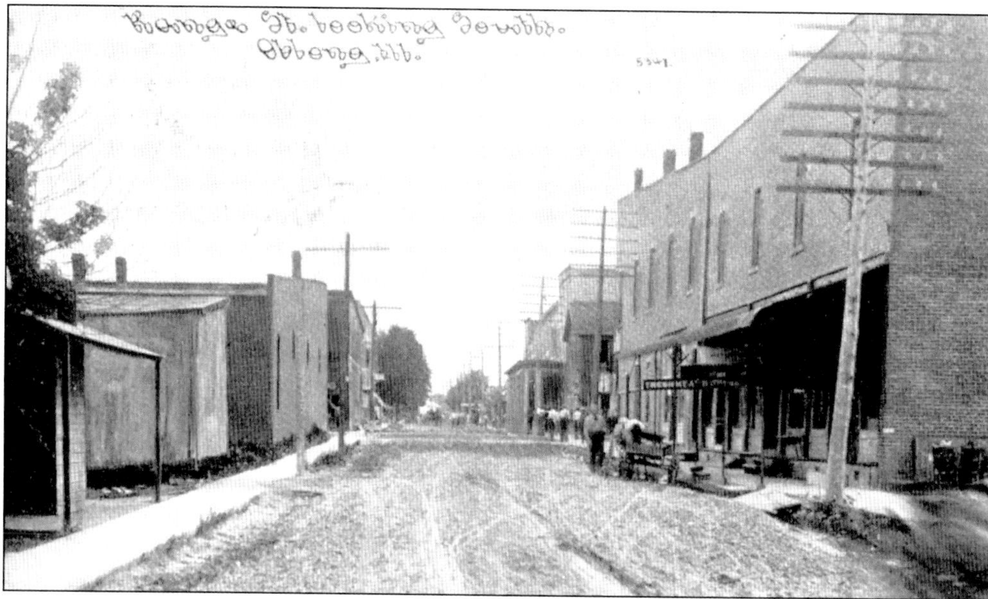

From the position of North Range Road looking south in 1906, the townsmen are gathered in front of what came to be known as the general merchandise store. It was originally built in 1860 and was begun by William Wood. A post office was located at this building during the Civil War, and it was torn down in 1919. This made way for the Oil Belt Bank, built in 1920. The corner is now occupied by the old First National Bank of Oblong building. (JF.)

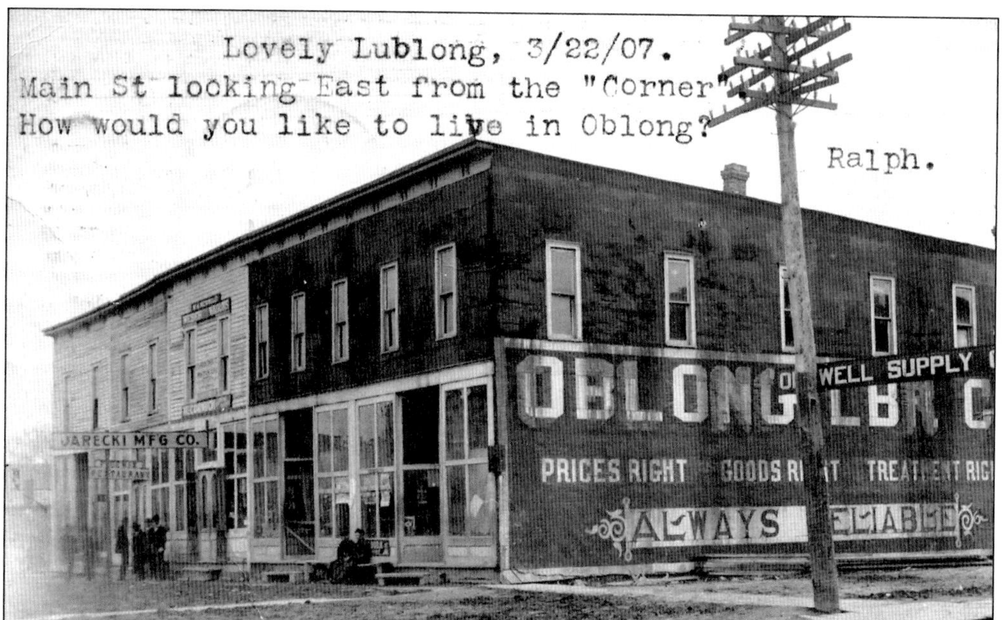

By March 1907, oil prospectors abounded, and Oblong experienced a serious housing shortage. Tents were put up in place of houses. It was not difficult to obtain oil and gas leases. In June 1910, this block of buildings situated on the southeast corner of Main Street burned to the ground and was rebuilt by James Herbert Wood with magnificent brick structures, some with corbelled bay windows, many of which remain. (JF.)

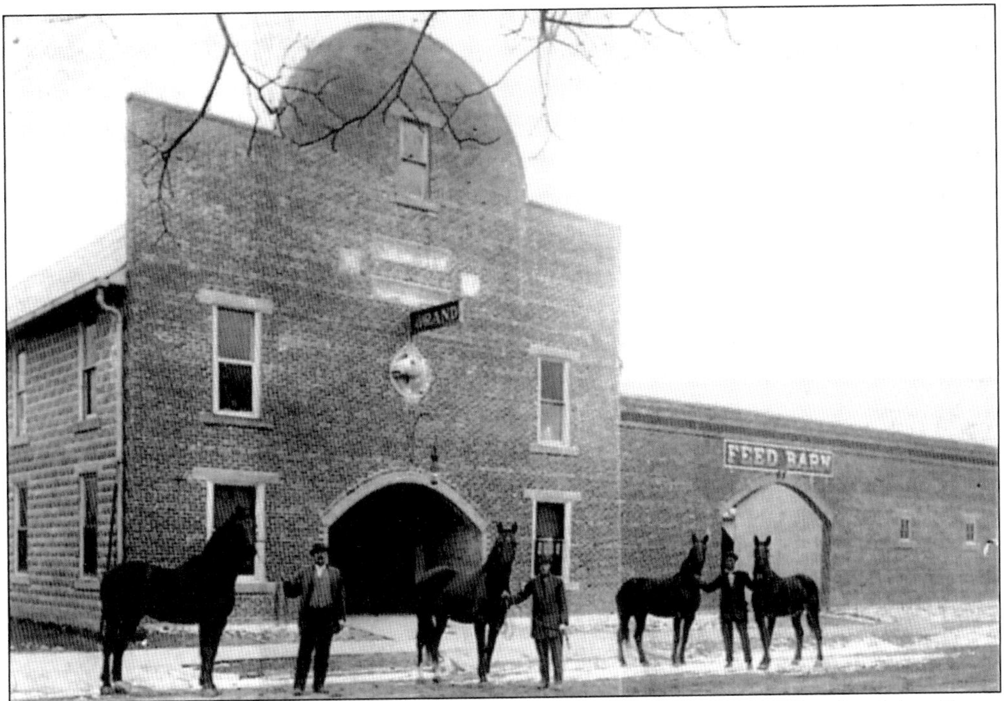

S. R. Grieves and Sons Livery Stable was located in the block east from Range Road on Main Street and was started around 1911. The horse's head above the arch is now placed as a memorial at the corner of South Adams and West Main Streets. The livery made way for automobiles by 1912, when the building was leased by George Larrabee, who eventually became a Ford dealer. (JF.)

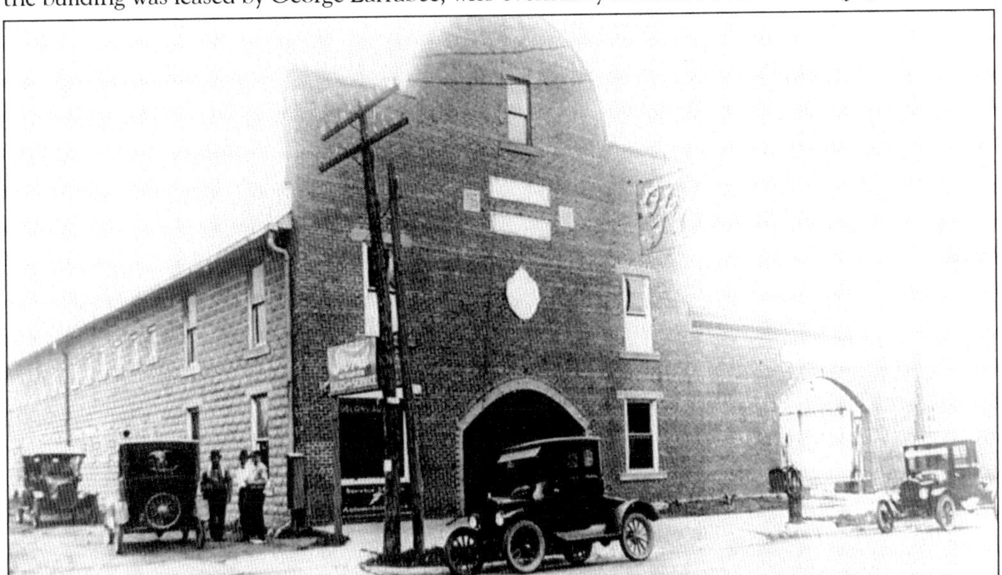

One of the men pictured in this photograph taken on August 8, 1920, is Enos Bloom. He came up with the idea for an oil field museum around 1961. His dream became a reality in June 1967, when he opened the museum at Oblong Park near the eastern edge of the lake. The museum has been moved, and a memorial to Enos Bloom has been erected at the site of the former museum. Pictured here from left to right are O. R. Smith, C. C. Oursler, and Enos Bloom. (JF.)

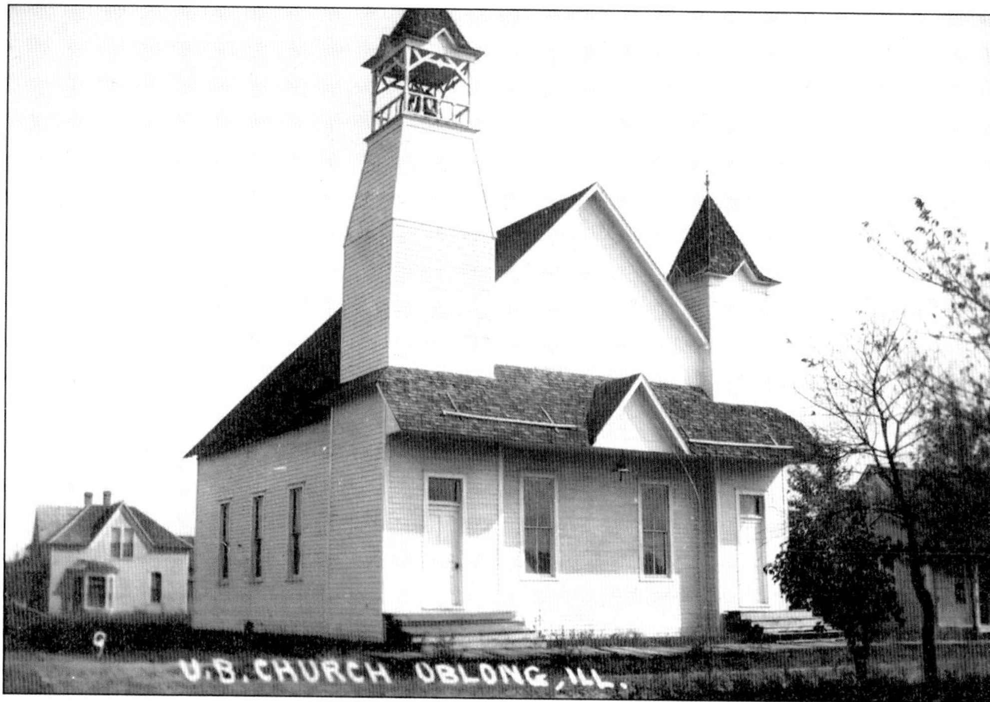

United Brethren Church in Oblong was organized under the ministry of Rev. J. C. Harbert in 1895, and this church was erected at that time. Today Oblong has no less than 13 thriving churches of various faiths. (JF.)

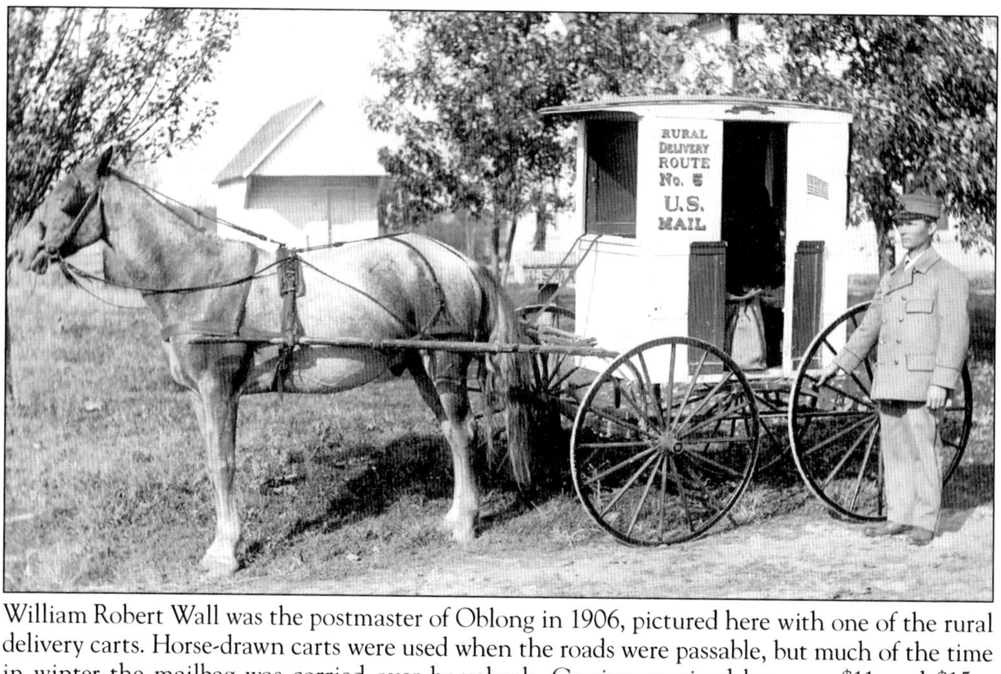

William Robert Wall was the postmaster of Oblong in 1906, pictured here with one of the rural delivery carts. Horse-drawn carts were used when the roads were passable, but much of the time in winter the mailbag was carried over horseback. Carriers received between $11 and $15 a month. (JF.)

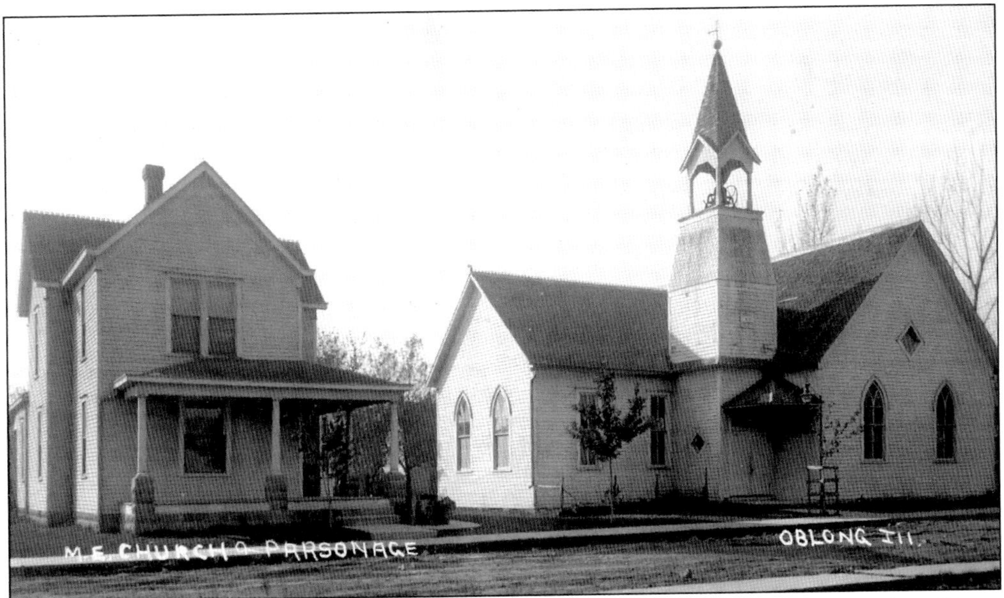

The old Methodist Episcopal Church and parsonage started here, later it became the Oblong Pilgrim Holiness Church. Oblong Wesleyan Church is located on the same corner of West Missouri and South Adams Streets, having been built a few years ago. (SJ.)

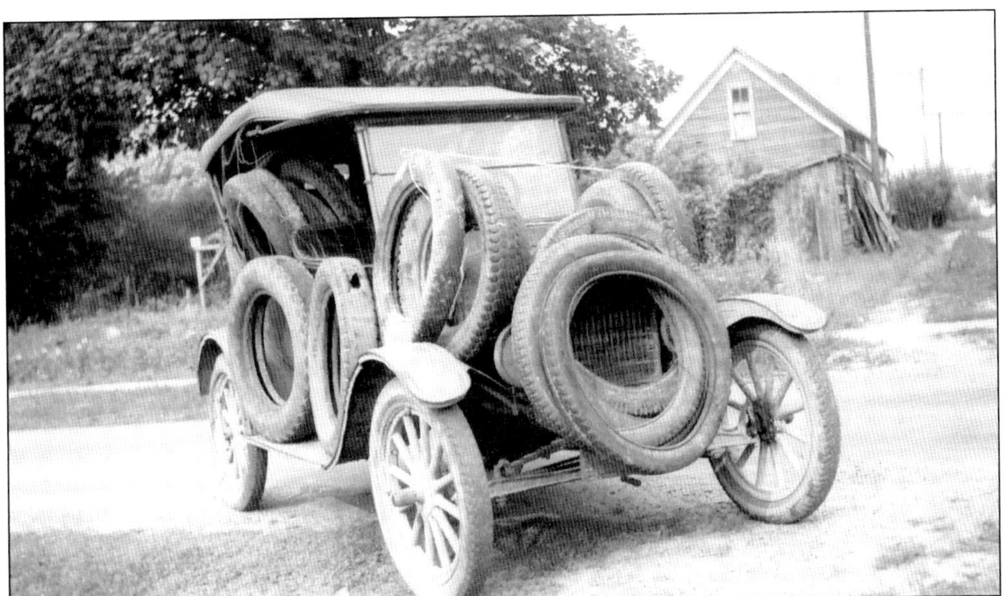

William Robert Wall was using this 1923 Ford for his mail delivery during World War II. Rubber was scarce and everyone was to hand in anything they could spare. When he delivered mail, many people left their old tires out by the mailbox. He would attach them to his car and when back in town, delivered the tires to a designated area. (JF.)

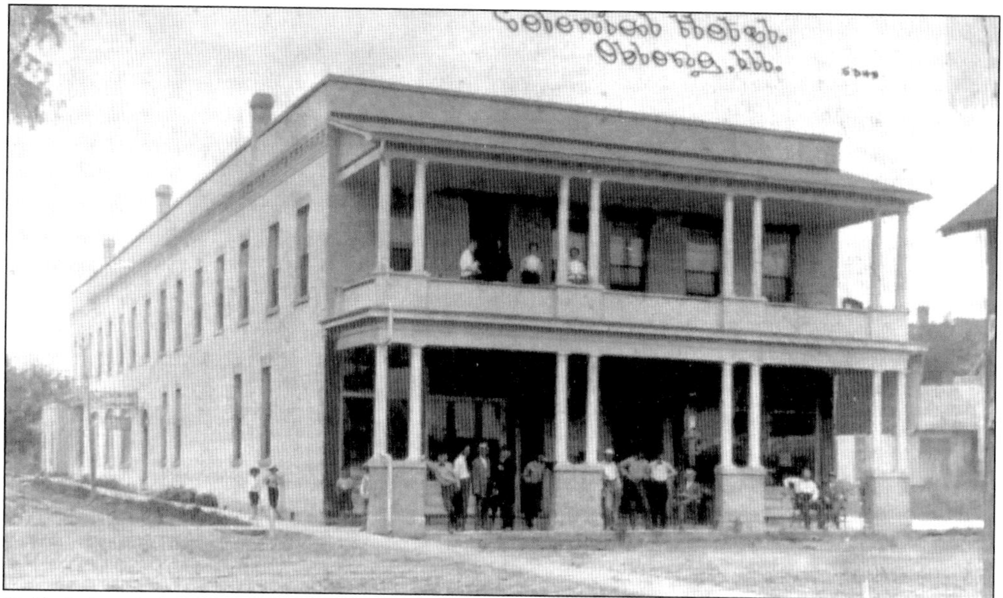

Called the Colonial Hotel and the Gem Hotel by turns, this beautiful building was erected in 1908 and was officially christened the Gem Hotel. The original owner was H. B. Smith. It housed the Oil Belt Bank and the Wood Investment Company. It held as many as 150 guests and was important to Oblong during the oil boom. It burned to the ground on September 6, 1918, along with its furnishings. The Oil Belt Bank was able to retrieve important documents and furnishings as that part of the building mysteriously burned slowly. (JF.)

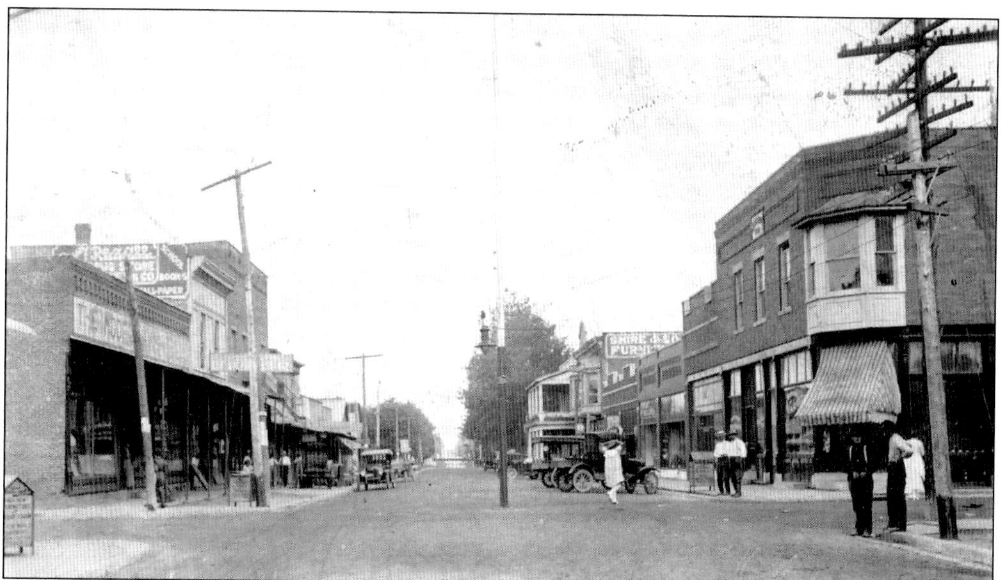

In 1918, the first block east of the Range Road and Main Street intersection was thriving with businesses. The buildings along the right side of the photograph included the block that James Herbert Wood rebuilt after the fire of 1910, and the left-hand side had a Rexall drugstore run by Robert and Myra June Edwards until 1946, when it was purchased by Ezra and Caroline Harmon. Today the third generation of Harmons runs an expanded and remodeled store close to the original location. (JF.)

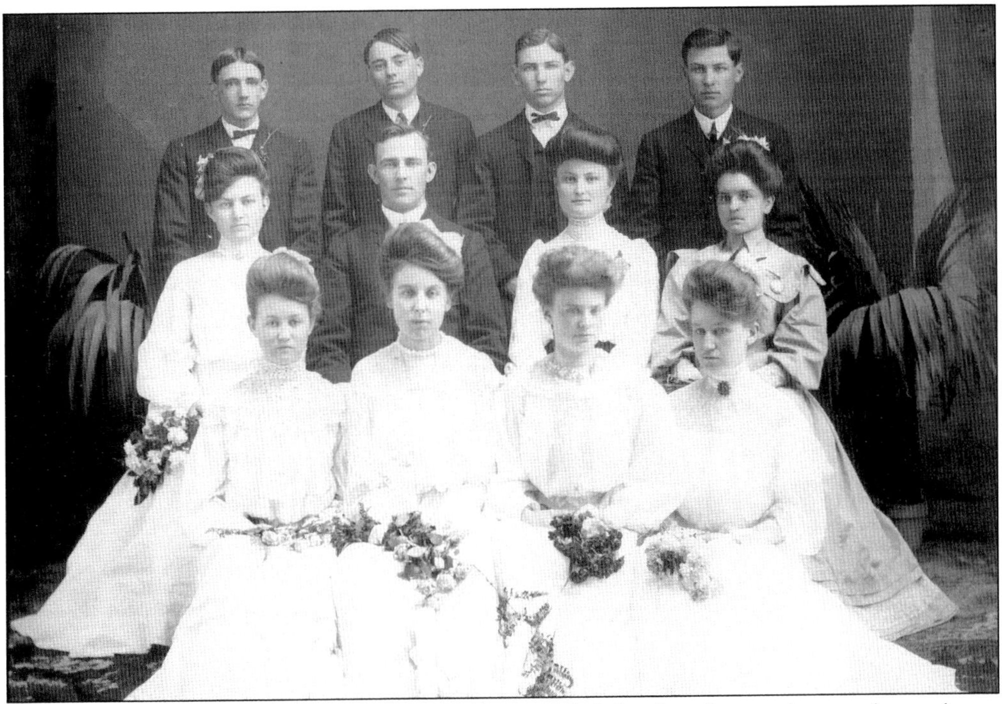

Pictured here are the debutantes and 1904 Oblong High School graduates. Among the graduates were young school alumni. The assistant principal, Cora Thrasher, who was a recent college graduate of Eddingham College, where she had been head librarian, is seated in the second row, far right. The principal, Prof. John T. Lindsay, is seated in the second row, second from the left. (RP.)

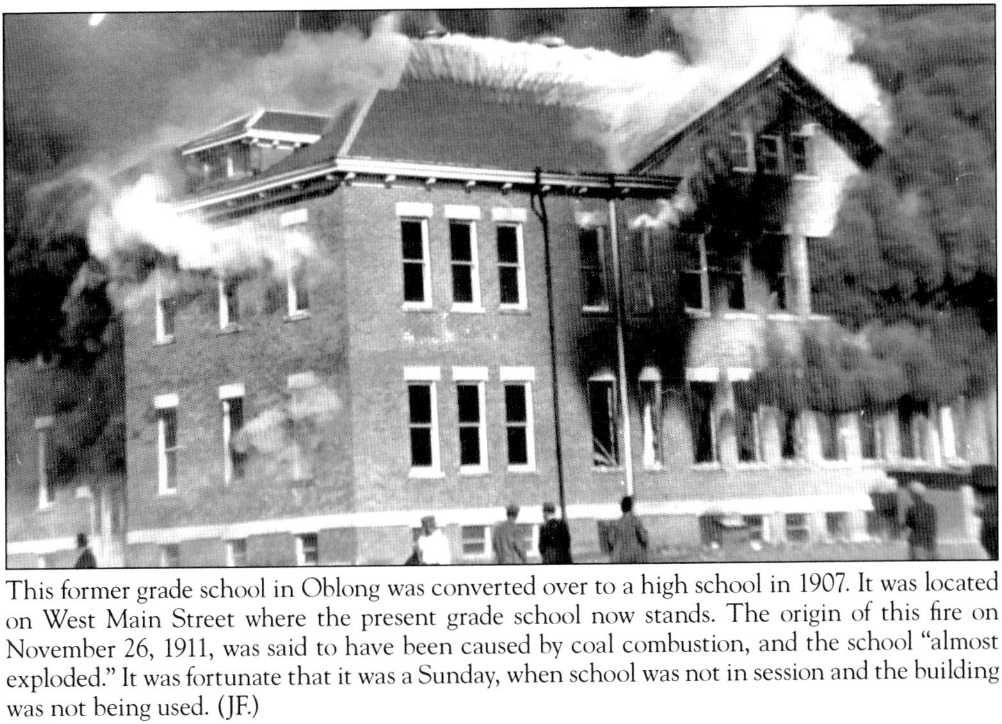

This former grade school in Oblong was converted over to a high school in 1907. It was located on West Main Street where the present grade school now stands. The origin of this fire on November 26, 1911, was said to have been caused by coal combustion, and the school "almost exploded." It was fortunate that it was a Sunday, when school was not in session and the building was not being used. (JF.)

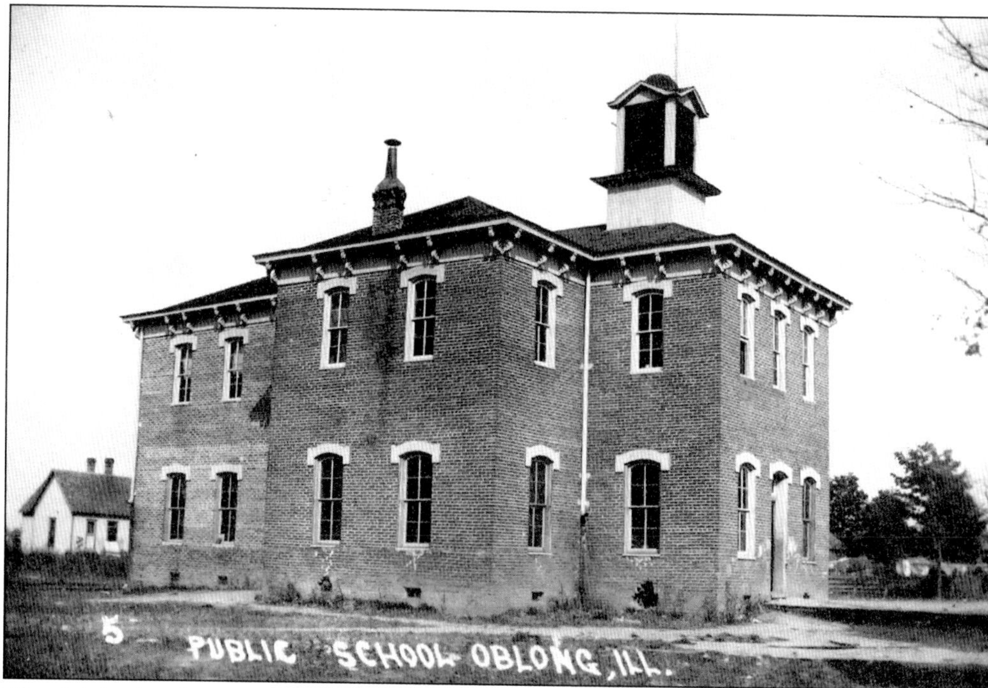

The third schoolhouse erected in Oblong in 1880 replaced Dr. Strohl's Livery barn. It stood where the Beulah Shipman home is located. In 1893, a two-story wing was added, making it a six-room building. At that time, William Wesner was superintendent of schools. (JF.)

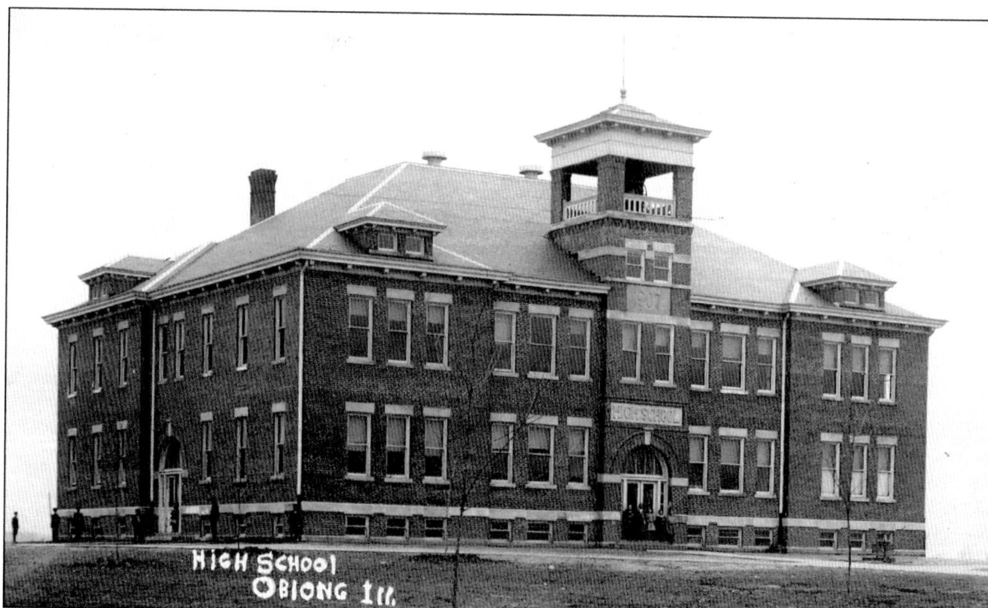

Oblong High School, before it burned in 1911, was an architectural milestone for Oblong. Its actual cash value was $9,000, but it was not insured for its full value. It cost $30,000 to build. Prior to this school building, the first public school was a log house with a puncheon floor and box stove, and the second, a frame building, was built in 1863, one block east of the Main Street and Range Road intersection. (JF.)

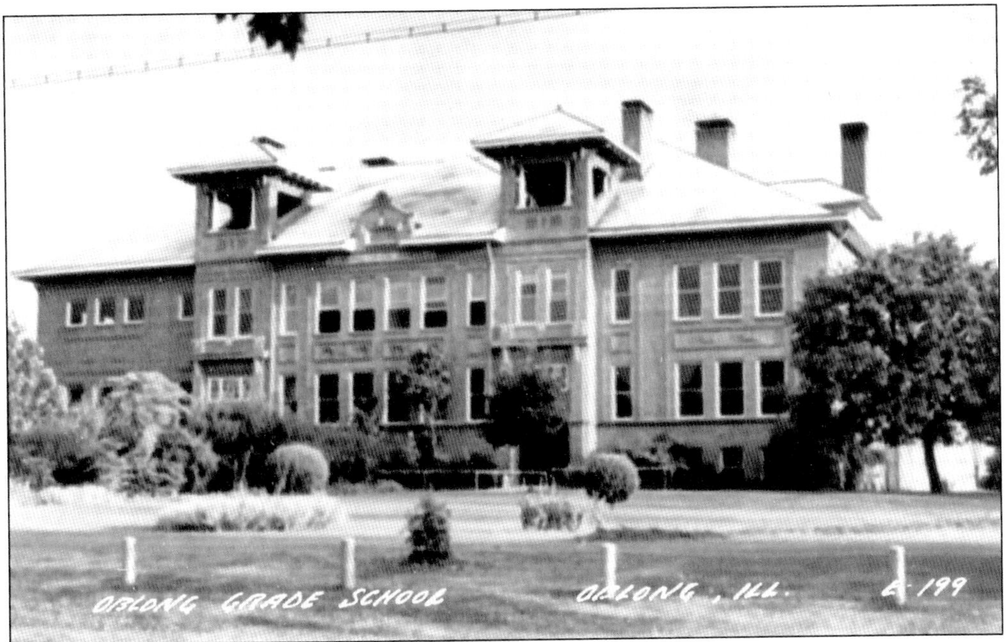

Oblong's current elementary school sits on the west end of Oblong at the former site of the high school that burned back in 1911. It has had a recent extension built on the west side. Lights are in the belfry, and the large bell is illuminated at night. (SJ.)

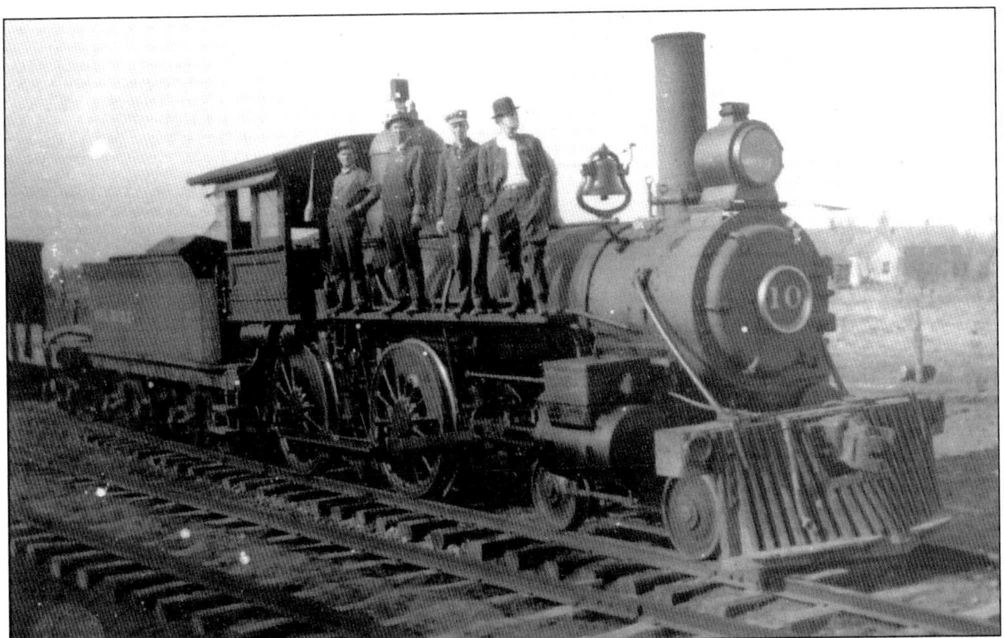

Trains ran sporadically from Oblong to Bridgeport in Lawrence County from 1910 to 1916. It was originally started to handle oil field equipment and various supplies. The Oil Belt Traction Company was incorporated on May 29, 1909, and came to be known as the "tri-weekly" because it was often sent down to Bridgeport on Monday and tried all week to get back to Oblong. From left to right are unidentified, Jed Barber, Howard Helvie, and C. O. Alexander. (BM.)

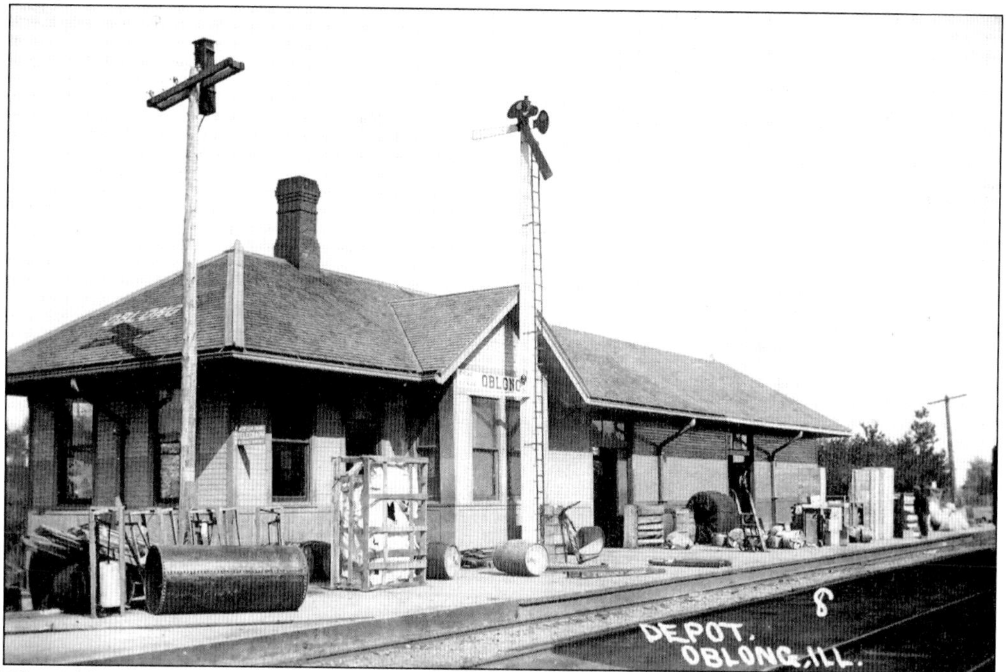

The Oblong railroad depot was demolished on Monday July 14, 1981, as the mayor, Art Farley at the time, ascertained that the building had become rat infested. It was part of a general town cleanup involving an overall desire to revamp the look of the city. (BM.)

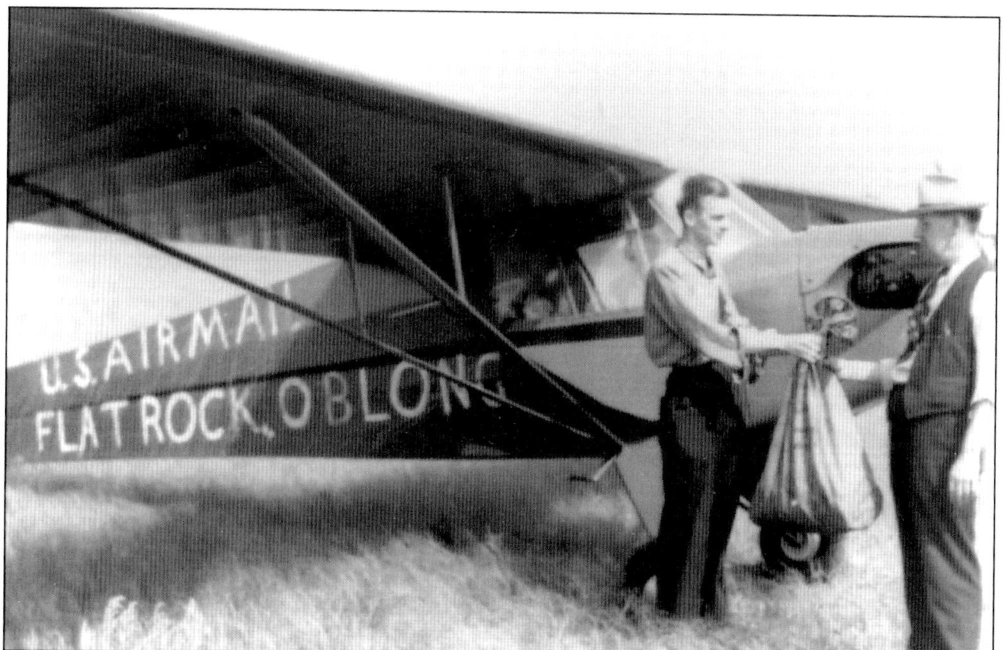

The "Red Plane" stopped on the Harve Parker farm, which was located southeast of Flat Rock, to pick up mail to take to the Effingham post office. In 1937, the plane would start at the O'Neal airport in Vincennes, Indiana, and stop at various places before winding up at Effingham. (JF.)

The old town hall, which was built in 1914, was torn down in 1985 to make way for a municipal center to be built on the old site. (OL.)

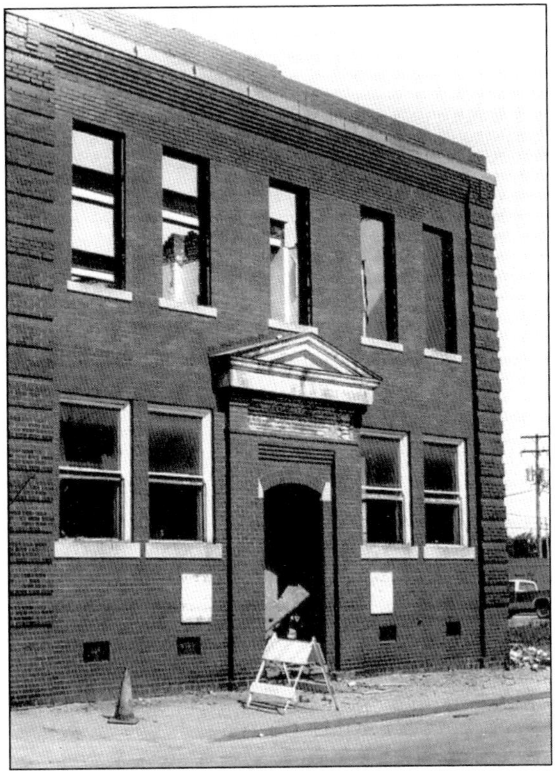

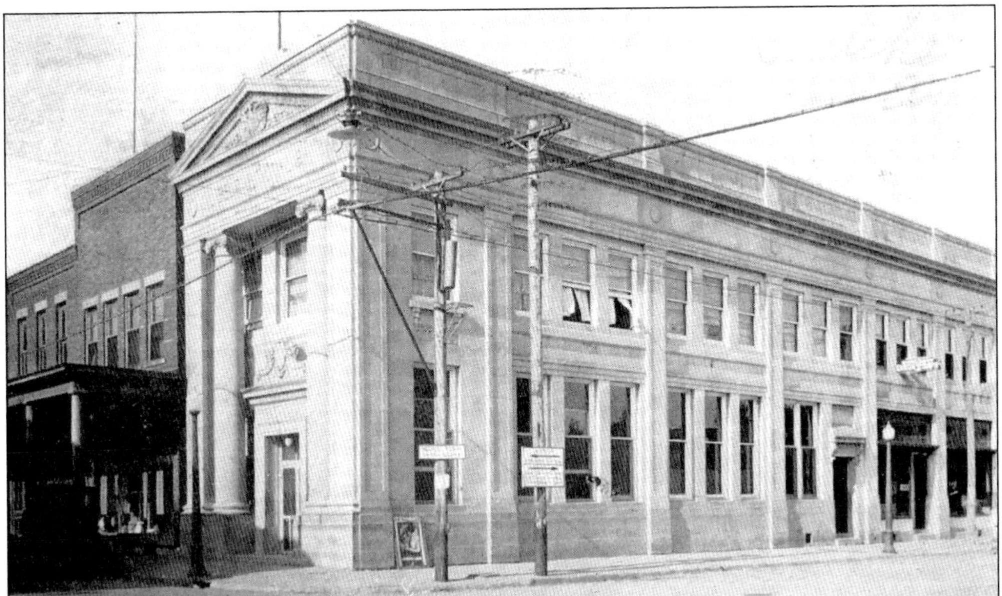

The O'Dells, Dennis J. and David W., started a private bank in 1900 at the back of Henry Brothers General Store. By 1907, it was chartered as the First National Bank of Oblong with capital stock of $25,000, and in a few months the stock doubled. First National merged with Oil Belt Bank, which originally sat at this location, and it was remodeled in 1961 to its present look. First National moved to a new modern facility in 1977 at 203 West Main Street. (SJ.)

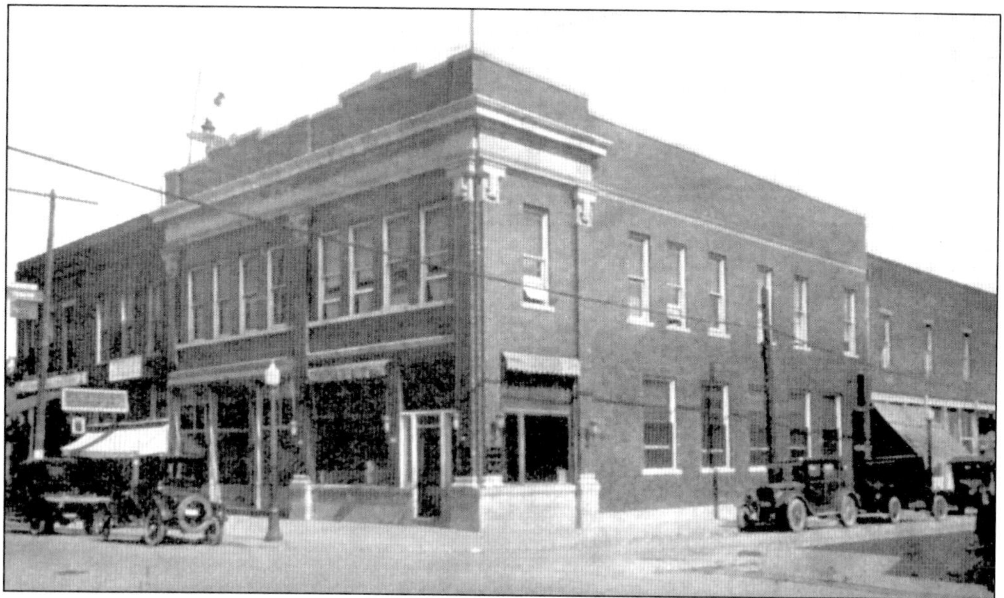

Banks were highly competitive in Oblong, and this bank started as the Peoples Building and Loan. Here it is situated on the northwest corner of Main Street and Range Road, directly south of the First National Bank. This corner was first occupied by the Economy Shoe Store, but when the store closed, the Peoples Building and Loan took possession. (SJ.)

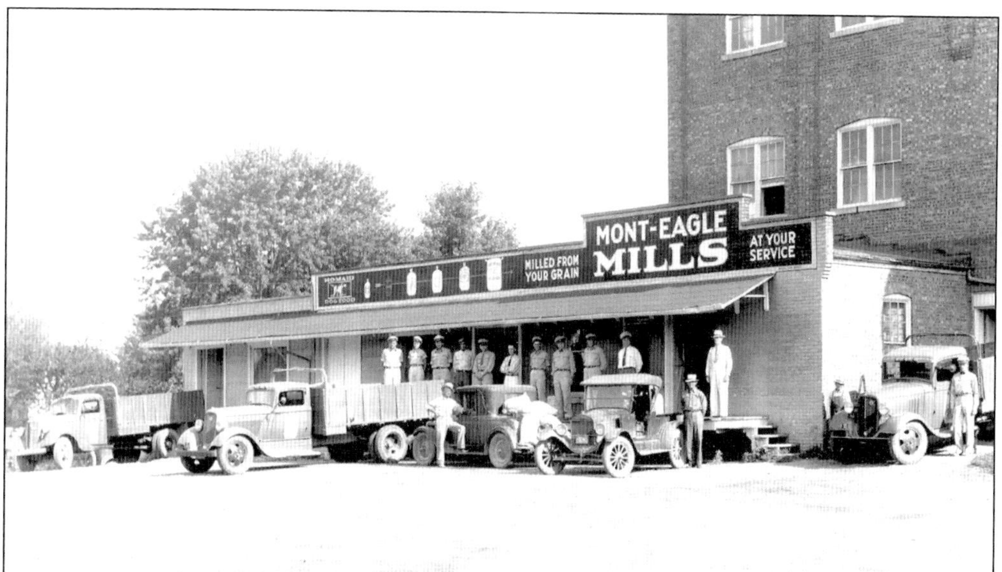

A partially completed steam mill, now known as the Mont-Eagle Mill, was purchased in 1869 by Capt. William Wood and Mr. Condrey. This was the first mill in the village and cost $3,000 to build. Captain Wood became the sole owner two years later and then sold the mill to Joel Ziegler. The Kirtlands bought it in 1879 and remodeled and placed modern machinery in operation by 1881. This building was erected in 1909 but faced demolition on December 13, 1989. (SJ.)

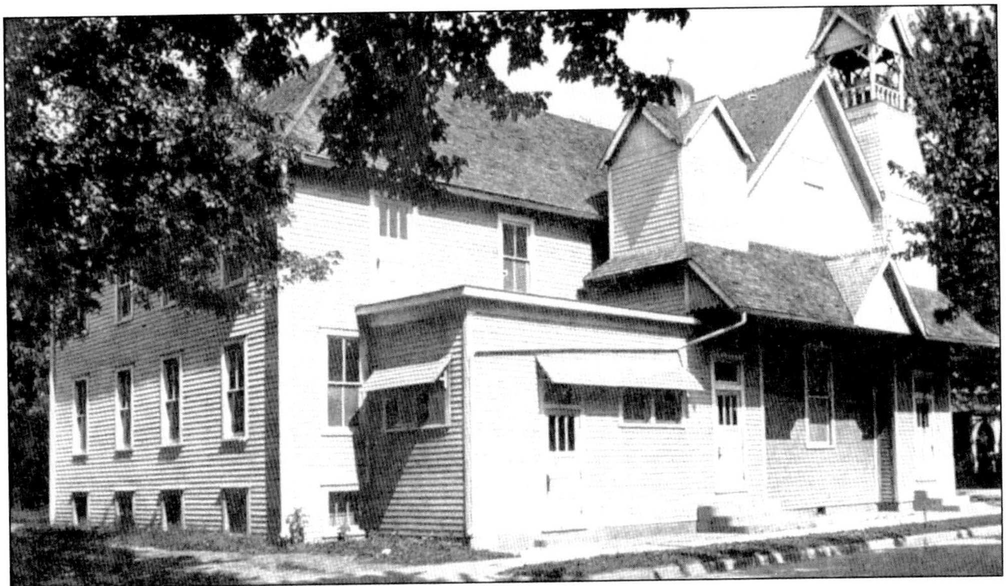

The First Christian Church of Oblong was one of many churches in the early history of the town. There were also Baptist, United Brethren, Pilgrim, and Catholic churches, and the Church of the Nazarene. All were active in the development of the town. (SJ.)

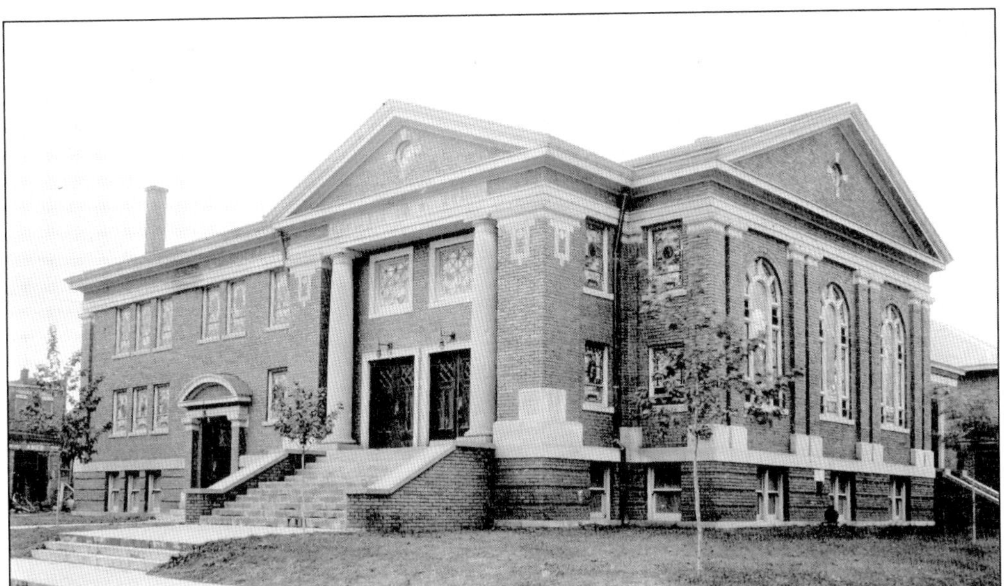

Central Methodist Episcopal Church on North Range Road stills stands and is now Central United Methodist. The building committee roster for the church was Dr. John W. Kirk, Clint J. Kirk, Dr. G. H. Henry, Jim Sheets, M. C. Foltz, and Guy Conley. (SJ.)

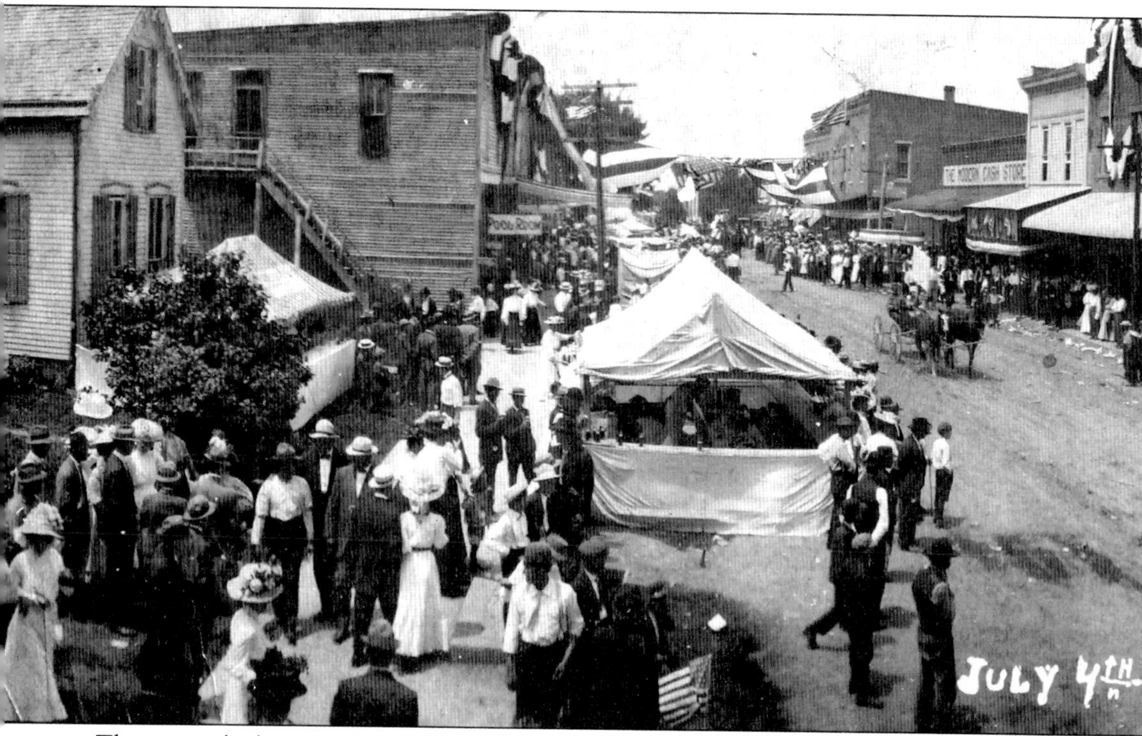

This view is looking southeast from the northwest corner of the center of town during the Mardi Gras parade in Oblong on July 4, 1909. Crawford County has many celebrations involving most of the towns, starting as early as the second Sunday in May for Southern Illinois Day, which honors the top county in the area, and extending throughout the summer into autumn. This one started with a parade with floats, then a carnival, a craft show, and fireworks on into the

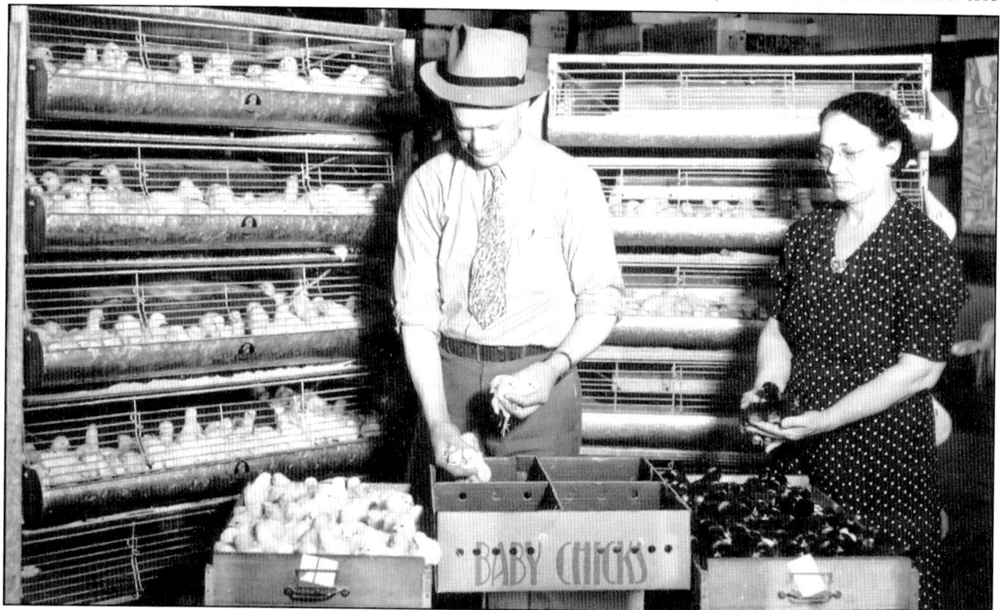

Sheets Hatchery was located on North Range Road and was run by Clarence Sheets and his wife, Edna. Before he started this business, he was an Oblong mail carrier. (KY.)

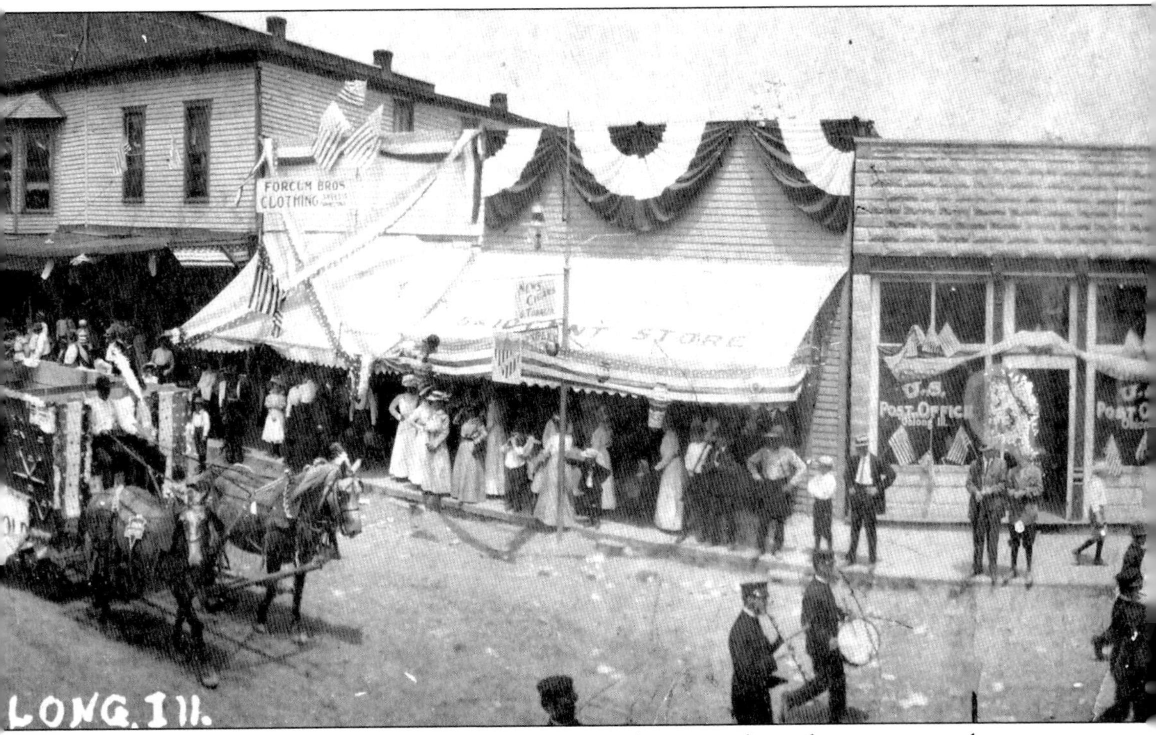

night. Many of the celebrations are traditional, but there are also a few unique to the area. Palestine hosts a Labor Day weekend festival that involves a rodeo each year plus the Civil War Debutante Ball, in which the town debutantes are introduced to society in authentic period costume, and the Civil War is reenacted the first Saturday in December. (SJ.)

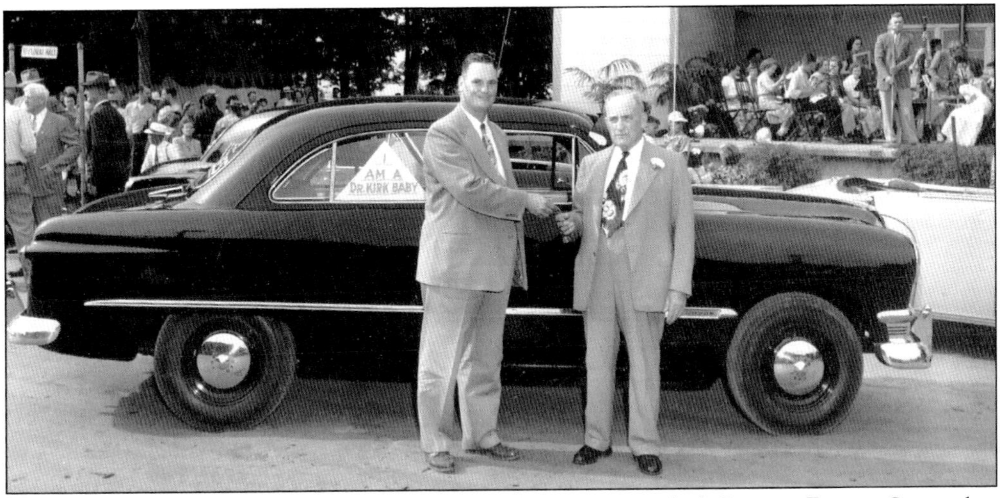

Dr. John W. Kirk was honored with a special day at a Crawford County Fair in September 1950. At the time, he had been in practice for 53 years, and he was presented with this car in appreciation. A float with several prominent citizens who had been birthed by Kirk was a part of the parade, and a letter written by Adlai Stevenson was read to the crowd by Bob Edwards, the master of ceremonies, and presented to Kirk. Kirk was known to have delivered 4,000 babies and never lost a mother in childbirth. (KY.)

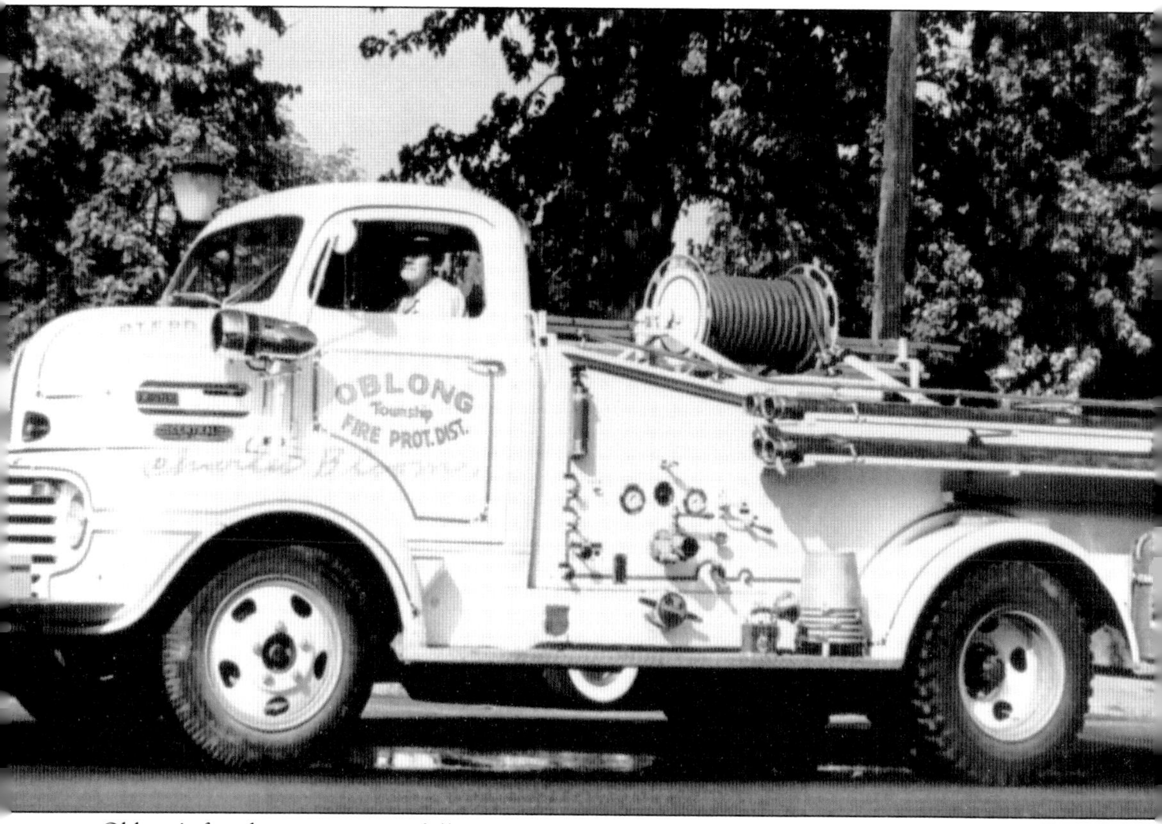

Oblong's fire department was fully equipped to handle any fire. Behind the wheel is Charles "Tubby" Bloom in his 1948 Ford fire truck. The current firehouse location is where the Odell Oblong House once stood. (SJ.)

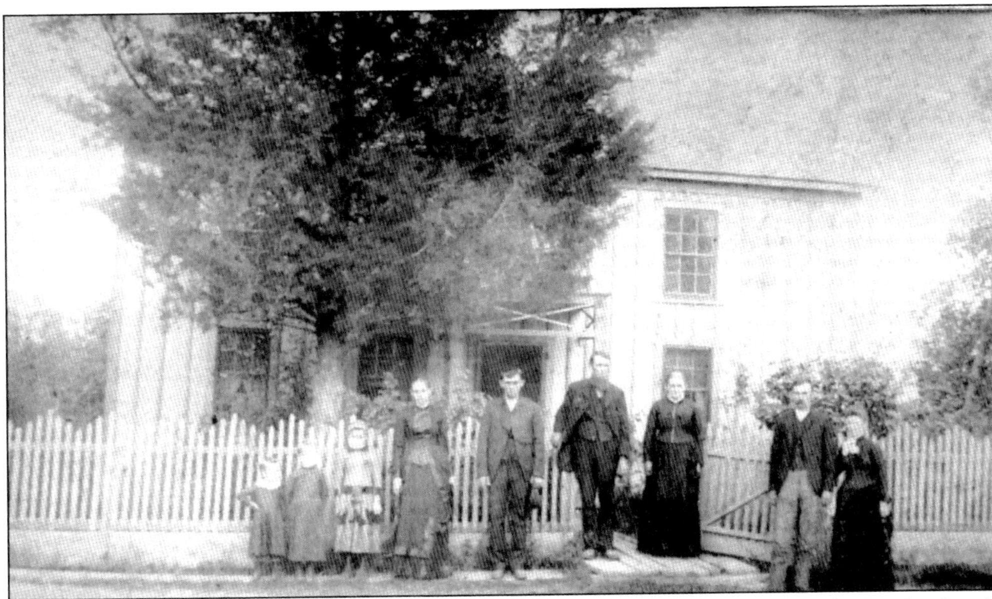

Log cabins outside of Hutsonville are nonexistent in Crawford County today. The Ziegler family cabin was built in 1865. It was located a half mile south of Oblong on South Range Road. From left to right are Edna Price, Edith Price, Ida Price, Anna May Ziegler Price, John T. Price, George W. Ziegler, Martha Virginia Muchmore Ziegler, Edgar Ziegler, and wife Drusilla Ping Ziegler. (RP.)

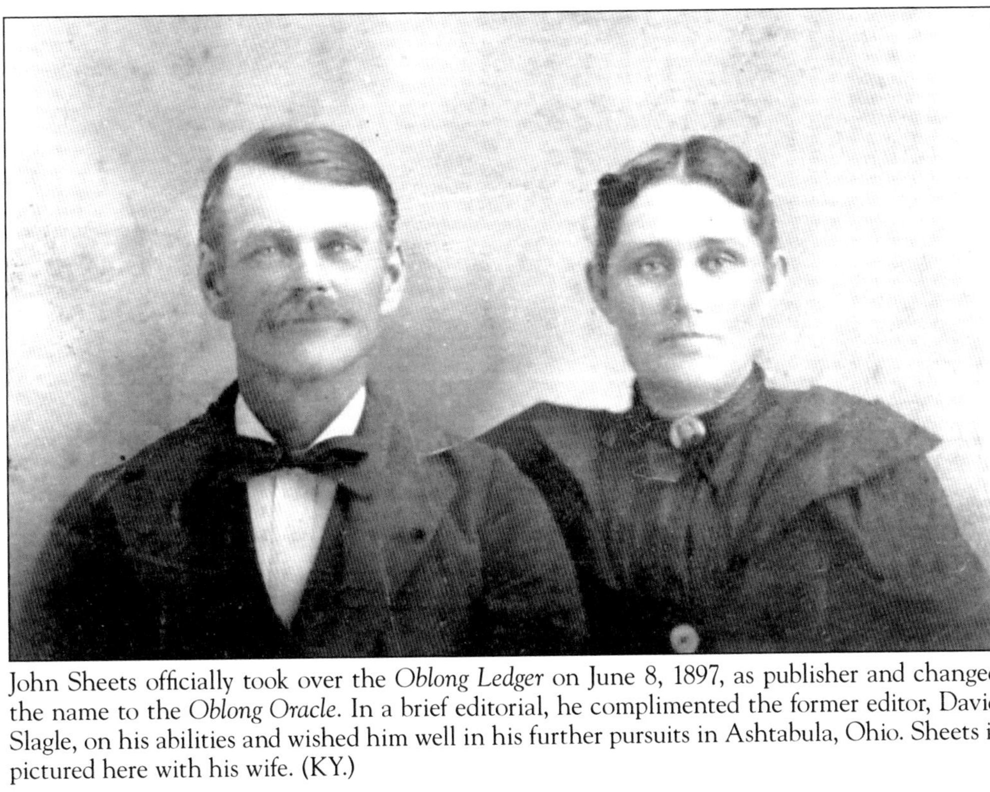

John Sheets officially took over the *Oblong Ledger* on June 8, 1897, as publisher and changed the name to the *Oblong Oracle*. In a brief editorial, he complimented the former editor, David Slagle, on his abilities and wished him well in his further pursuits in Ashtabula, Ohio. Sheets is pictured here with his wife. (KY.)

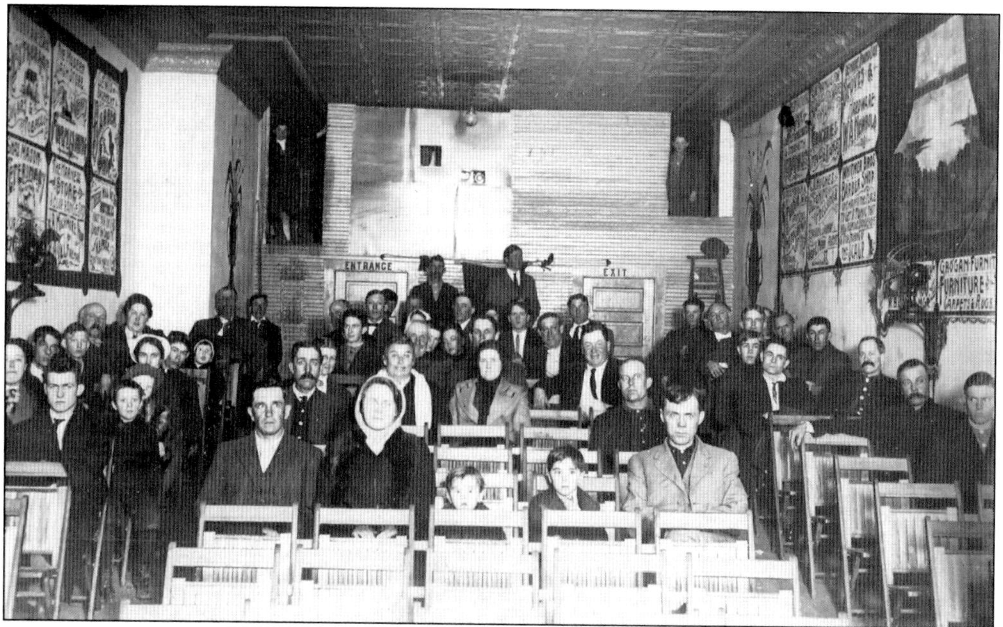

The Majestic Theatre was originally built on the west side of North Range Road. The Central Methodist Episcopal Church replaced the theater after it was torn down, and it was rebuilt on the east side of Range Road and was then torn down for the Oblong Masonic Lodge. (JF.)

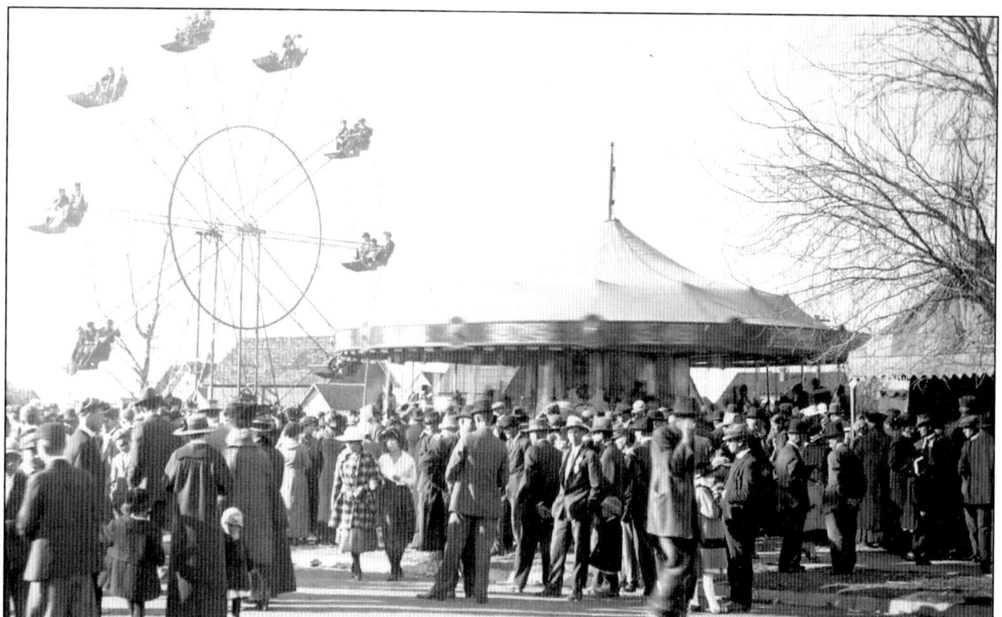

The Oblong Carnival for Mardi Gras in 1916 was held on Oblong's fairgrounds. Mardi Gras celebrations drew people from other towns all over the county. This was followed up with fireworks after the sun went down. (SJ.)

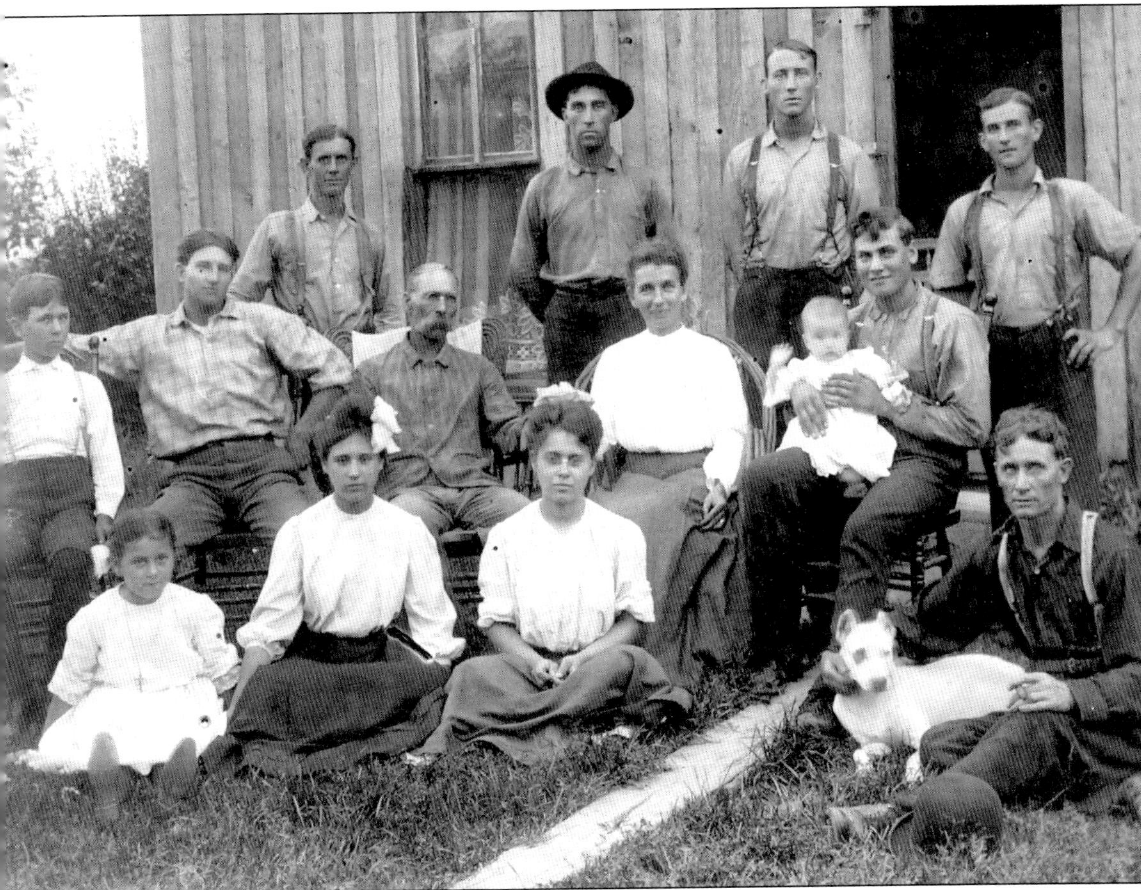

During the oil boom, Jackson's Boardinghouse provided shelter for these people in the vicinity of Hardinville, which is halfway between the southern border of the county and Stoy. (RP.)

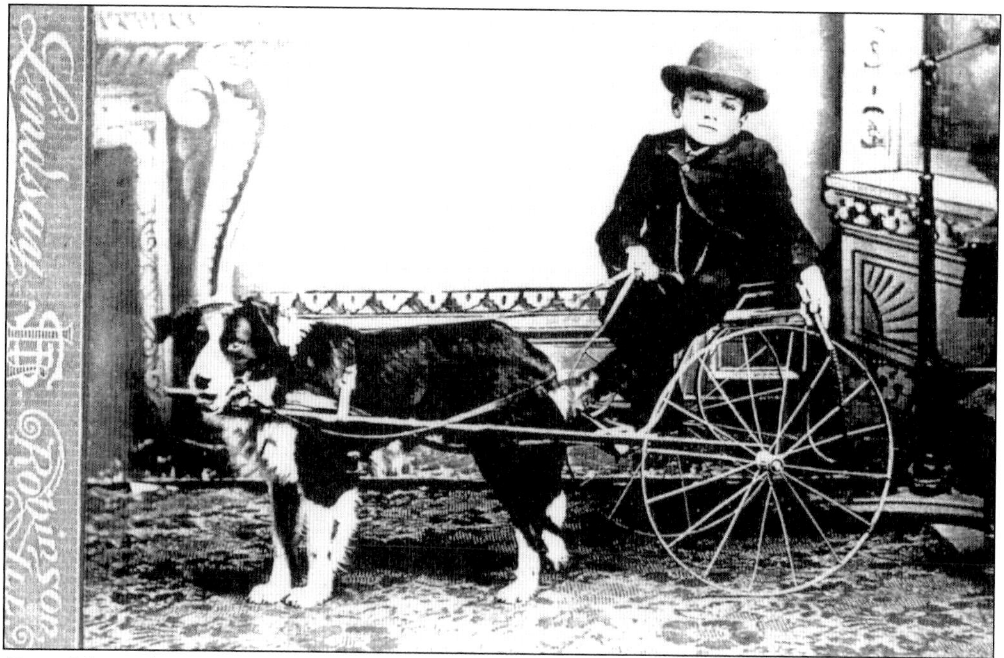

One of the earliest pioneer families was the Wood family. There were also the Eatons, Salisburys, Yorks, Smiths, and McCrillises. Darrel Wood, pictured here, was the son of Capt. James Herbert Wood, who fought in the Civil War; his mother was Susanna Price. (RP.)

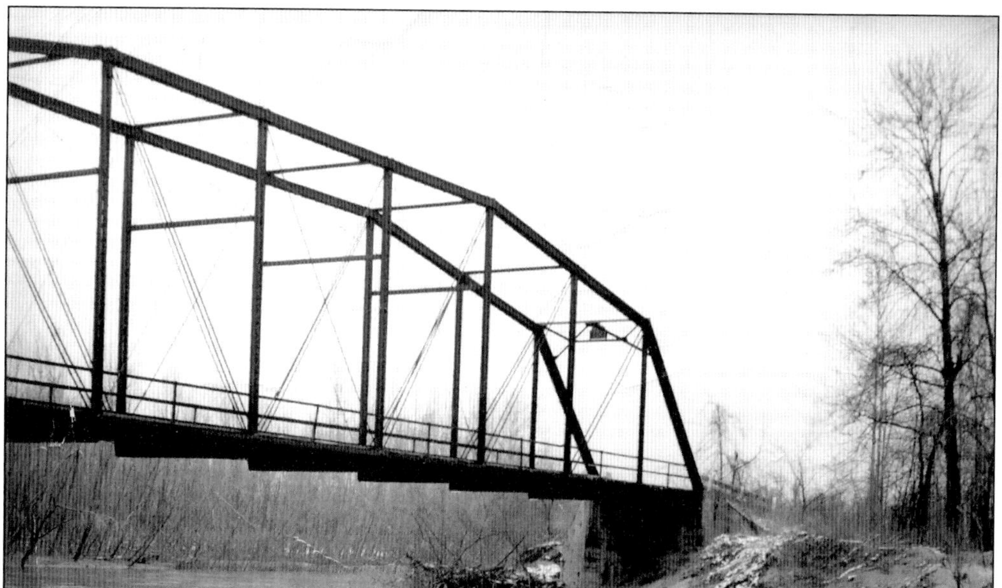

Like the Gibson Bridge, the Spencer Bridge was constructed over Embarras River in the area known as the Dark Bend. Today it is a modern, sparsely populated area with nice country homes, but more than 100 years ago, it had a reputation for being littered with chicken and horse thieves, bootleggers, and a few notorious criminals, such as the counterfeiter Cornelius Taylor. Taylor owned a ferry in the 1820s. He was put under surveillance and was tracked to a shack that contained counterfeiting equipment. (KY.)

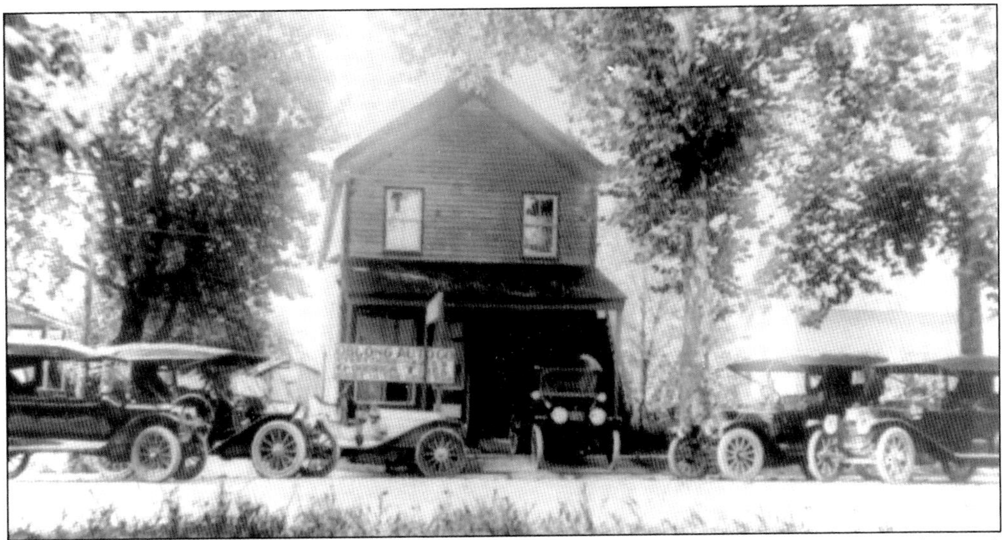

Oblong Auto was located on the east side of Oblong where the American Legion is now located. This was the location that George Larrabee added when he started selling automobiles. The first models he sold were made by Coles and were manufactured in Indianapolis. When he became a Ford dealer, the company insisted that no other makes could be sold along with Fords, and he moved remaining Coles stock to this location. (SJ.)

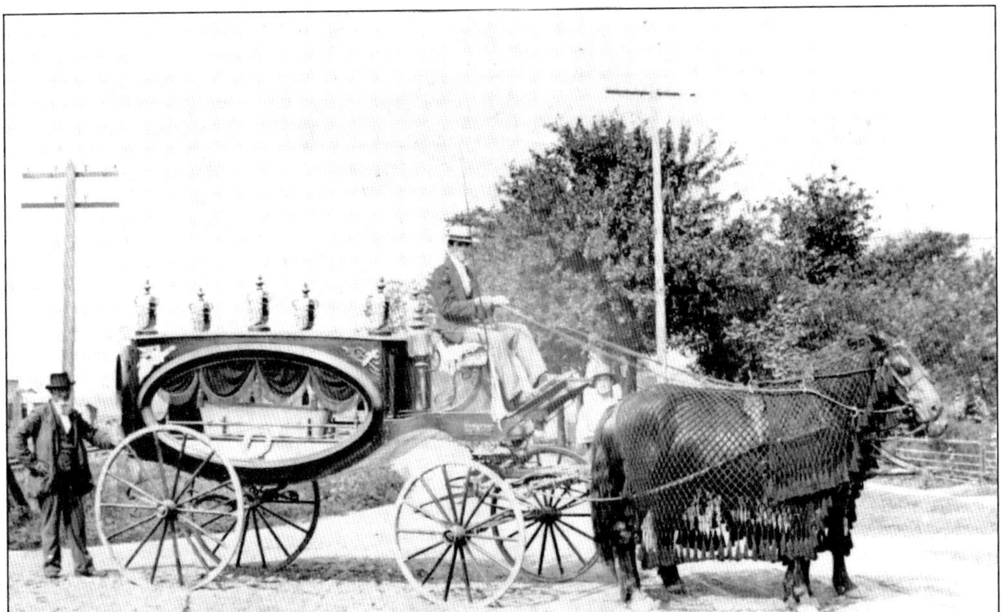

In 1898, James and Hall Funeral Home was located on South Adams Street. M. L. James was a Civil War veteran, and during the war, he learned how to embalm the deceased in preparation to be sent home. His son-in-law Harry Hall joined him in the business some years later. (SJ.)

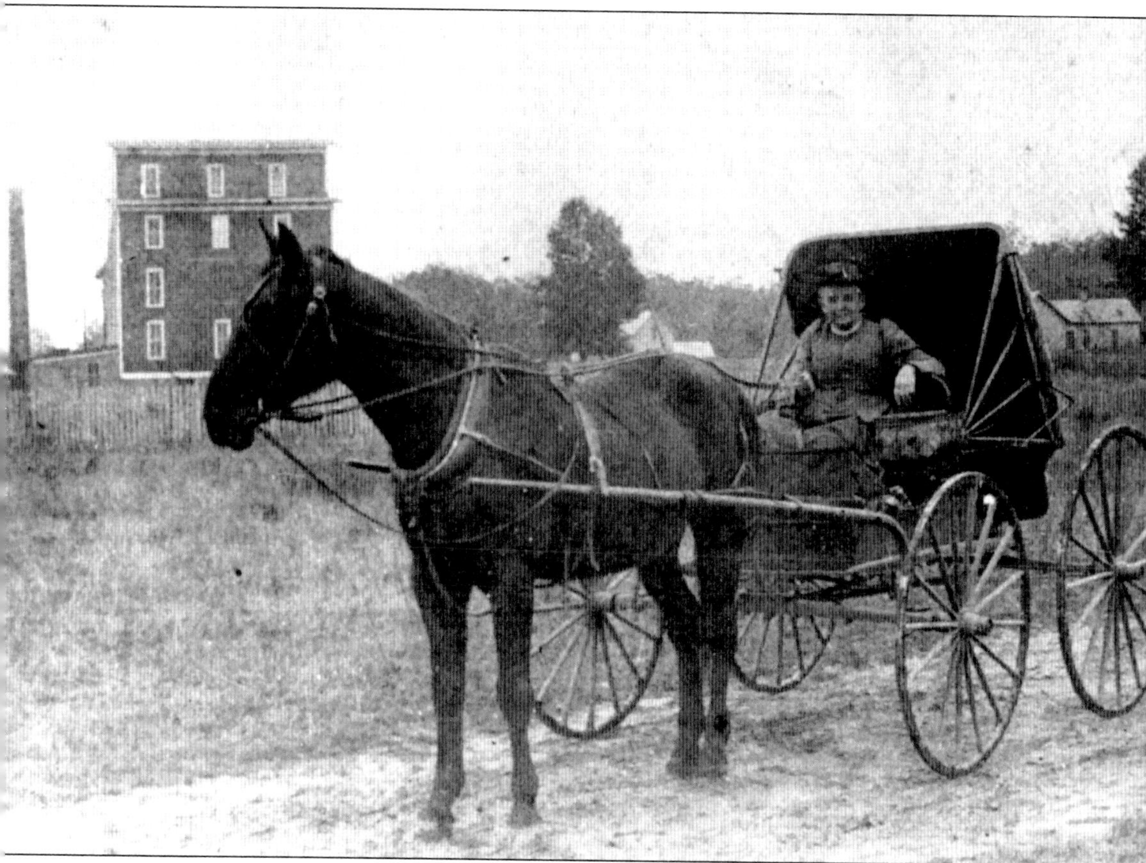

Martha Virginia Muchmore Ziegler was a familiar sight in Oblong as she sold butter from her buggy. Back at this time, cream separators came into vogue, and people would take their cream into town to sell. Much of the milk (which would be bluish in color) left over from separation was often mixed with bran and fed to the hogs. (RP.)

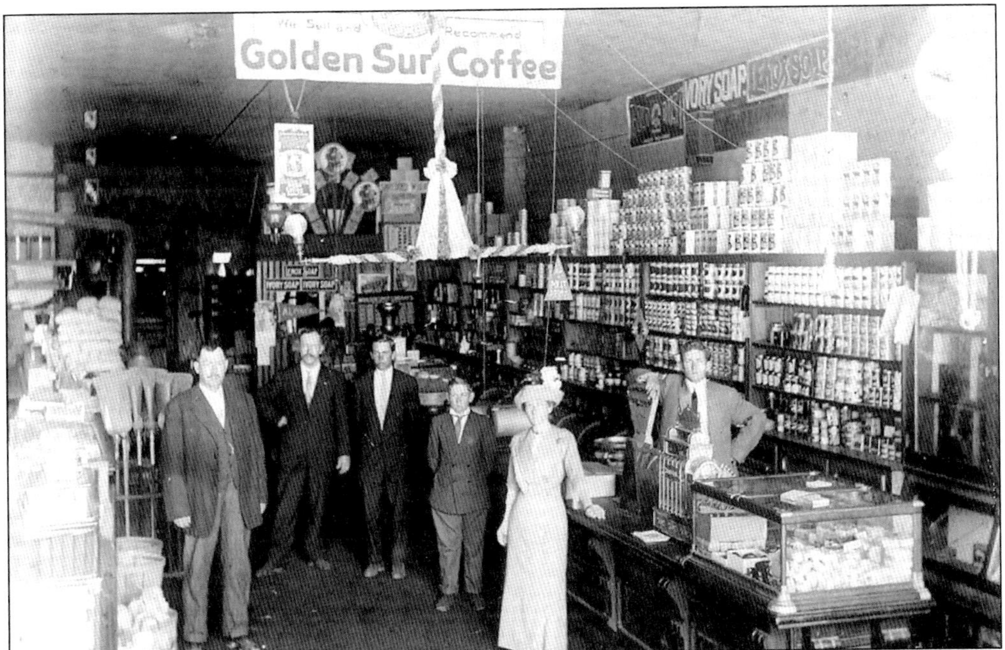

One of Oblong's early general stores was Wirt Brothers. During the boom days in the town, there were about 28 grocery stores in the area. Zach and Henry Wirt located their store on the northeast corner of Range Road and Main Street. They had a dry goods store on the west side of the building, with an archway connecting their grocery store. (SJ.)

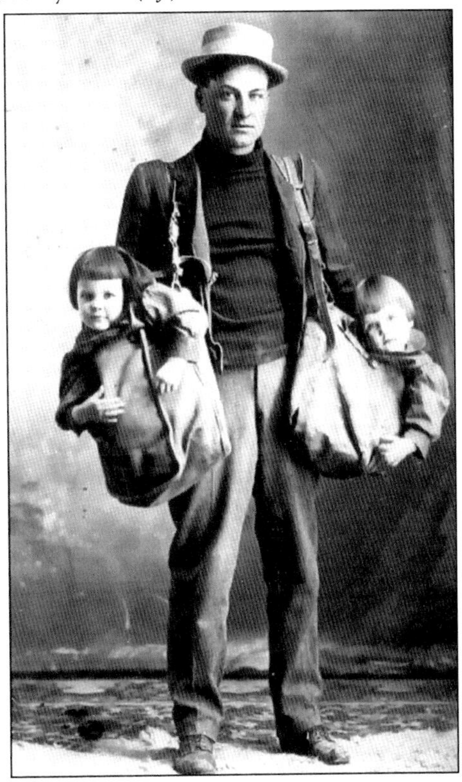

Thomas Jefferson Price II was an Oblong mail carrier. This is a playful moment between him and his two daughters, Marie and Imogene. (RP.)

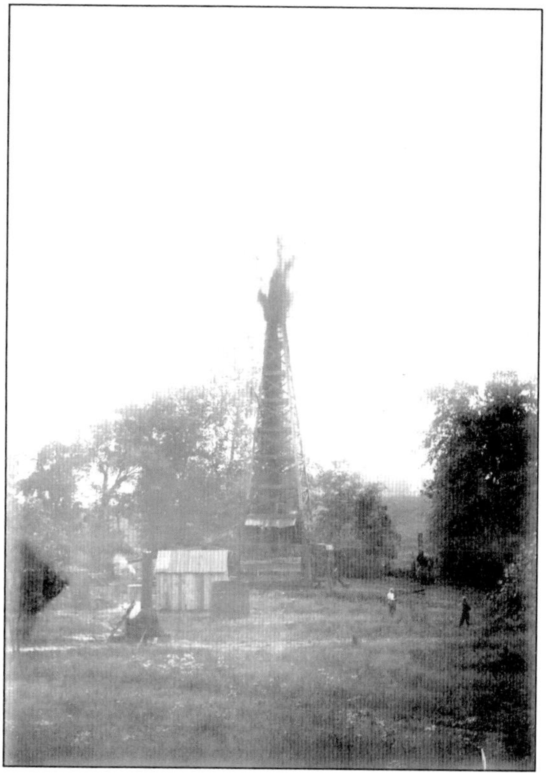

Oil derricks in the earliest stages were built of wood, and the cable tools were transported by teams of horses. Even so, rig building contractors and their crews could erect a derrick complete from the mud sills to the crown block in a single day. This oil derrick would be anywhere from 30 to 50 feet high. The Illinois Oil Field Museum started humbly on the edge of Oblong Lake at the park on the northeastern extremity of Oblong in 1967. Enos Bloom conceived the idea even though he was not a rich oil man. He was a mechanic who worked on broken derricks and oil field equipment and understood the importance of saving the history and original artifacts. (Seyferths.)

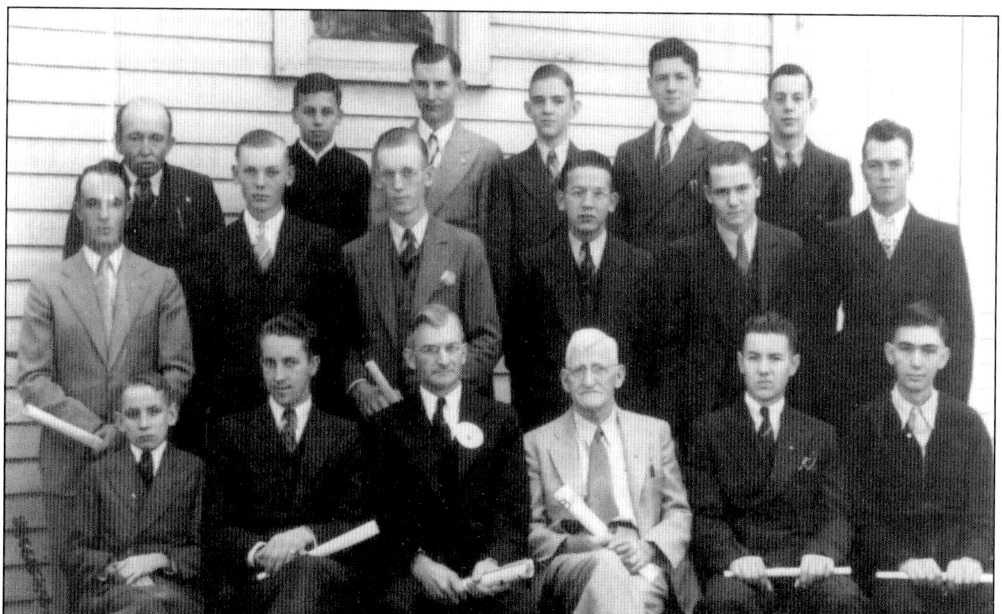

The Young Men's Class of First Christian Church of Oblong are, from left to right, (first row) Robert McKnight, unidentified, Rev. W. H. Elliot, Clark Courtelyou, Harry Randolph, and unidentified; (second row) Ralph Goodwin, Robert Utterback, Mervin Utterback, Kent McKnight, Jim Caywood, and Millard Mikeworth; (third row) Clifton Barker, Warren Dillman, Harold Jacobs, Hal Keith Leggitt, Claire Shumaker, and Glen Smith. (JF.)

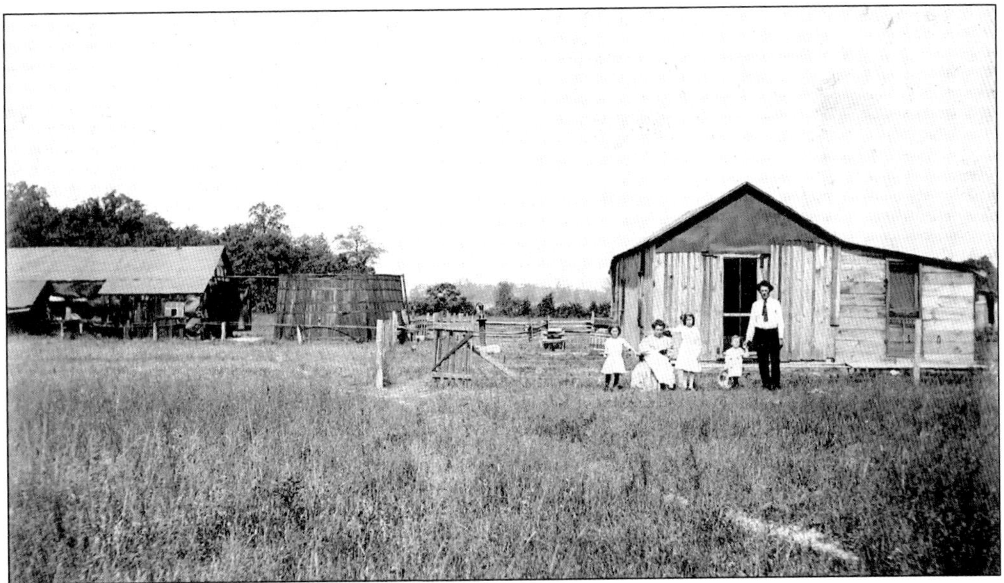

Joe Ames Farm was located less than a mile from town on the northeast side. Oblong is a large soybean, corn, livestock, poultry, and dairy producing community. In 1906, Ames discovered oil on his farm like many other farmers. In 1910, the Joines Lease was established on his farm. The buildings held the machinery to run it. From left to right are Violet Maus, Evalina Rice Maus (holding baby Forest Maus), Nina Maus, Donald Maus, and Frank H. Maus. (RP.)

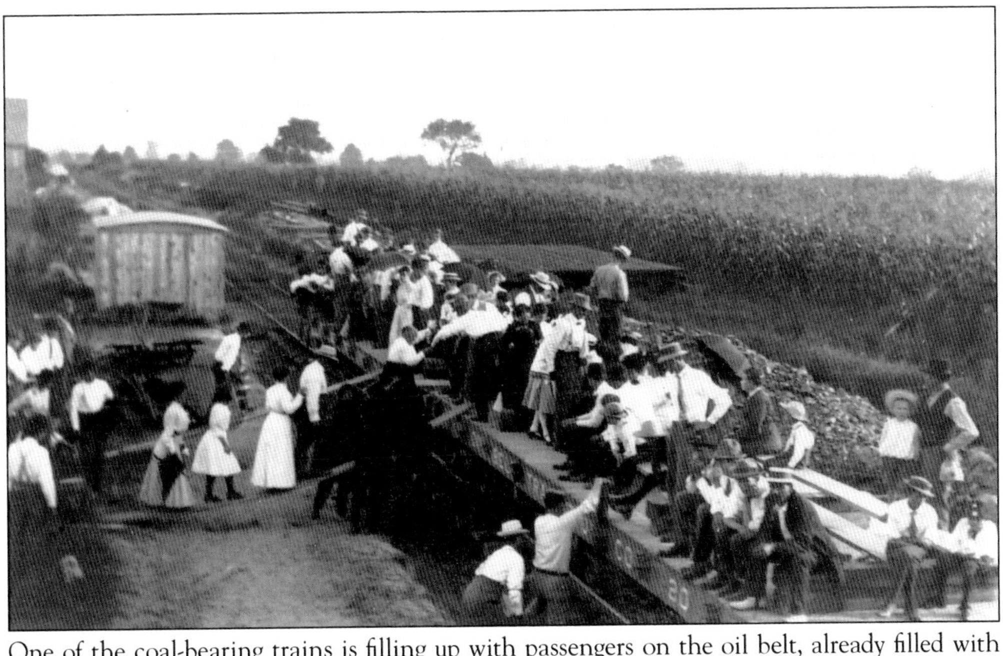

One of the coal-bearing trains is filling up with passengers on the oil belt, already filled with coal. This was a Sunday excursion with festively dressed travelers. Traffic between Robinson and the oil fields in Oblong, Martin, Prairie, and Licking townships relied heavily on the Illinois Central Railroad. The number of patrons was so great that some would be hanging on the steps, and others boarded freight trains and cabooses. (JF.)

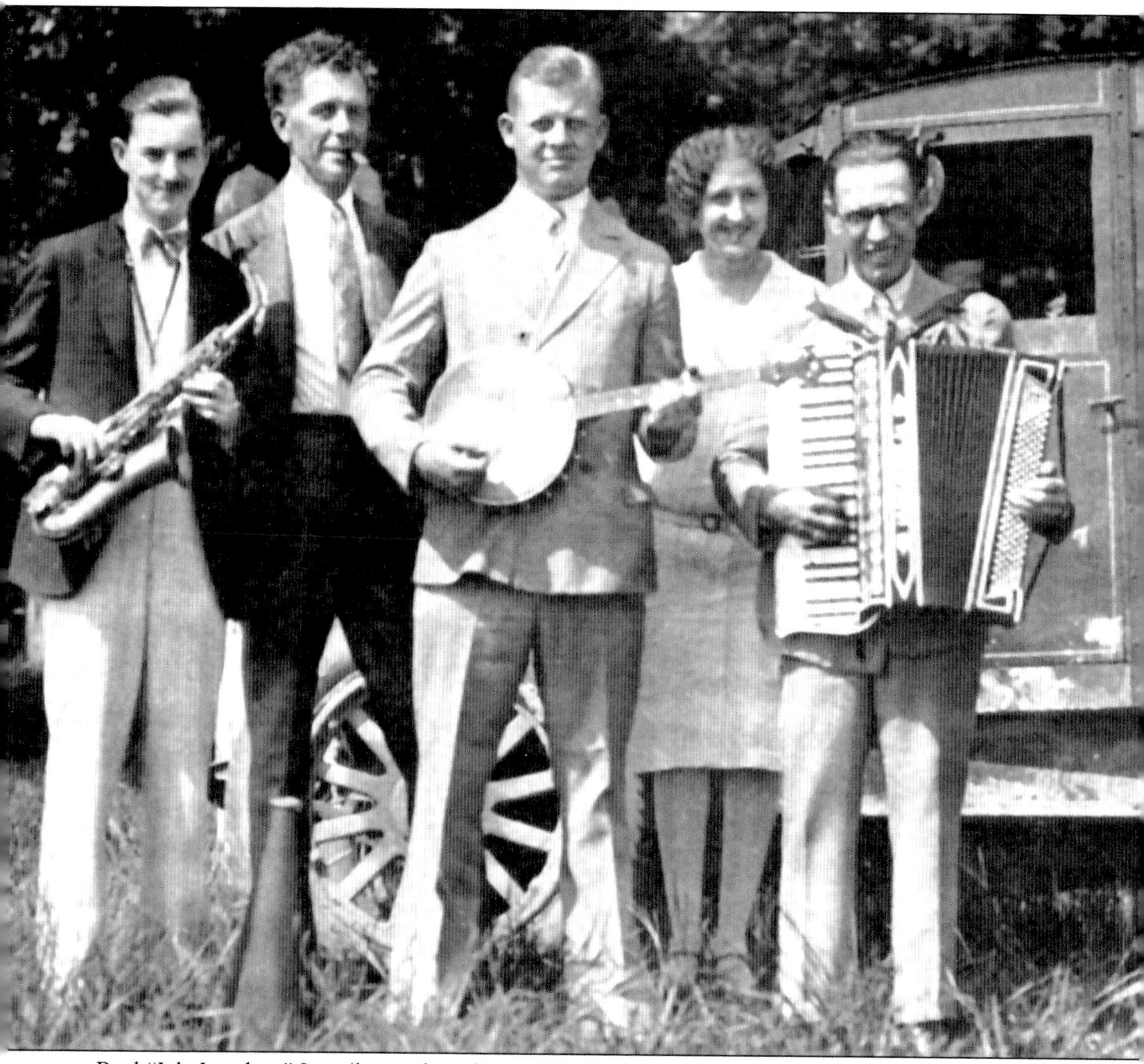

Burl "Icle Ivanhoe" Ives (located in the center, holding his signature banjo), was born to Frank and Della Ives on June 14, 1909, in Hunt City just over the Crawford County border. Best known for his Academy Award–winning role in *The Big Country*, he grew up performing with his siblings in churches and county fairs. They were known as "those singing Ives." He attended Willow Hill High School in Newton and Eastern Illinois State Teachers College at Charleston with an aspiration of becoming a high school football coach. Instead he dropped out and went go on to make 45 movies and television appearances. He died on April 14, 1995, in Anacortes, Washington. (SJ.)

Five

Smaller Towns and Townships

Crawford County borders a few more towns than 20, which is understandable considering most of the central southeastern Illinois region is primarily farmland. Barring a few bank robberies and holdups, there have not been any major economic failures except during the Great Depression.

For all that, the history, even outside the major towns, has been lively and diverse. In the southeastern corner, the Wabash River was the site of the only naval battle fought on the river during the Revolution. This is very close to Flat Rock and Heathsville, where Elizabeth Reed, the first woman hanged in the state of Illinois, is buried. There is an Amish community in the Villas region of the southern border, and closer to the southwest corner, the Embarras River slips through the area known as the Dark Bend, which has been warily considered by the county inhabitants as a harbor for a criminal element. That was more prevalent during the early 1900s, however.

Robinson, Palestine, and Oblong along Route 33 have dominated the county largely through their placement along the Lincoln/Vandalia Trail, which was primarily a trade route. In the northern area, Trimble has quietly sat next to its Hutsonville neighbor close to the Crawford County Historical Museum, and most of the northwest region is farmland and conservation areas. Illinois's oldest continuous Quaker community also sits in the northernmost region close to State Highway 1, and it has long been believed that a Civil War–era underground railroad existed in the West York settlement.

Another farmland area that is not as well known is the Richwoods area, which sits south of Palestine. Large land ownerships for farming are existent south of Palestine. Richwoods has enjoyed an abundant prosperity here for many years.

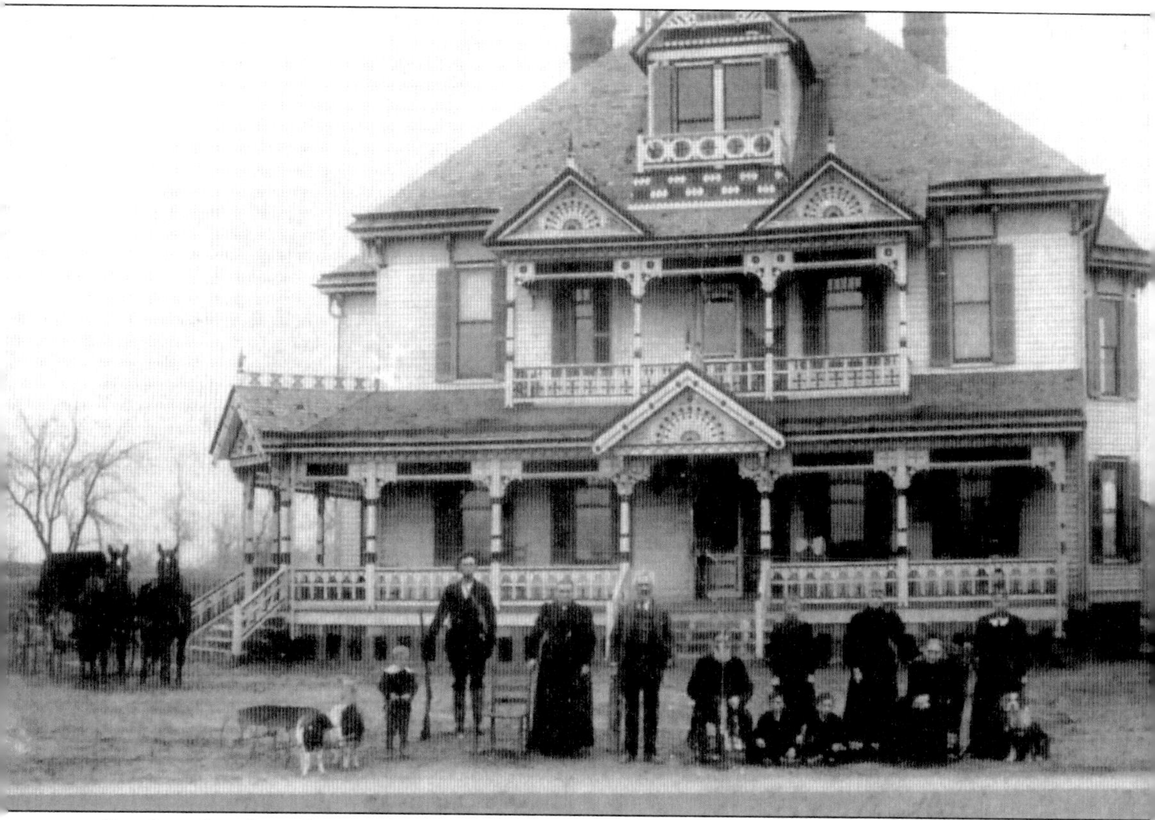

Goodwin has long been a family name associated with the farming community of Crawford County. John Goodwin moved to Montgomery Township from Coshocton County, Ohio, in 1851. His son Elisha was a landowner in the Richwoods vicinity, which is southwest of Palestine. Elisha married Sarah Ellen Adams and had three children, twin sons who died and Ray, the youngest. Elisha bought this home in 1895. He went to Valparaiso College and was a teacher for several years. Wendel, his grandson, said there was a swing on the third floor of the house for the kids to swing on. From left to right are Ray Goodwin (Elisha's surviving son), Uncle John Adams, Sarah Ellen Goodwin (née Adams), Grandfather Elisha, Grandpa Adams (Elisha's father-in-law), twin sons, and aunts Lela, Carrie, and Stella. Seated is mother-in-law Lowdskey "Lowdie." (Wendall Goodwin.)

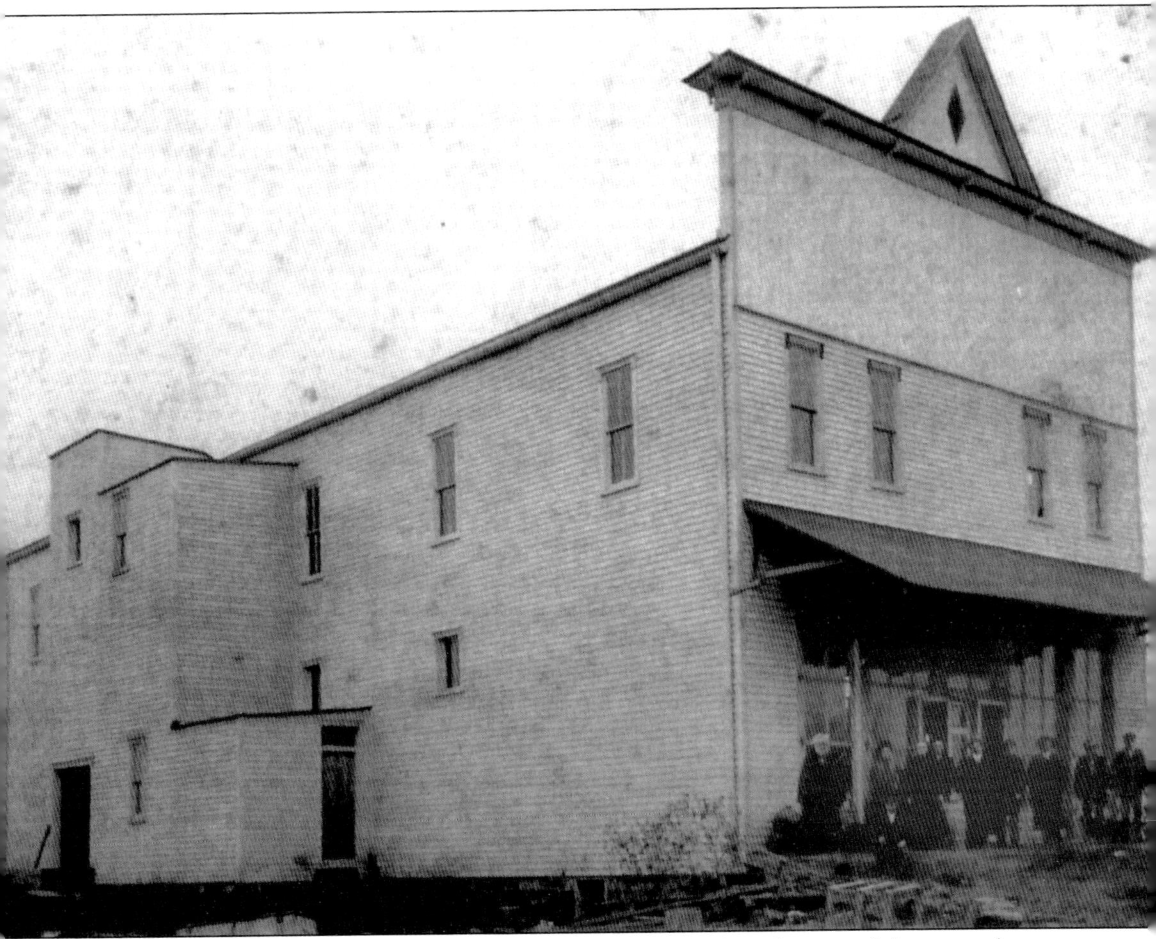

Elisha Goodwin was a landowner in Richwoods, and he also built and operated this general store where his wife, Sarah, worked as postmistress. He ran it as a general store and had an elevator in the back side entrance, which led up to the upper rooms. Inside, on the ground floor on the left-hand side, a stairway also led up to the second floor. Elisha had wanted to rent it out as a public house but never did so. His son Ray (1890–1965) continued farming in the Richwoods area, and he married Mary Buser of the Green Hill neighborhood. They had four children, Reo, Wendel, Glen, and Reva. Wendel is also a farmer in Richwoods, and he married Ruth Evelyn Espy in 1946. They moved to a farm north of Richwoods and have three grown children, Marcia Reardon, Marilyn Holmes, and Lois Kay Goodwin. (Wendall Goodwin.)

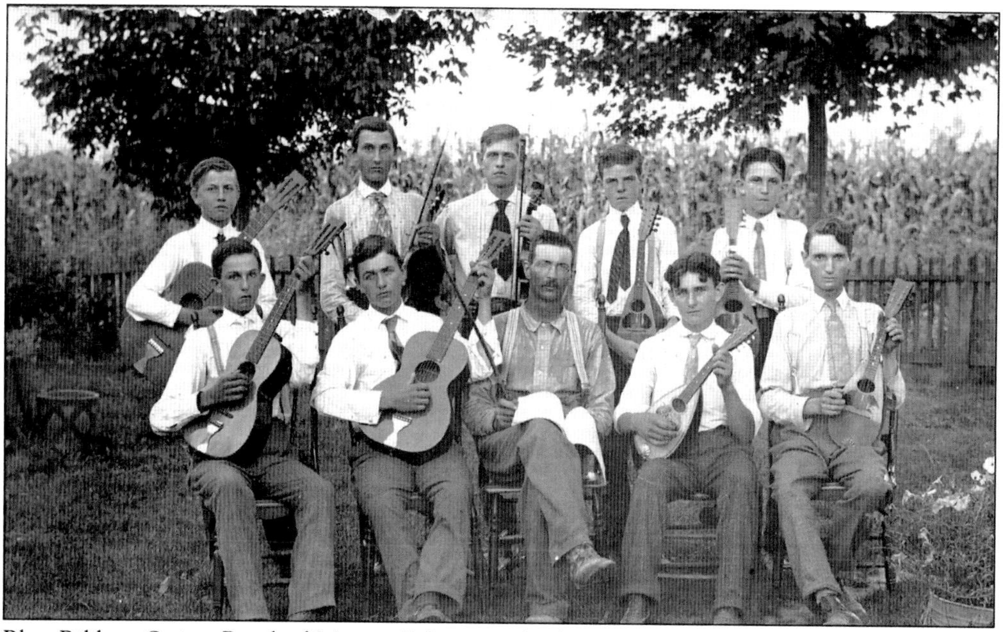

Blue Ribbon String Band of Mount Ephraim, which was located north of Trimble, met on Sunday afternoons and played for their own enjoyment for years. Their meeting place was at the home of Jim Goodwin who resided west of Mount Ephraim. Pictured are, from left to right, (first row) Allan King, Ellis Correll, Elder Boyd, Atlas Correll, and Lester Correll; (second row) Noble McCain, Noble King, James Scotton, Raymond Scotton, and Harvey King. (SW.)

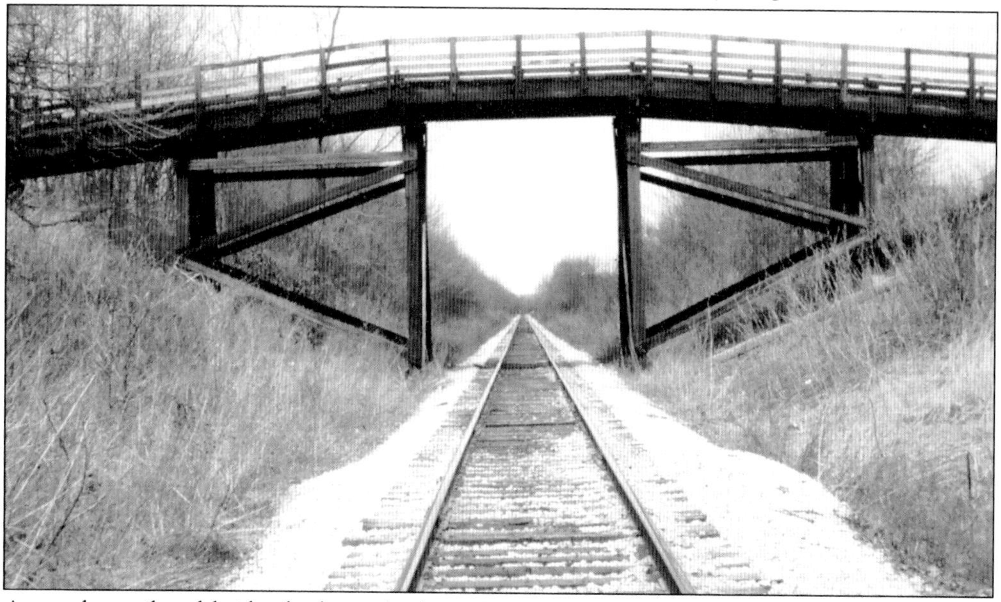

A wooden railroad bridge built in the late 1800s was located one mile north of Trimble on Route 1. It had an angled approach toward the west that angled northeast and, near the top, straightened out and went straight down on the other side. Viewing oncoming trains was impossible from either side. There were 50-gallon drums buried on the south side of the bridge to collect rainwater just in case the hot ashes from the train engine ever set the bridge on fire. The bridge was torn down around 1950. (SW.)

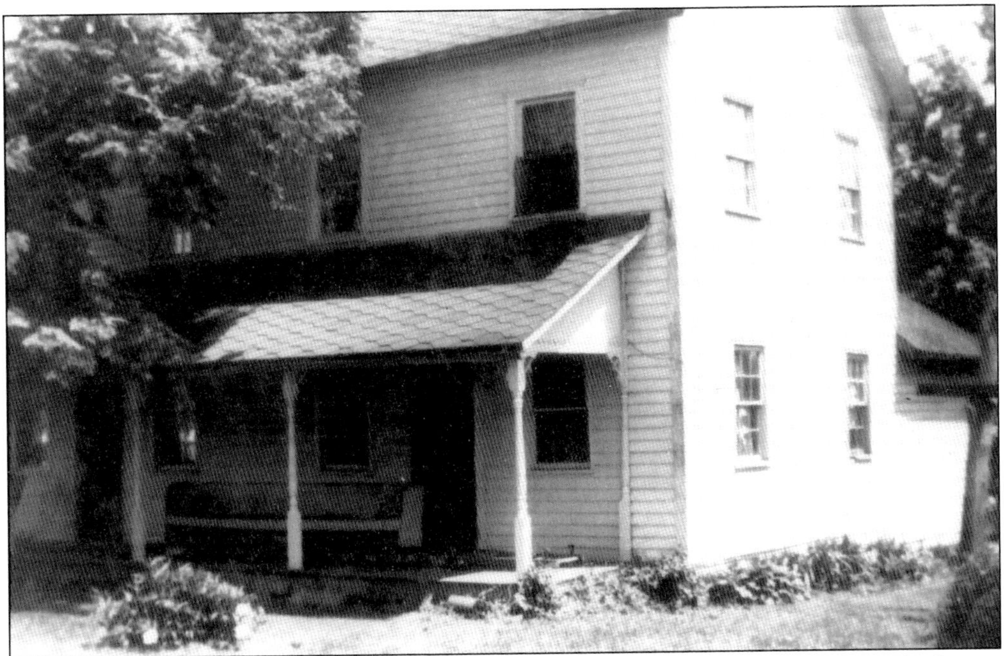

In 1927, Bud Burress purchased the Elisha Goodwin store building in Richwoods. It was dismantled and the lumber, windows, doors, and hardware were saved to build the Trimble store, known as Burress Exchange. It opened on January 1, 1938. In 1932, he started hauling eggs and poultry to Chicago and brought back used furniture. He sold the store merchandise to Walter and Ola Knapp, and they rented the building for 22 years. There were living quarters in the back with apartments upstairs. Today it is abandoned. (SW.)

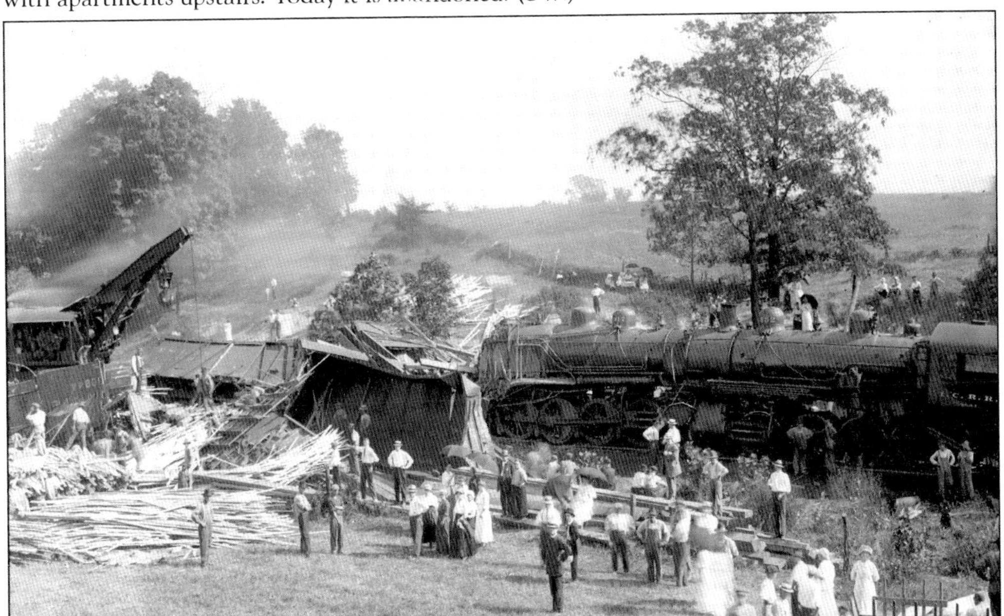

A head-on collision of two 280s on the same track occurred in the early 1900s, involving one train pulling lumber and undetermined freight on the other. This was the run from Oblong to Robinson, and the trains collided in the vicinity of Stoy. (BM.)

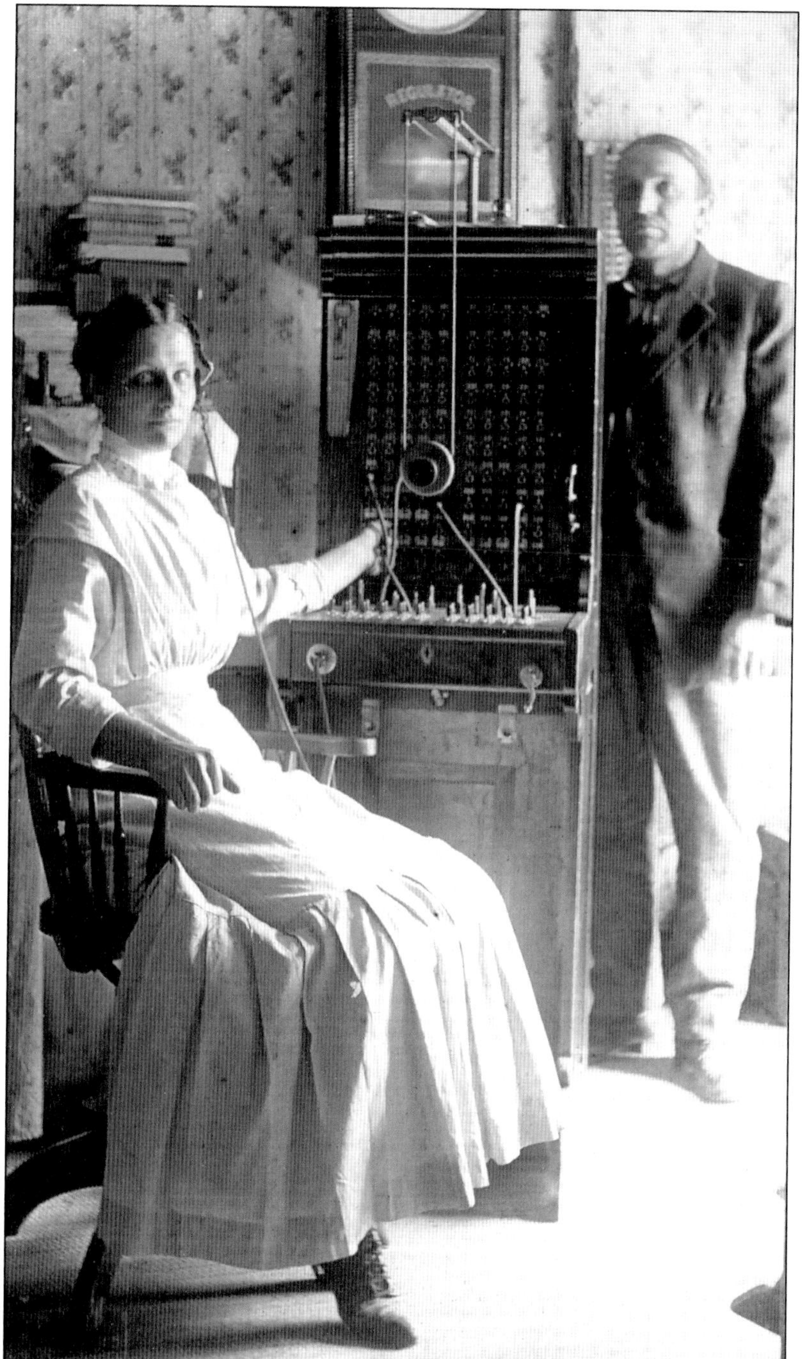

Frank and Estella Millsap ran Porterville's first telephone operation in their home. They also ran a general store and later, the local hotel. They rented out rooms to the oilmen during the boom. In August 1960, Porterville's telephone operation was purchased, most likely by the Continental Telephone Company, as well as Hutsonville's and some smaller towns in years previous. Like Estella, many young women of the community around the Palestine area worked as "telephone girls" until 1957 when direct dialing was introduced to Palestine. (BM.)

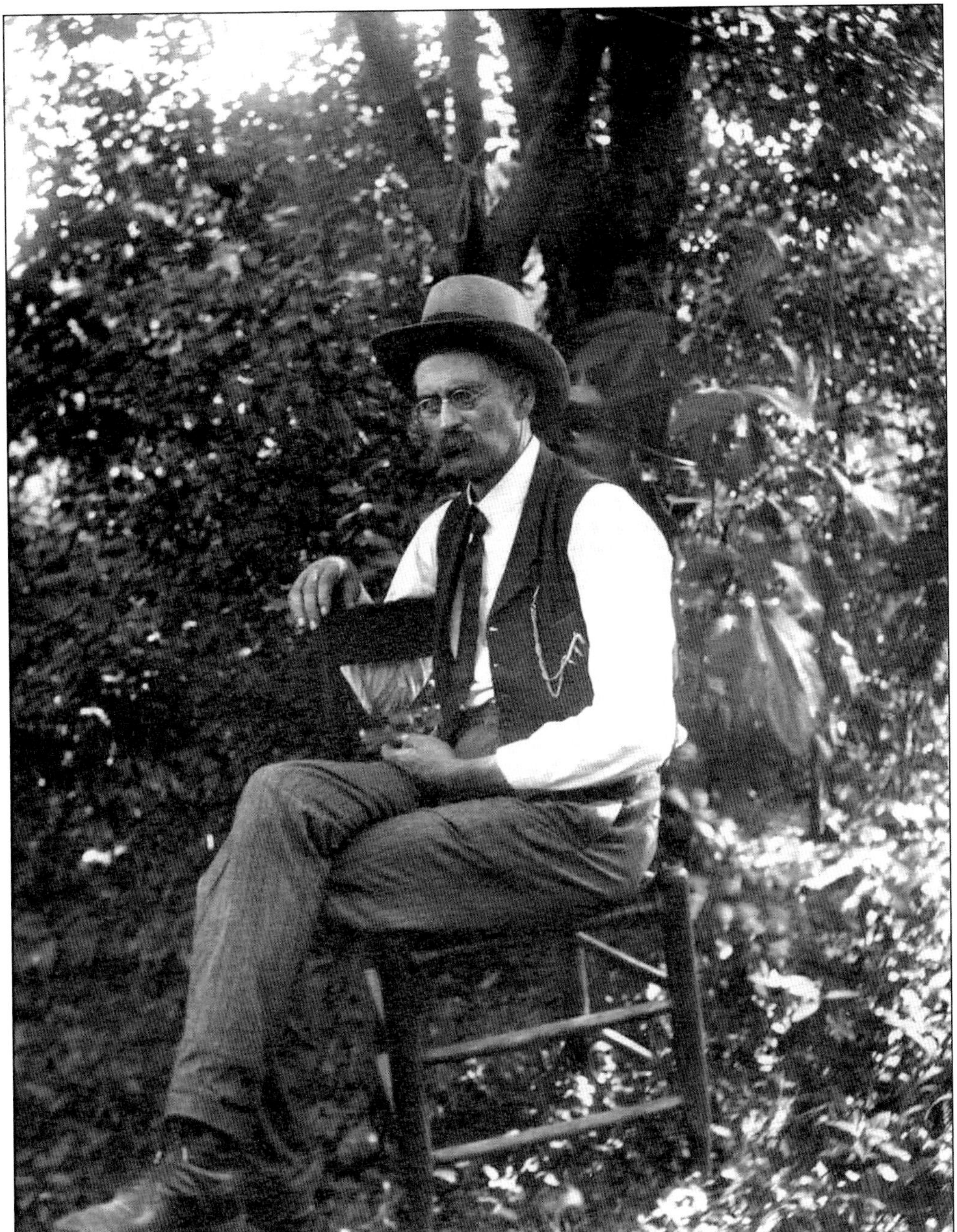

Dr. Charles D. Ryerson, who was born in 1854 and graduated from a medical college in Cincinnati in 1881, became a well-known doctor who worked most often in the West York area. Before that, he had offices in York and West Union for one year, and he was in medical service for a total of 47 years. During that time, he was a pioneer doctor in the truest sense of the word. He was on call day and night and traveled by buggy, on horseback, and on foot if roads were impassable to get to patients. He died on his 74th birthday on June 14, 1928. (SJ.)

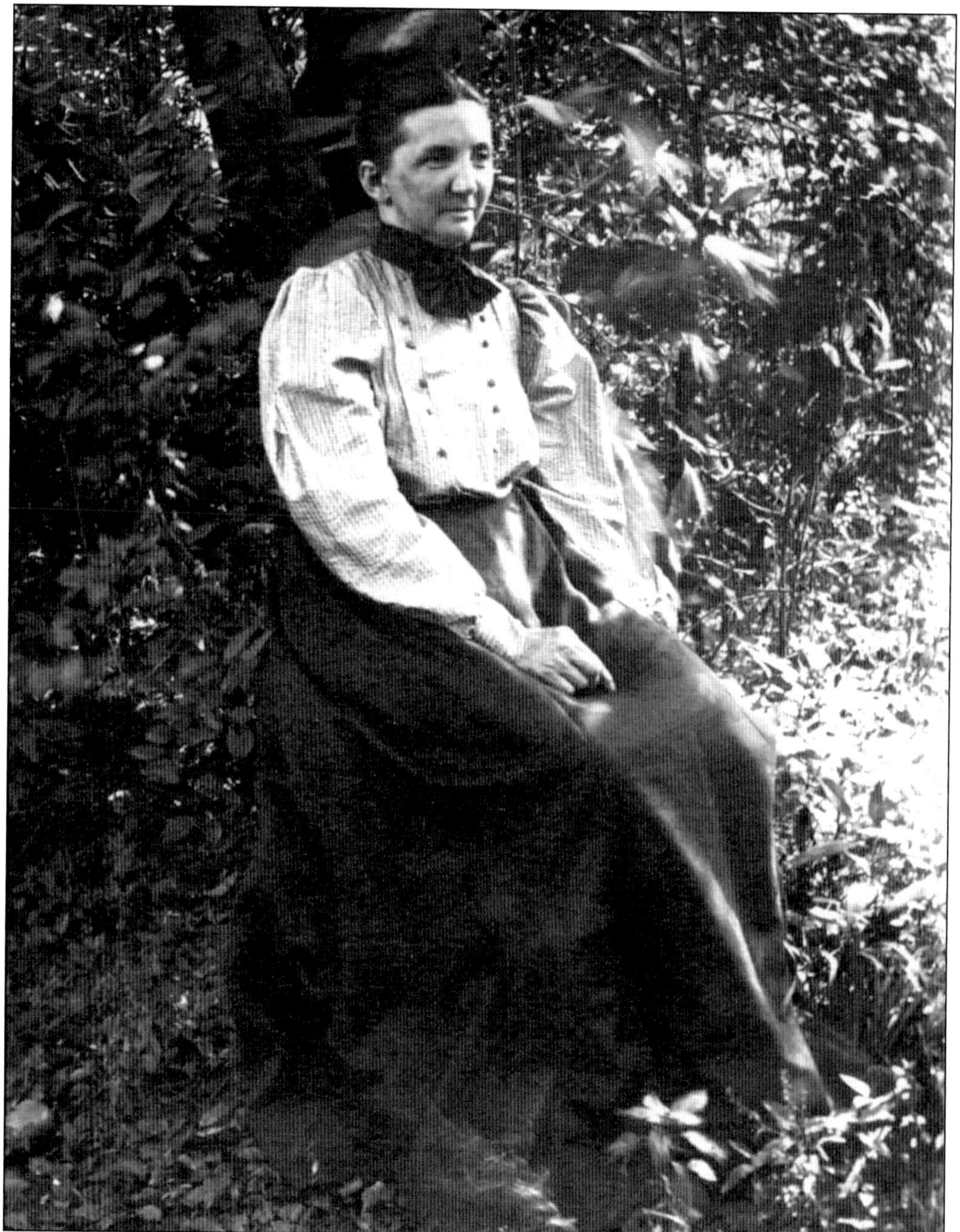

Emma Myers, born to George F. Myers and Margaret Myers (née Murphy) in 1857, married Charles D. Ryerson on May 19, 1881, a month and a half after Ryerson received his medical diploma. They had seven children. Emma died on August 10, 1932, at the age of 75. (SJ.)

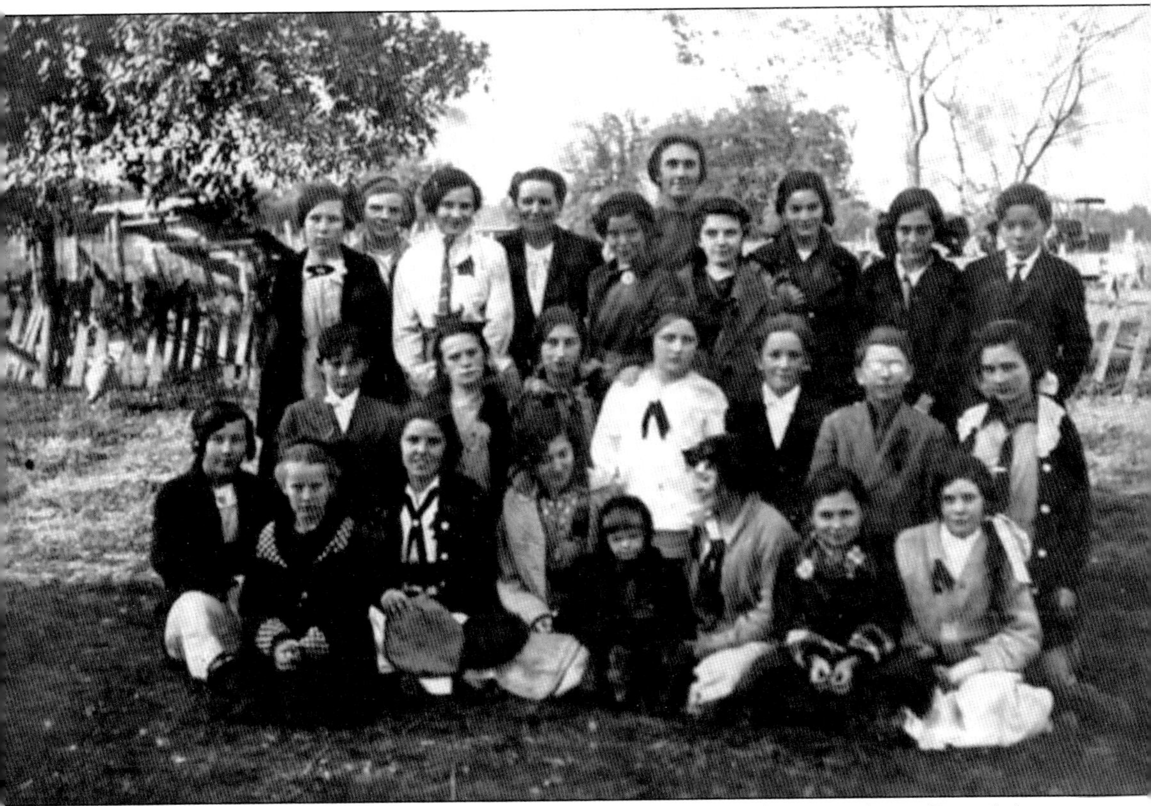

Porterville's Sunday school class gathers to honor the birthday of Kate Webster. From left to right are (first row) Clara Ballard (Conley), Edna Godsey (Conover), Mary Hills (Mitchell), Myrtle Faught (Burcham), Edytha Beabout (Wilson), Jewell Gowner (Newlin), Leona Smith (Wood), and Florence Lindsay (Newlin); (second row) Virgil Bonham, Myrtle Kinney (York), Ollie Hampsten (Mills), Cleda Leo (Millsap), Leonard Bonham, Kenneth Price, and Clysta Howard (Faught); (third row) Mary Myers (Conley), Soy Kinderdine (Mitchell), Bertha Flick (Wood), Kate Webster, Lena Holloway (Holmes), Alice Wilson, Clara Grossman (Wilson), Stella Barrick (Holmes), Opal Doty (Wilkin), and Luther Bonham. (SJ.)

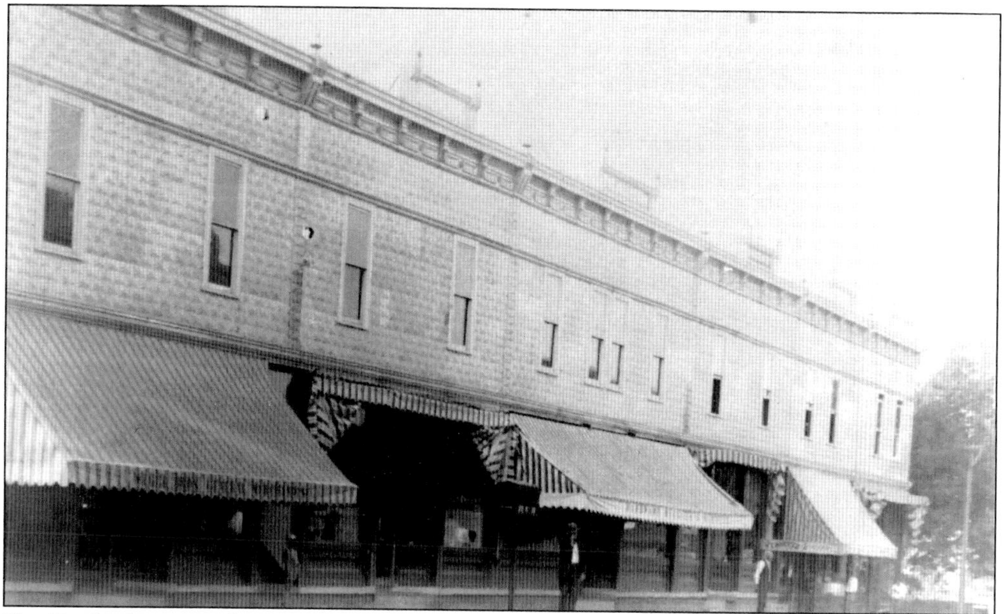

Flat Rock's business district in 1912 proliferated with a variety of stores and services. All of the buildings were made of wood, and when a fire broke out that year, it was devastating. This photograph was taken before the fire of the south side of Main Street, which consisted of a hardware store and Weber's General Merchandise. Twenty-four businesses burned to the ground before Robinson's fire department, which was sent down on a train, showed up to contain the fire. It was finally extinguished without a single loss of a home. (SJ.)

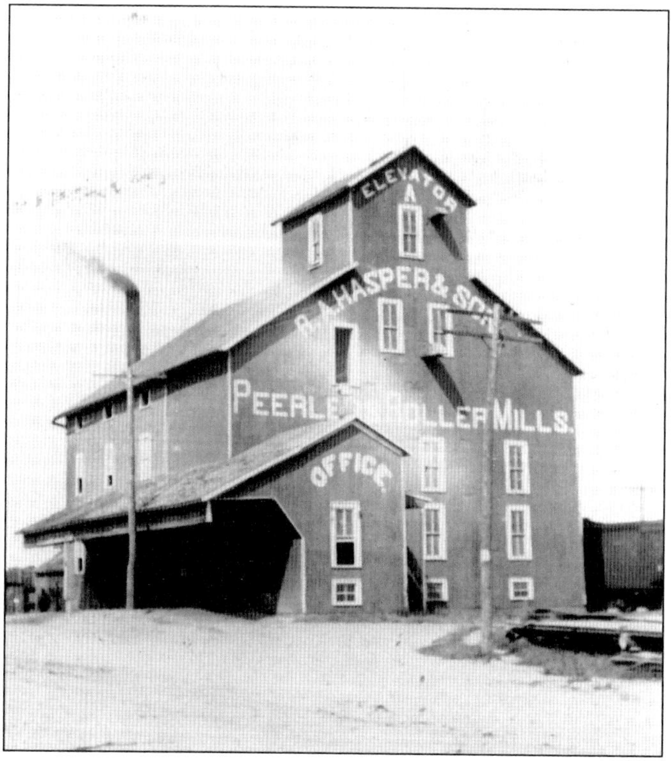

Peerless Roller Mills was bought out by R. A. Hasper around the time of the Civil War from G. T. Taylor. They expanded business to include selling coal and fuel, and sold feed for livestock. They were well known for their square dealing with the farmers and townspeople in Flat Rock. Hasper's Best flour had a strong reputation for the best quality. (SJ.)

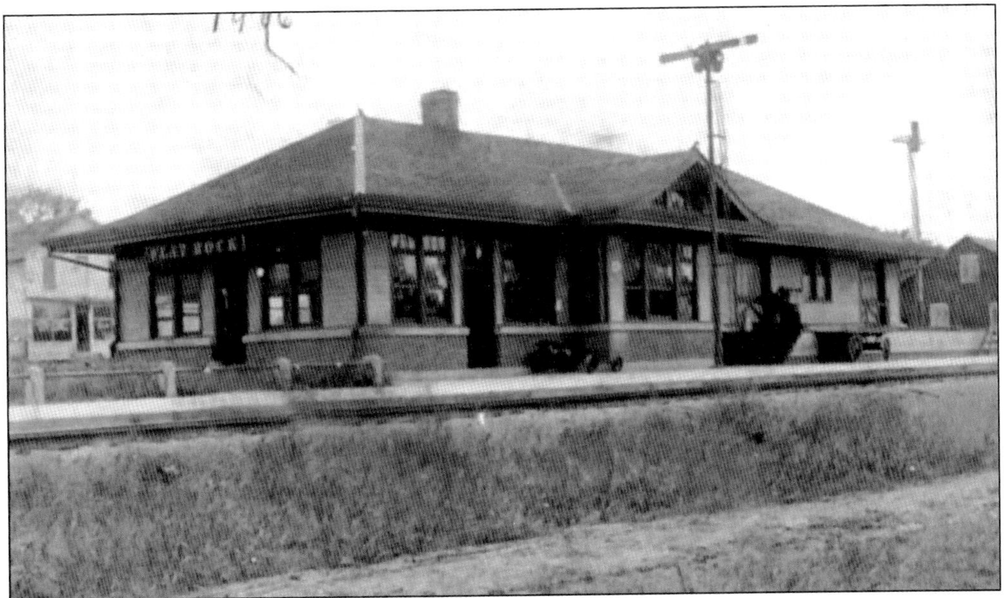

The Flat Rock depot played a significant role in the future of Flat Rock in 1912, as one of the worst fires in the history of the county broke out involving mostly the businesses. The loss for Flat Rock was financially considerable, but it would have been much worse had it not been for the timing of the Big Four Railroad. A special train was sent from Robinson with the chemical engine and about 50 men. There was a serious delay at Duncanville because of a long freight, and they managed to get to Flat Rock before the fire spread to the east side and the lumberyard. (SJ.)

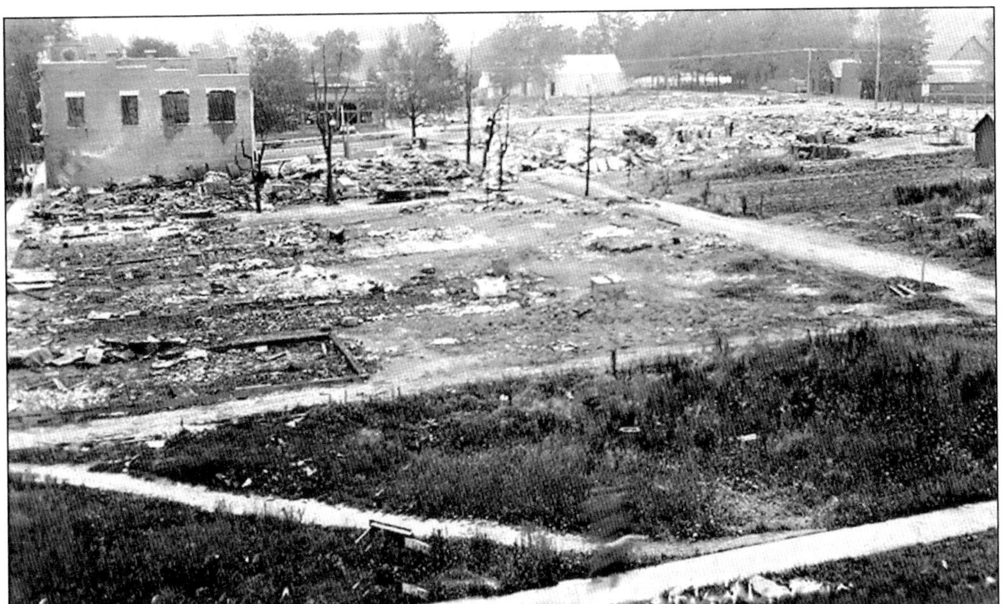

The origin of the fire was never determined, but it was reasonably certain that Bill Brown's undertaking parlor above McClure's bakery was likely at fault from someone laying a smoking pipe down. The original blaze broke out there in the W. E. Bond building. The east side of the square was spared heavy damage, but many of the businesses south (west of the bank) and north were destroyed. (SJ.)

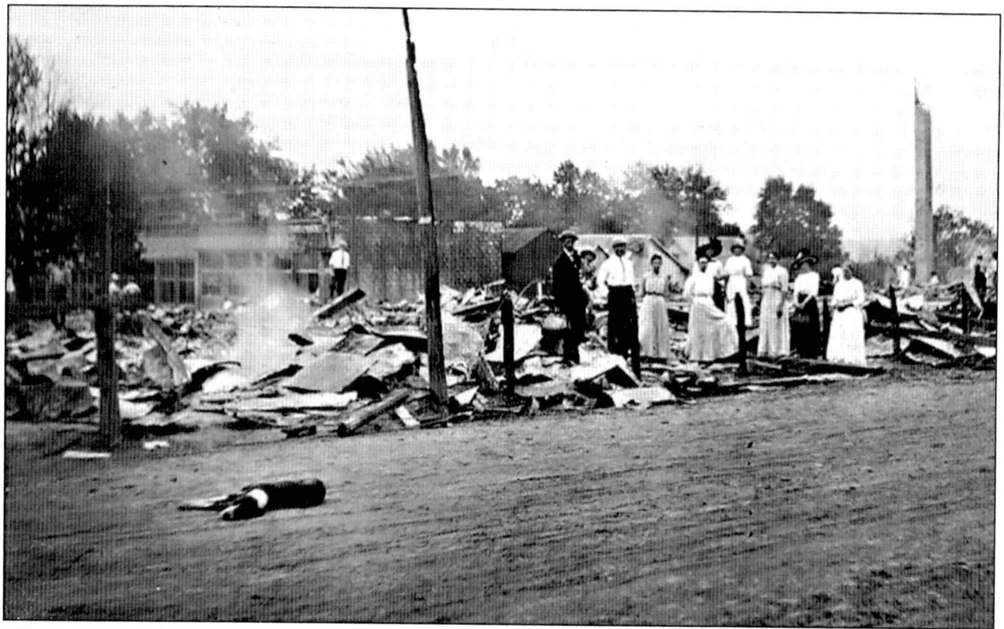

The citizens of Flat Rock acted fast in saving important stock. Dr. Hardin carried his stock of drugs into the street, while the bankers at Flat Rock Bank gathered their money, valuable papers, and books and placed them in a hearse, which was drawn to the edge of the village where it was guarded until the danger was over. Dr. Hardin's store was restocked later as his building was the only brick building in the district. (SJ.)

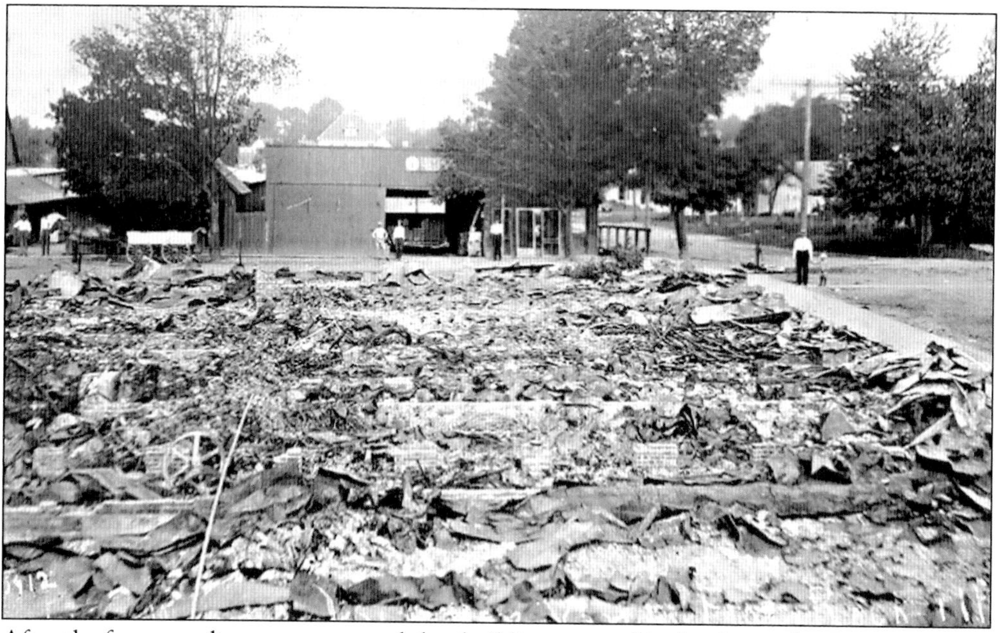

After the fire, an ordinance was passed that buildings erected had to be made of stone or brick. Additionally, the town put in concrete everywhere to offset any future fires. At one time, the town had more concrete per capita than anywhere in the nation. One of the first concrete roads in Illinois was built for Flat Rock. The road is referred to as the Lost Slab and was built between 1915 and 1916 between Honey Creek Township and Flat Rock. (SJ.)

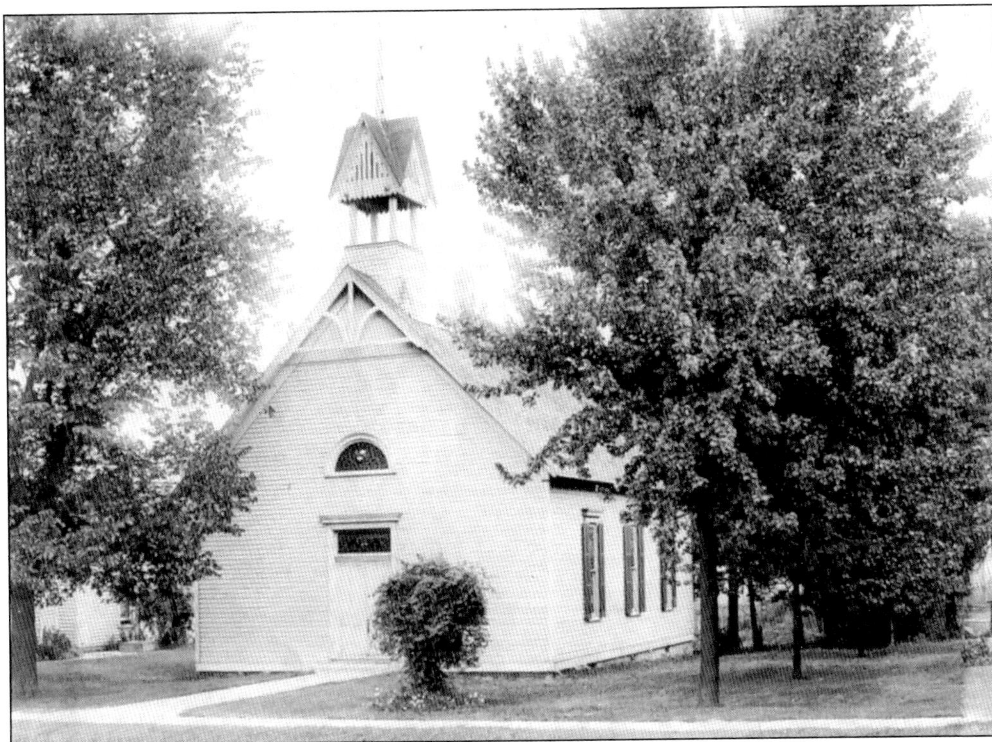

Flat Rock Primitive Baptist Church was started and built by the Swedenborgen Church Society. Eventually the Baptist Church took it over. (SJ.)

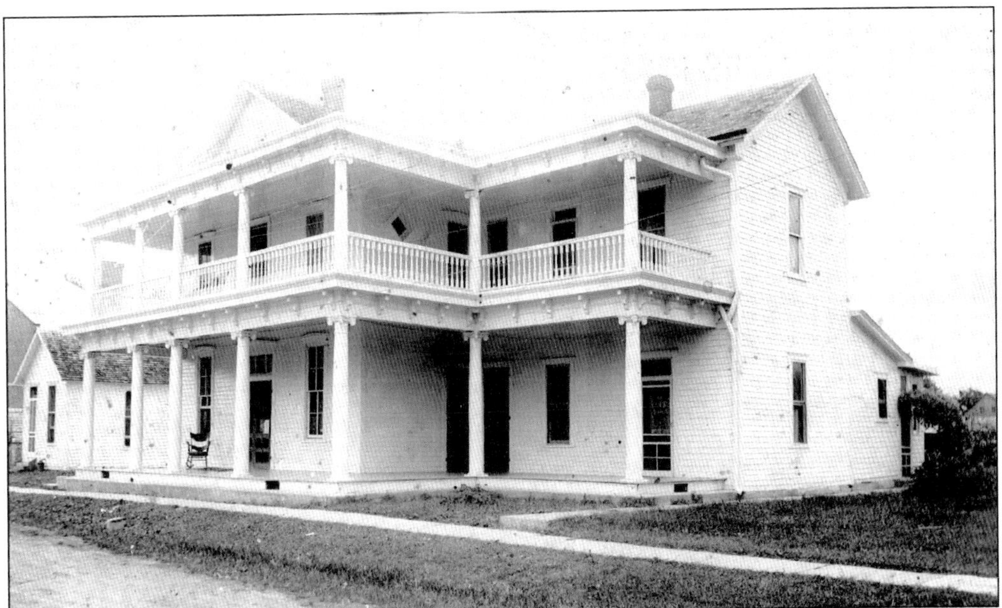

The Ford Hotel in Flat Rock was started by Mrs. L. W. Ford in 1907. She provided more luxurious accommodations during the oil boom than was usual. The Ford Hotel had a more homelike atmosphere, and the two-story structure was richly furnished, providing dining rooms and kitchens. (SJ.)

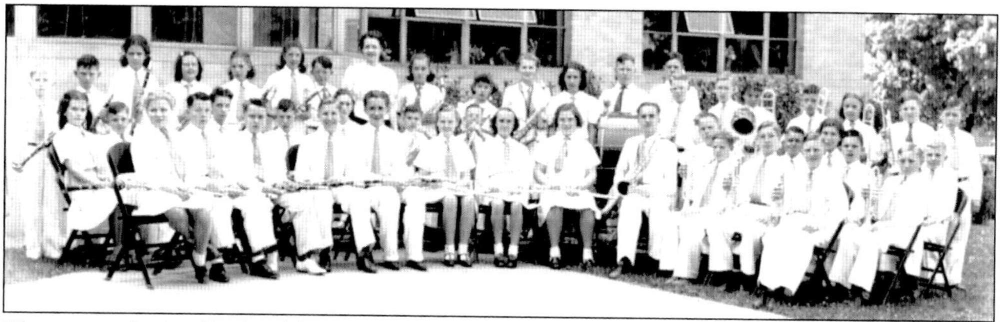

This junior high all-school band was photographed around 1939, with some future notables. Mary Ann Jones, James Jones's sister, is sixth from the left in the back row. In later years, when the Handy Writer's Colony was established, she became one of the aspiring authors of the retreat in Marshall, Clark County, Illinois. Others in this photograph are Bob Heath, Jim Woodworth, and David Steel. John H. Lockhart acted as president of the Chautauqua Association for two seasons. The Chautauqua was held in a big tent each summer on grade school grounds. Many good lectures, concerts, plays, and educational entertainments were presented at these events. (SJ.)

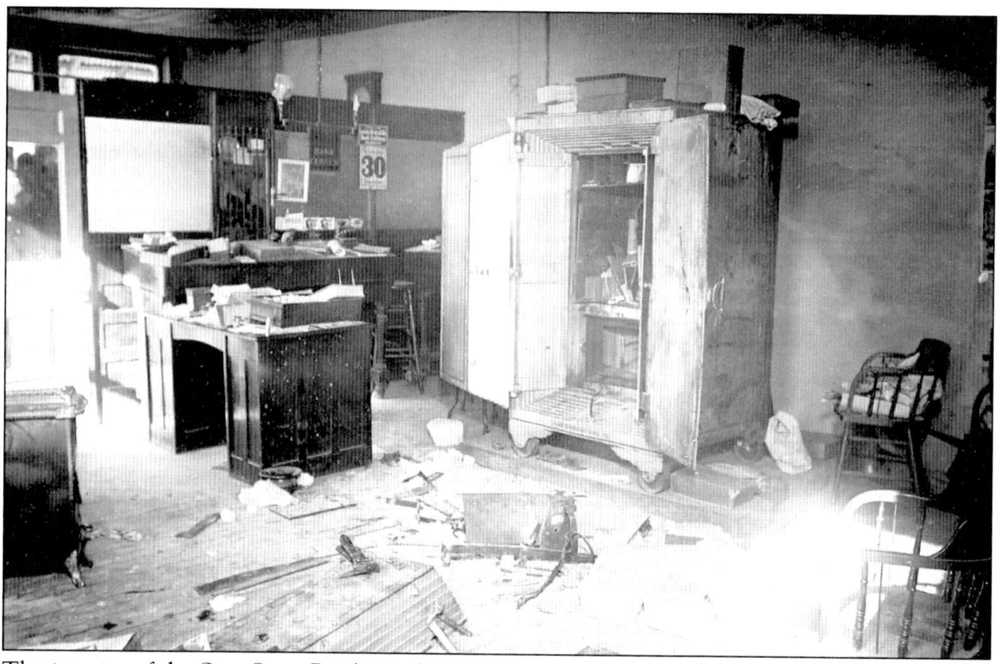

The interior of the Stoy State Bank was left askew after burglars had used nitroglycerine to blow the vault. The explosion took place on November 30, 1911, during the heyday of the oil boom, when exploration and drilling was still taking place. As a result of the noise level that was almost constant, nobody took notice of the explosion, and the crooks took off with $1,500. They were never apprehended. (Seyferths.)

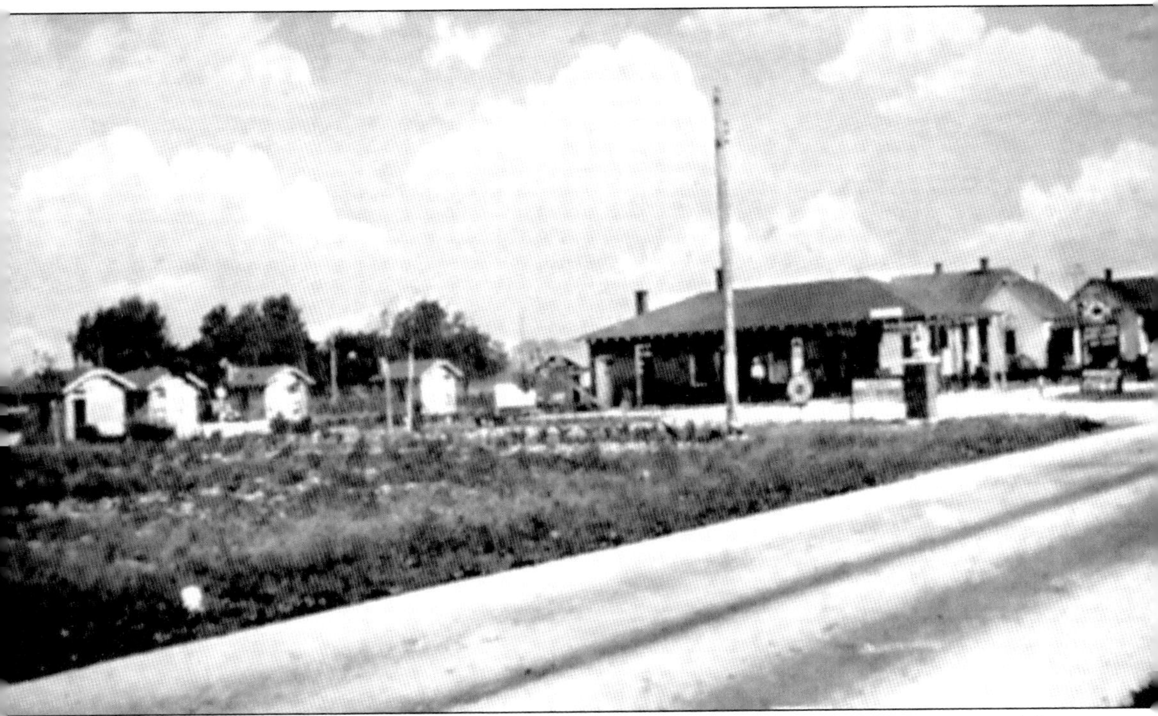

Gordon Junction sits at a crossroads where Highway 1 meets with Route 33. It was named for the Gordon family that settled in the area. This was a motor court established in the 1900s and was the first of its kind in the area. Today it is a traffic stop with one store on the southeast corner. (SJ.)

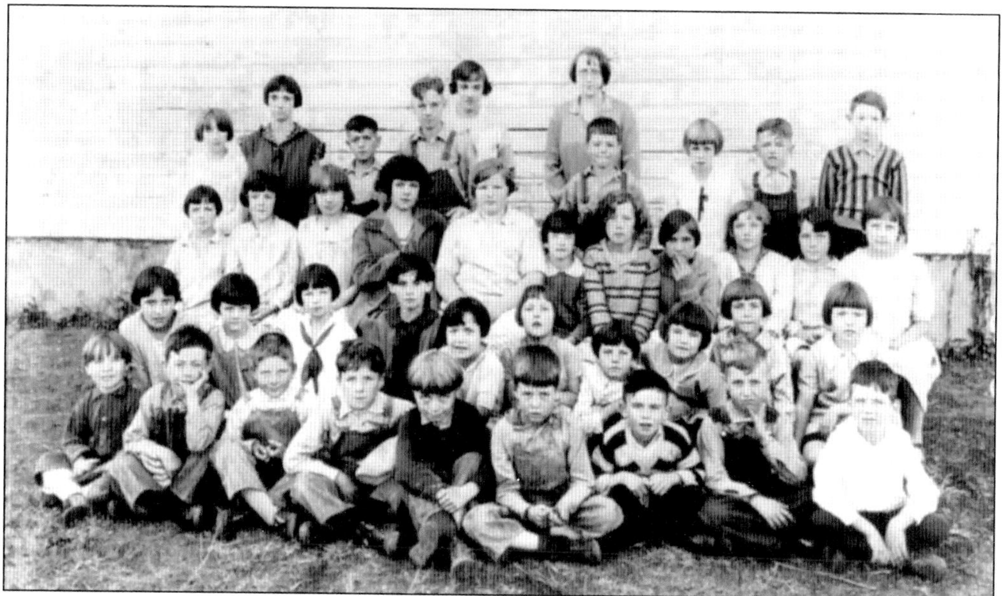

A Trimble grade school class in March 1922 consists of, from left to right, (first row) Vincent Brock, Stanley Williamson, Paul Knapp, Harold Stephens, Wayne Brock, Robert Trimble, unidentified, Harrison Correll, and Frank Johnson; (second row) Alma Matheny, Frances Johnson, Avis Creed, ? Champlain, Nola Matheny, Esther Gayer, unidentified, Martha Ray Conrad, Marjorie Burress, and Dorothy Knapp; (third row) Elizabeth Brownlee, Elizabeth Trimble, Audrey Creed, Louise Trimble, Eva Knapp, Vivian Johnson, Velma Stephens, Fannie Beard, ? Champlain, Irene Matheny, and Eunice Matheny; (fourth row) Scythia Champlain, unidentified, Henry Brownlee, Mervyn Correll, Richard Trimble, Anna Trimble, Randall York, and Eldredge Matheny; (fifth row) Ruby Correll and Belva Correll (teacher). (Ruby Correll.)

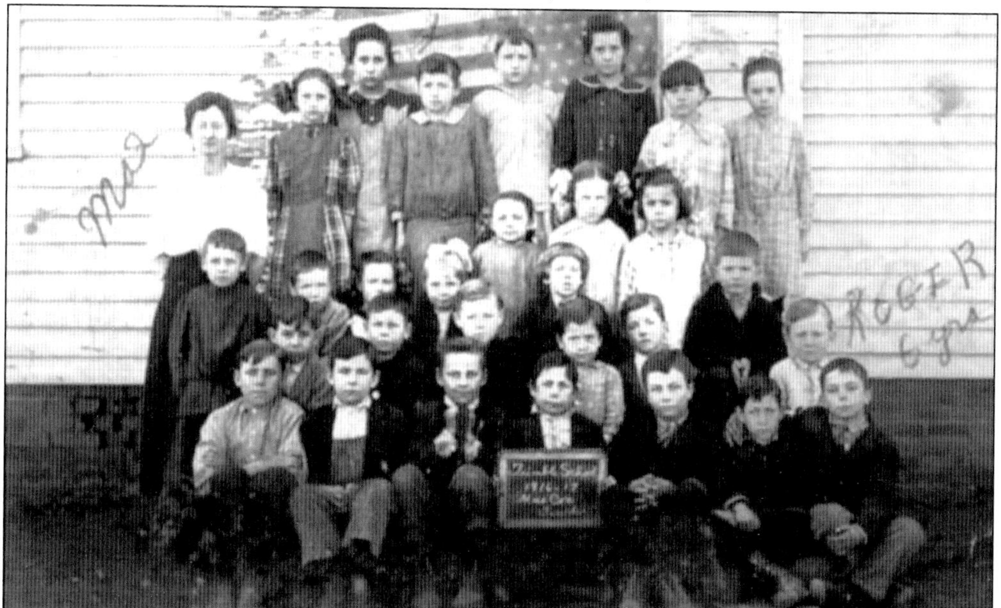

An earlier Trimble class during the 1916–1917 school year was taught by Mae Cox, on the far left side. Cox's second cousin Roger is among the students, in the second row on the far right. (SJ.)

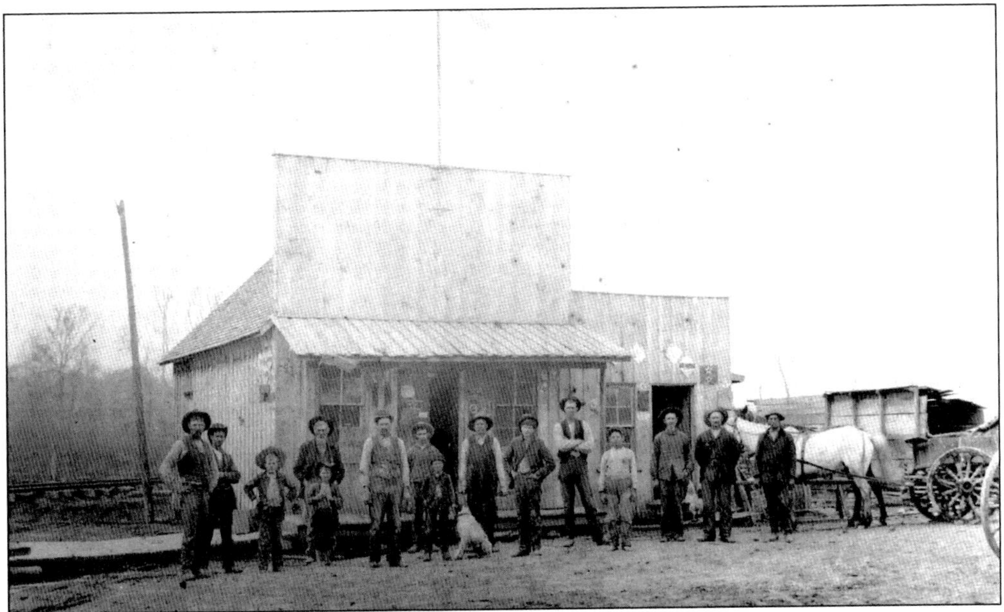

McClain Station in 1889 had a post office established, which gave Stoy its official name. Charles Keiffier was the postmaster. A little later, Purcell's general store was established in 1893, becoming the longest-running business for Stoy, spanning 78 years and not closing until June 1971. The store was always owned and run by the Purcell family. The post office for Stoy resided at Purcell's and continued there for some time after it closed. (BM.)

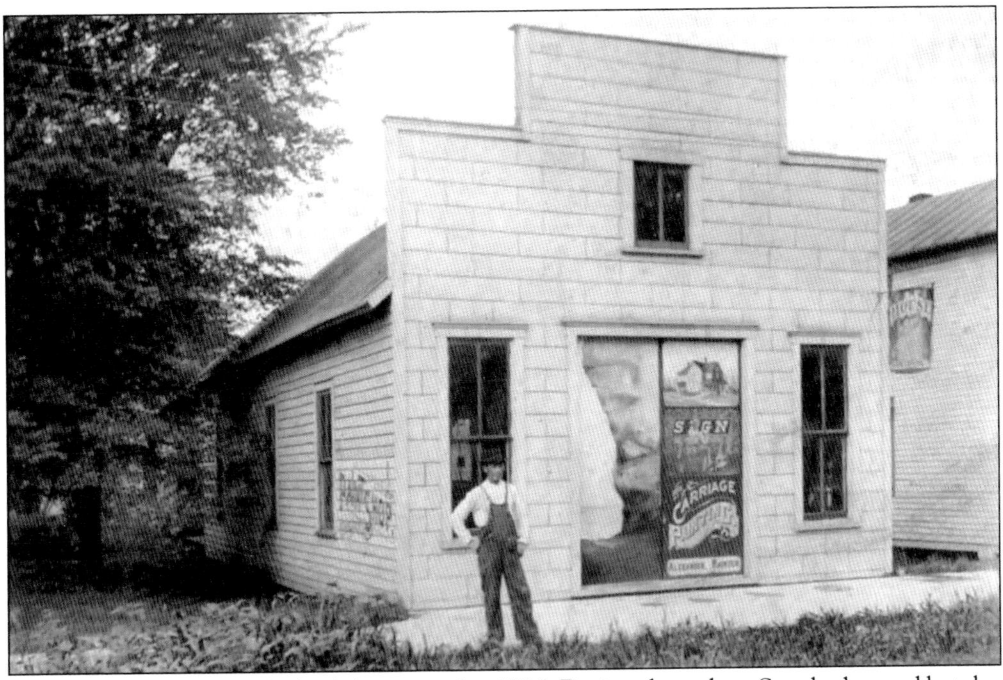

Stoy's Paint Shop enjoyed a brisk business after 1906. During those days, Stoy had a good hotel, a bank, barbershops, a number of restaurants, a meat market, a drugstore, and 13 saloons (a record for Crawford County). (SJ.)

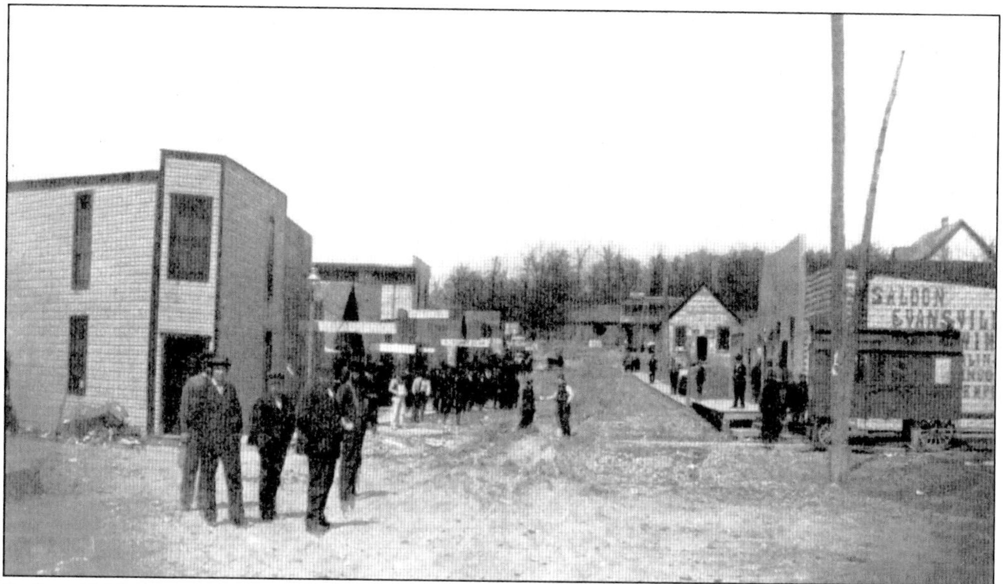

Before 1900, Stoy was rather insignificant as far as the economy of the county was concerned. By 1909, the Effingham branch of the Illinois Central Railroad, which had been doing less than $100 a year in business, reported boxcar receipts of over $25,000 to its credit in the first month. The Ohio Oil Company put in a pipeline and a pumping station, along with storage tanks, in anticipation of continued success on the wells. (SJ.)

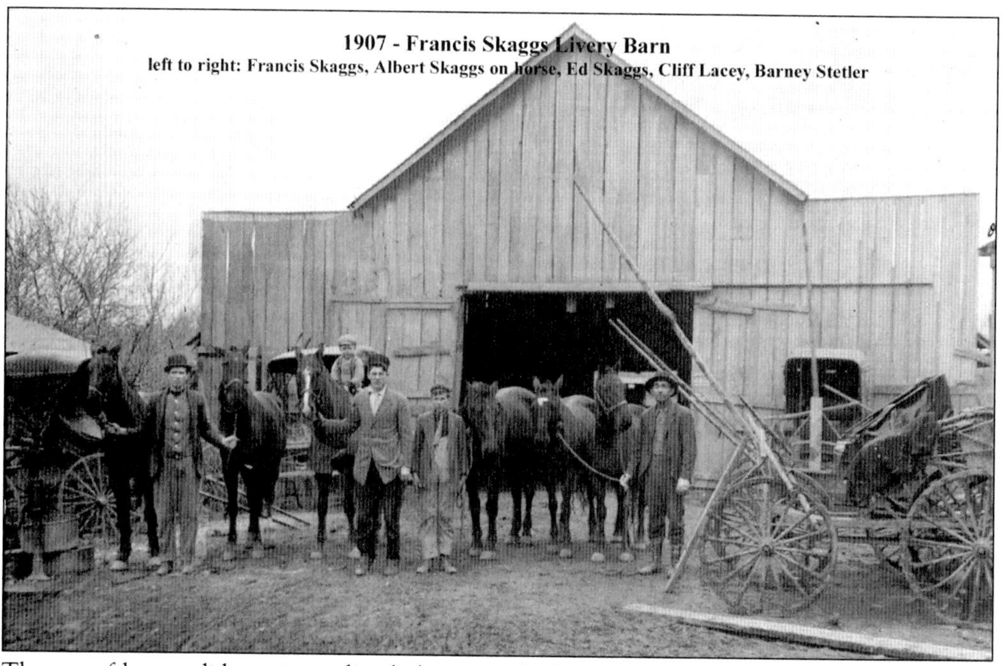

The use of horses did not immediately become obsolete in Stoy, but not long after 1907, this livery stable's use became limited to short-term transportation. Service was often made to the railroads. Skaggs's Livery Barn employed, from left to right, Francis Skaggs, little Albert Skaggs on a horse, Ed Skaggs, Cliff Lacey, and Barney Stetler. (SJ.)

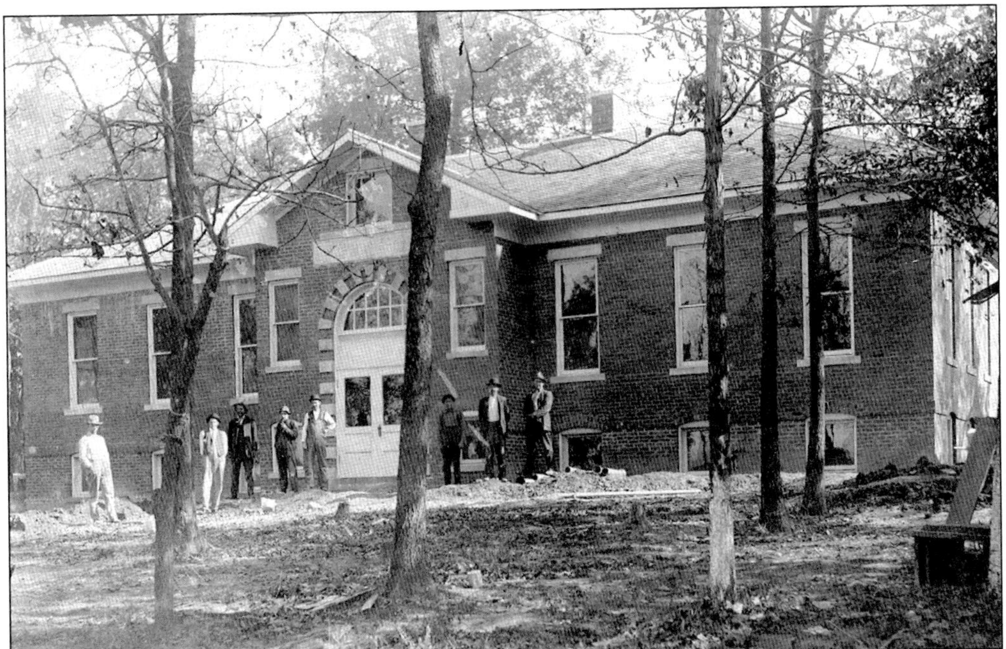

Stoy School was in its final stages of being built in this photograph. It is now a private residence and is one of the finest buildings in Stoy. The oil boom made it possible for this building to be erected, and Stoy was even visited by tycoons such as John D. Rockefeller. (SJ.)

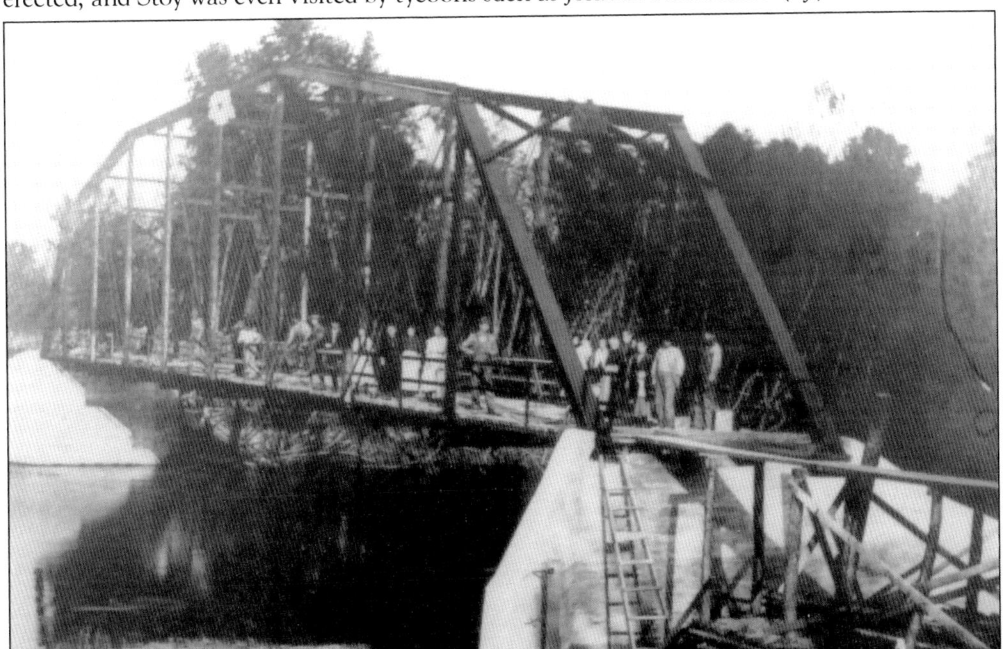

Gibson Bridge was built over the Embarras River far south of Oblong in Southwest Township. William Gibson owned farmland south of the bridge on both sides of the road. It came to be called the Gibson or Stoltz Bridge by turns. Nearby, the area was known as the Dark Bend, which is now a part of Jasper County, termed so because it fell on a bend along the river and was grown over with dense trees and ground vegetation. (SW.)

Bibliography

Ford Times. March 1957.
http://www.rootsweb.com/~ilcchs.
http://www.wikipedia.org.
Historic Palestine 1811–1988. Book 1. Palestine, IL: Palestine Preservation Project Society.
Historic Palestine 1811–1990. Book 2. Palestine, IL: Palestine Preservation Project Society.
"Lost Slab, a Brief History." *Honey Creek Times* VIII, no. 3. Published by Philip L. Young.
Robinson Argus. Souvenir and Business Edition. Compiled by Annette B. Haskett. Republished by Victor L. Smith, July 30, 1973.
Sangamon State University. "Reveille to Taps." VHS.
Wilson, Dorothy C. *Lincoln's Mothers, a Story of Nancy and Sally Lincoln*. Garden City, NY: Doubleday, 1981.

INDEX